Chester Noyes Greenough
Collected Studies

Collected Studies by
Chester Noyes Greenough

Selected and Arranged by
FRANK WILSON CHENEY HERSEY

With an Introduction by
WILBUR CORTEZ ABBOTT

Essay Index Reprint Series

BOOKS FOR LIBRARIES PRESS
FREEPORT, NEW YORK

First Published 1940
Reprinted 1970

INTERNATIONAL STANDARD BOOK NUMBER:
0-8369-1879-7

LIBRARY OF CONGRESS CATALOG CARD NUMBER:
78-128253

PRINTED IN THE UNITED STATES OF AMERICA

Contents

[vii]

CONTENTS

Introduction

ONE of the lesser misfortunes of those whose lives are spent in the world of letters and scholarship is that their occasional essays, studies, and reviews are so frequently buried in the proceedings of societies and academies, and in the pages of periodicals, often unknown or inaccessible to many who might otherwise profit by them. The paths of literature, history, journalism, even science, are strewn with such materials, among which are often to be found some of a man's most important and interesting productions. Fortunately, that part which finds its way into periodicals has been made available by the patient industry of those obscure but useful servants of society known as indexers. But in too many cases it has been difficult to trace the work of an individual through these various indexes without an expenditure of time, energy, and ingenuity beyond the reach of most of us.

This is the more regrettable in that many scholars and writers have distributed their contributions so widely that the sum of their work and its particular quality, as well as their individuality, have been too little known even to many concerned with the same problems as those to which they addressed their talents. For it is the nature of many such men to take small account of these productions and to keep neither copy nor record of them, much less to publish them in one collection. Like Nature they scatter their seeds widely and generously, hoping that, though some may fall on stony ground and some be eaten by the birds, some may take root and grow and bring forth fruit in due season. In this, like Nature, they are seldom disappointed, for many times in the most unlikely quarters and at unpredictable times and seasons, it happens that the seeds they have scattered produce crops even beyond their hopes.

Yet if, as sometimes happens, a kindly hand takes time and trouble to gather a part or all of a man's contributions in one place, he and the world at large are the more fortunate for that circumstance. For such labors of love serve two important purposes. They make materials, always useful and often interesting, more accessible, even to those outside the particular field of study which they represent; and they give a picture of the mind of the man who cultivated that field, which is not seldom as important as his factual contributions to knowledge. The way in which a man's mind works is often as significant and as interesting as the product of his mental processes and may be a guide and inspiration to others following in his steps. To these purposes there may be added a third consideration. It is the revelation of the fact that there are so many organizations interested in the activities of that obscure body of men known as "scholars," on whom, in the last resolution, depends much of what we call "culture" or even "civilization," and the added fact that amid the material things of life there are so many men who have a concern for life's more enduring if less practical interests.

It is in such a spirit as this, that from time to time—though not, perhaps, as often as we should wish—there appears a collection of papers, whether, as we say, "occasional" or even "fugitive," such as this volume contains. As to their character and their value, they speak for themselves, nor is it necessary here to labor the patient, accurate, minute, and ingenious scholarship which they reveal. What is of even greater importance is that they provide, as it were, a portrait of the man who wrote them: his careful intellectual honesty, his attention to detail, his painstaking scholarship, his earnest search for truth even, to use an old figure, at the bottom of the deepest well. In this latter respect, if in no other—and there are many others—they may well serve as a model for all those who, like him, seek truth and ensue it. Nor is this collection less to be noted as a memorial to the interests which filled so large a part of his life, to those friends and colleagues among whom he spent his days, to the societies in which he was active, and to the journals which he and other scholars maintained. It is in fact a memorial to the whole of that intellectual movement of which he was a part, and which finds reflection in his contributions to what some of us must always regard as one of the greater influences and products of the world in which we live.

WILBUR CORTEZ ABBOTT

Chester Noyes Greenough
Collected Studies

Some Prerequisites for
Research in Literature

WHEN the undergraduate really becomes a graduate student—which he cannot do by merely enrolling himself in a graduate school—he changes principally in that he narrows his field of study and broadens his conception of study. The second of these two changes furnishes at once the necessity and the compensation for the first. It is my purpose to suggest to you certain considerations which should help to determine the attitude of the graduate student toward that which he renounces and that which he principally selects. For various reasons, I limit myself to a single field, the field of literature.

Before we go on to consider the special problems which meet advanced students of literature, and to ask what equipment is necessary to solve them, let us touch upon two qualities which every advanced student is expected to have—industry and accuracy. Without these qualities nothing can be accomplished. With them it is at least certain that work of one sort or another will be regularly turned out and that the workman will deserve the credit of being a faithful copyist or cataloguer or bibliographer.

But, although the absence of industry and mechanical accuracy means failure, the presence of them does not insure success. The words of Francis Parkman upon this point are as applicable in the field of literature as in that of history: "Faithfulness to the truth of history involves far more than a research, however patient and scrupulous, into special facts. Such facts may be detailed with the most minute exactness, and yet the narrative, taken as a whole, may be unmeaning or untrue." It remains, then, to discover, if we can, what is positively necessary (in addition to patient and scrupulous research, be it observed, and not in place of it) in order that the products of research in literature may be marked by this larger significance and truth—to ask what equipment of information, what point of view, what spirit, what qualities of temperament and of character, will furnish the most substantial guarantee of success.

Literary history is not the history of facts; it is the history of certain ideals which can be dimly seen in some facts, though not in all, and which, in different degrees at different times, may be conditioned by facts. Working in this exceedingly difficult material, we wish to accomplish three things. First, we wish to acquire and test facts. When this is done, we have a considerable heap of information, each bit of which should be equally true. But, though equally true, it can hardly be equally significant. Hence, our second process is to arrange our facts—to decide what to throw into high relief, what to subordinate, what to omit. Some very admirable scholars have never learned what to omit. Finally—and this is the most difficult of all—we have to face the task of communicating to others the effect which all this has made upon our own minds and sympathies. When, as frequently happens, the thing to be communicated is not what is ordinarily termed a fact—not, for example, what a certain person did, but what he aimed to do—this final task of representation and embodiment is bound to make us realize to our sorrow the clumsiness and inadequacy of the materials which we are forced to build with.

It is a commonplace to say again that the student of literature needs for the solution of these difficulties all the light that can be thrown upon his subject by history, ethnology, economics, and philosophy, as well as the historical study of political theory, architecture, and every other form to which men entrust their thoughts and their emotions. And yet we who study literature are in permanent danger of forgetting how very small is, and has always been, the literary class, and how very great, in consequence, is the danger of interpreting the past by the evidence of its literature alone. We shall do well to recall often the wise saying of that English physician whom Lord Acton quoted in his memorable inaugural address: "An educated man cannot become so on one study alone, but must be brought under the influence of natural, civil, and moral modes of thought."

Next after these great influences from without comes a great influence from within, and yet from aloof—the influence of the literatures of Greece and Rome. They are indispensable in forming the taste, in training the powers of discrimination and criticism, and in acquainting us with many of the canons, types, and devices of modern literature. To the absence of this classical training, I think, is largely owing one of the most apparent infirmities in our teaching of modern literature. The average student, even the average graduate student, is almost wholly unable to express himself naturally and significantly when he tries to write down his opinion of what he has read. And, for once, it is not defective instruction in English composition that is chiefly to blame. The difficulty mainly arises because the ordinary student has little or no knowledge of the precise nature of the various types of literature and of the canons of excellence in each. So, not knowing just what to look for within the book, he naturally repeats his little version of what, from his teacher, from one or another of a host of manuals, or from the introduction to some heavily equipped edition of the prescribed book, he has been given to understand that he is expected to think about the point in question. Hence, the study of modern literature—philological study excepted—is in the gravest danger of losing the disciplinary value which it ought to have.

One way out lies in a revival of the study of those critical statutes which were fixed so admirably by the ancients. When Aristotle made his famous saying in the *Poetics* about pity and terror in tragedy, when Longinus wrote that a noble work marred by technical flaws might well be placed above an ignoble work which is flawless, when Cicero perceived that the test of a great oration is that it shall appeal with equal force to the learned few and to the unlearned multitude, critical canons were formulated which, for their historical influence and their inherent good sense, better deserve our study than almost any similar utterances of modern times. Besides having diligence and accuracy, then, the apprentice at research in literature must be grounded in the humanities, and particularly, in order that he may make certain indispensable preliminary measurements, he must know some of the great canons and definitions that he cannot well get except from the classics.

It can hardly have escaped your notice that the three processes to which the materials for our study must be subjected —accumulation, correlation, and representation—are not alike. The first is purely scientific; the second is partly scientific, partly artistic; the third is purely artistic. Yet hardly anyone finds it equally easy to accomplish the scientific and the artistic; too commonly, indeed, those who hold to the one despise the other. No argument is needed, however, to show that complete success at research in literature must be withheld from those who do not in some degree unite these two qualities so difficult to reconcile and combine.

Yet this reconciliation is only one of many that are demanded by our study. In the very nature of its progress the history of literature, if it is to be comprehended in any large way, makes a similar demand. For progress in literature, historically considered, is not progress in a straight line. It is not, that is to say, brought about by a steady increase of understanding and of technical skill applied by each generation to the attainment of those ends that were almost attained by the generation immediately preceding. It is rather progress by reaction. Each generation, disrespectful of the good qualities of its immediate predecessors and overconscious of their failings, reverts to an older fashion, modifies it, often unconsciously incorporates with it something in the manner of the period which it seeks to improve upon, and so fits its reading of the past to its own time, until it in turn is built upon by a new generation, which usually takes for the headstone of the corner some principle that the earlier builders had wholly rejected. A commonplace illustration will suffice to show how human all this is. We are all conscious of the feeling with which we regard the style of furniture that was in vogue about 1840: it irritates or bores us, and makes us turn for solace to the fashion of a remoter period—perhaps to the severe outlines of Revolutionary days, perhaps to the pseudo-mediaevalism of the so-called mission style. By a precisely similar change of heart it comes about that classicism in literature, beginning in a useful reaction against uncontrolled fancy, waxes so strong in its own conceit that a romantic revolt presently triumphs for a while, only to lead in its turn back to the quieter days of the Victorian period.

For students of a history which progresses by such steps as these, a very marked difficulty arises. Each of these bygone epochs, honestly and usefully differing from that which precedes or follows it, finds among scholars its eager champions. There results the danger that if, as should be the case, we are able to acquire the point of view of our special period and in some degree come to make its grievances and triumphs our own, we may buy our knowledge of a particular epoch at the price of a loss of due respect for the ideals which it overthrew and for those to which it reluctantly gave place.

To keep the balance level is also difficult when we weigh

against each other the merits of certain conflicting methods of studying literature. We find one group interpreting literature, as Carlyle interpreted history, by the lives and works of a few great figures. Another school reminds us that a great number of minor writers, less inspired but closer to the mass of people who never write at all, more fairly represent their time. Still another learned group makes less of persons, whether great or small, than of forms, types, and tendencies. This school instructs us that it is "in the air" that certain literary effects shall be brought about at certain times; it cautions us against the biographical method and bids us be historical; it urges inductive study, based upon large masses of minor work, as a corrective for our enthusiasm over "The Hero as Man of Letters."

There must, furthermore, be "periods"; and there must be fairly distinct boundaries between periods. Yet it is also necessary to remember that on the morning after the death of John Dryden, in 1700, citizens of London did not greet each other with the prophetic observation that the Age of Dryden had passed and the Age of Pope begun. Again, it will undoubtedly save us from some absurdities if we make it our rule to prefer simple and obvious explanations; but we shall run squarely into other and no less regrettable absurdities unless we constantly remember that human nature has also been known to manifest a dislike of the obvious and an obstinate preference for the longest way around. We shall do well, therefore, even while reminding ourselves that after all literature is to a considerable degree a hand-to-mouth affair, and that consequently we must not be in haste to ascribe to men of letters niceties which as economical craftsmen they would hardly employ, to remind ourselves in the same breath of a perverse, monastic habit which leads a certain type of man to hide away his finest work in dark corners, there to be worshipped by himself alone.

These contrasts are rather sharp. There remains no end of minor difficulties, no end of moods, devices, points of view, mannerisms, pet phrases and aversions, each of which, though a valuable part of our critical individuality, may so easily deprive us of a due understanding or appreciation of that opposite which is for each the sovereign corrective. And yet, it is better to be something of a zealot and a sectary in these matters than to clothe ourselves with a perfunctory habit of eclecticism, to deny ourselves all favorites and enthusiasms, to trace the ups and downs of ideals with never a share in them, and to chronicle changes of fashion with no pleasure in the good work or regret at the bad.

And what, finally, should be the attitude of those who study the literatures of the past toward the writings of their own day? Considered aright, contemporary literature seems to me to enforce for the student of literary history, as politics enforces for the historian, the truth of Sir Walter Raleigh's observation that "the end and scope of all history" is "to teach us by examples of times past such wisdom as may guide our desires and actions." One way in which contemporary literature rewards consideration may be seen from Professor Turner's brilliant and influential discussion of *The Value of the Frontier in American History*. Always, he shows us, there is to be found upon the edges of civilization the reproduction of conditions which elsewhere have long since perished. Hence the vital relation of Parkman's *Oregon Trail* to his *Montcalm and Wolfe* or *The Jesuits in North America*. The same method may be applied to the study of some fields of literature. We all know, for example, how exceedingly difficult it is to conceive the actual conditions under which, by processes of communal composition, popular ballads seem to have taken form. Yet something like these conditions are even now being studied by an American scholar who is collecting the songs and ballads of Texan cowboys.

[9]

Even if it did not thus reward our study, however, we should feel bound not to stand aloof from the writing of our own time. And in our attitude toward it there should be something downright. Our feeling about the conflict between romanticism and classicism, and other battles long ago, may well be, with no lack of enthusiasm for either side, one of well-balanced appreciation, since both were in the same degree human and useful. But there are certain sharp and permanent distinctions which we must neither ignore in our study of the past nor fail to bring to bear upon the present. Such is the difference between work which is honest and work which is dishonest, between work which is noble and work which is ignoble. To be silent upon these matters, to distribute praise and blame without reference to them, is to withhold from the present the deepest lesson of the past, to confuse information with wisdom, to accept a definition which I know you will never accept—the definition that proficiency in the field of letters (whether that proficiency be creative or interpretative) is merely an accomplishment instead of being one of the manifestations of character.

The Oriental Tale in England in the Eighteenth Century[1]: A Review

BETWEEN 1684 and 1786 Miss Conant finds a pronounced tendency both in France and in England to orientalize—sometimes very slightly, sometimes as thoroughly as might be—the novel, allegory, tale, vision, drama, and fictitious correspondence. This material she very effectively divides into four main groups,—imaginative, moralistic, philosophic, and satiric. A rather long chapter on each of these groups, together with a final "literary estimate," an introduction, appendices, and an index, make up the work.

Miss Conant's book will certainly be useful; she has brought together French and English literature at many points, she has shown the presence in a period which was prevailingly classical, of an influence more than slightly romantic; she has spoken of books in a way that makes one wish to read them, and she has delighted those who love a phrase by dubbing the *Arabian Nights* the fairy godmother of the English novel. In her final chapter she sums up clearly and justly. She is particularly to be commended for the good judgment with which she handles her point (on the whole perhaps the most salient in the book) that the material with which she has been dealing was popular chiefly because it was pseudo-romantic. Just as Bishop Hurd, a pseudo-romantic in criticism, prepared the way for Coleridge, or as Thomson, a pseudo-romantic in landscape poetry, prepared the way for Wordsworth, so "less obviously, but none the less truly, the translators and writers of the oriental tale, together with historians and travelers, were forerunners of Southey, Moore, Byron, Matthew Arnold, Fitzgerald, and many others, on to Kipling in the present day." Such results as these should go far toward convincing those not already under conviction that—notwithstanding all of its enemies and many of its friends to the contrary—the literature of the eighteenth century is quite sufficiently complex and inconsistent to be interesting.

With the heartiest thanks to Miss Conant for what she has done, we venture to suggest some additional facts and considerations which seem to us to enlarge or modify the subject.

In the first place, we doubt if it can be too clearly kept in mind that the oriental movement in fiction extended rather more generally than Miss Conant makes us realize to most other arts, and that as a cult it was regarded by its enemies as no less inimical than the "gothic" to all that was orthodox and "just." Scores of passages show this: for a single instance let us take a part of the fifty-sixth letter in Dr. John Shebbeare's *Letters on the English Nation: By Battista Angeloni, a Jesuit, Who resided many years in London. Translated from the Original Italian*, etc. (1755),—a work which Miss Conant has, strangely enough, neglected to include in her list of pseudo-letters after the manner of Goldsmith's *Citizen of the World*.

The simple and sublime have lost all influence almost every where, all is Chinese or Gothic; every chair in an apartment, the frames of glasses, and tables, must be Chinese: the walls covered with Chinese paper filled with figures which resemble nothing of God's creation, and which a prudent nation would prohibit for the sake of pregnant women.

In one chamber, all the pagods and distorted animals of the east are piled up, and called the beautiful decorations of a chimney-piece; on the sides of the room, lions made of porcelain, grinning and misshapen, are placed on brackets of the Chinese taste, in arbors of flowers made in the same ware, and leaves of brass painted green lying like lovers in the shades of old Arcadia.

Nay, so excessive is the love of Chinese architecture become, that at present the foxhunters would be sorry to break a leg in pursuing their sport in leaping any gate that was not made in the eastern taste of little bits of wood standing in all directions; the connoisseurs of the table delicacies can distinguish between the taste of an ox which eats his hay from a Chinese crib, a hog that is inclosed in a stye of that kind, or a fowl fattened in a coop the fabric of which is in that design, and find great difference in the flavor. . . .

To my unpolite ears, the airs which are sung at present have no longer the imitation of anything which would express passion or sentiment, and the whole merit lyes in the Gothic and Chinese closes and cantabiles, frithered into niceties and divisions, which, like minute carvings, are the certain characteristics of a little taste, that delights more in difficulties than truth, that would rather see a posture-master in all bodily distortion than the graceful attitudes of Dupré on the French theatre of the opera at Paris, in the most exalted manner of dancing.

The Chinese taste is so very prevalent in this city at present, that even pantomime has obliged harlequin to seek shelter in an entertainment, where the scenes and characters are all in the taste of the nation.

A glance at almost any book on the furniture, the gardens, the music, or the cookery of 1750 and thereabouts will confirm the essential truth of Shebbeare's amusing picture. Something is said (pp. 223–225) by Miss Conant about this aspect of the matter, but hardly enough.

Again it is to be observed that this rage for things oriental, and particularly for things Chinese, was partly due to actual contact with the east. Exploration, travel, trade, war, and the great number of books which these brought into being,—all give us help which we must not neglect if we are to understand the full complexity of English interest in the orient. Turn where we will, we meet it; for example, in that curious "Essay upon all sorts of Learning, written by the Athenian Society," which is prefixed to the *Young-Students-Library* (1692) we find in the chapter devoted to history, which is decidedly enlightened,[2] a strikingly large number of books of travel and the like—most of them pointing eastward—set down among the sixty-three "best books" for the historian. There are Chardin's *Voyages into Persia*, *The Embassie of the Five Jesuits into Siam*, Chammont's *Embassie into Siam*, Dapper's *Description of Africk*, Tavernier's *Travels*, a *History of Barbadoes and the Caribbee Islands*, Ogleby's *History of China*, his *Japan*, his *Asia*, and his *Africa*, Rycaut's *History of the Turks* (which Addison makes Will Honeycomb quote in *Spectator*, No. 343), Knowl's (*sic*) *History of the Turks*, *An Historical Relation of the Island of Ceylon in the East Indies*, and *The Travels of Monsieur Thevevot into the Levant*. Thus the trend of serious writing was largely in the paths of trade and travel, and the trend of fiction followed that of serious writing. A part of an essay in *The World* (No. 102, December 12, 1754) bears upon this point:

Besides those words which owe their rise to caprice or accident, there are many which having been long confined to particular professions, offices, districts, climates, etc., are brought into public use by fashion, or the reigning topic on which conversation has happened to dwell for any considerable time. During the great rebellion they talked universally the language of the scriptures. . . . In our own memory the late war, which began at sea, filled our mouths with terms from that element. . . . The peace taught us the language of the secretary's office. . . . With the rails and buildings of the Chinese, we adopted also for a while their language. A doll of that country, we called a joss, and a slight building a pagoda. For that year we talked of nothing but palanquins, nabobs, mandarins, junks, sipoys, etc. To what was this owing, but the war in the East Indies?

At the same time it is true, and particularly true in the case of the material which Miss Conant treats in her fourth chapter ("The Satirical Group"), that the orient was used largely as a point of view. The popular attitude toward neighboring nations was unfavorable; the seventeenth-century "characters" of France, Spain, Ireland, Scotland, and Italy are adverse; and the Frenchman or Dutchman in the drama of the period is, like the Irishman or the Welshman, usually a butt for ridicule. The oriental had the advantage of remoteness,—his habits of thought were quaint and fresh, and there was nothing against him. Moreover, he had other advantages than mere remoteness; he lived in the chosen abode of magic, wealth, wisdom, and gravity. In a romantic period—and in the more imaginative writings of any period—the magic and the fabulous riches of the east would be emphasized; in the eighteenth century, particularly by the moralist and satirist, constant use was made of oriental wisdom uttered with oriental gravity. As these characteristics were developed, the unskilful erred on the side of excess; long before the *Citizen of the World*, Dr. Johnson commended Father Lobo's *Voyage to Abyssinia* because the eastern people described in it were not "either devoid of all sense of humanity, or consummate in all private and social virtues; here are no *Hottentots* without religion, polity, or articulate language; no *Chinese* perfectly polite and completely skilled in all sciences." The oriental in literature very early acquired his characteristic manner of speaking in similes and parables, and this manner was applied with little discrimination to Turks, Chinese, and American Indians. As early as 1706 Charles Gildon, in his *Post-Boy Robb'd of his Mail*, introduced some letters from one Honan, an Asiatic, but of just what country even his friends did not know. As these letters are about to be opened,

"Now shall we (said *Grave*) have Metaphors, Allegories, Exclamations and Interrogations in abundance. Right (pursu'd Church,) for that is the style of the Asiatic Virtuoso's. At least (pursu'd *River*,) if we may credit all that goes in our Language for such."[3]

This sameness of thought and language serves well enough when the oriental is merely, as he so often was, a prodigy constructed for didactic purposes. In such cases the main care of the writer is to take a good long jump away from England. He does not always land in China, or even in the orient. Sometimes he finds his foreign observer among the South Sea islands,[4] or the American Indians.[5] So later, we find American authors (for example, Wirt in his *British Spy* and Jacob Duché in his "Caspipina's Letters") using the eyes of Englishmen, and Matthew Arnold, in *Friendship's Garland*, resorting to a German, the notable Arminius, Baron von Thunder-ten-Tronckh. Primarily, in this species of satire, the search is for a representative of that people who would be most unfavorably struck by the particular faults which it is desired to correct.

Little praise can be given to Miss Conant for her investigations into the oriental material in periodical publications. Indeed the mere existence of such lists as those of the periodical publications in the British Museum, Nichols,[6] Drake,[7] and the Hope Collection,[8] should suffice to check one from venturing to apply the word "complete" (p. xi) to a list of oriental material in periodical publications which includes nothing except English periodicals, and of English periodicals only the *Spectator*, *Guardian*, *Freeholder*, *Rambler*, *Idler*, *Adventurer*, *World*, *Connoisseur*, *Babler*, *Lounger*, *Mirror*, and *Observer*.[9] Ten minutes' use of Drake's *Gleaner*—the work to which one would naturally turn after exhausting Chalmers and the other familiar collections—would have revealed several additional papers of importance. Much more might be found by a careful search through the *Gentleman's Magazine*, in which a great many important periodicals are summarized. Even then there would still remain the British Museum and the "Nichols Newspapers" in the Bodleian. Meanwhile, let us note:

Le Babillard, Vol. III, Nos. 25 ff.
The Champion, I. 300.
Common Sense, July 23, 1737; August 5, 1738.

Flying Post, No. 1.

Free Thinker, Nos. 84, 128, 129.

Friend, No. 8.

Hyp-Doctor, No. 10.

Lay-Monastery, No. 18.

Loiterer, No. 25.

Looker-On, i. 372.

Meddler, No. 11.

Muscovite, Nos. 1–5.

Pharos, Nos. 11, 12.

Philanthrope, No. 24.

Prater, Nos. 13, 15, 28.

Visitor, Nos. 17, 24, 25, 26.

The handling of the *Citizen of the World* device also leaves a good deal to be desired in the matter of completeness, although here the omissions are less conspicuous than in the case of the periodical publications. The device of a foreigner visiting the country to be satirized, and writing letters about it which are accidentally translated and made public, is still vital and effective, as is shown by Mr. Howells's *Traveller from Altruria* and *Through the Eye of a Needle*, Mr. Dickinson's *Letters from a Chinese Official*, and—with a certain difference—Mr. Irwin's *Letters of a Japanese School-Boy*. Miss Conant follows this interesting little genre down from Marana (or whoever wrote *The Turkish Spy*) through Montesquieu and the rest to Goldsmith's *Citizen of the World* and beyond, not forgetting to mention Lord Lyttelton's *Letters from a Persian in England* and Horace Walpole's *Letters from Xo Ho*, as well as the Marquis d'Argens's *Chinese Letters* and others, and Madame de Graffigny's *Lettres d'une péruvienne*. She even goes so far afield as to include Defoe's *Consolidator* and his *Tour through Great Britain*.

She fails, however, to mention several examples; and so it is perhaps worth while to arrange chronologically some instances of the genre which occur before 1787 and which are not noticed in this book:

(1) 1704. Swift's hint given opposite the title-page of his *Tale of a Tub*.

(2) 1706. Charles Gildon's *Post-Boy Robb'd of his Mail; or, the Pacquet Broke Open, Consisting of Letters of Love and Gallantry, and all Miscellaneous Subjects; In which are Discovered the Vertues, Vices, Follies, Humors and Intrigues of Mankind*.

(3) 1714. *The Muscovite*. (See the catalogue of the Hope Collection, page 29, No. 108.)

(4) 1728. *The Flying Post*, No. 1.

(5) 1731. *The Hyp-Doctor*, No. 10.

(6) 1744. *The Meddler*, No. 11.

(7) 1749 or 1750. Dr. William Dodd's *The African Prince now in England, to Zara at his Father's Court and Zara's Answer*. (Watt dates this work 1750; the *Dictionary of National Biography* gives 1749.)

(8) 1752. *Lettres iroquoises*.

(9) 1755. John Shebbeare, *Letters on the English Nation: By Battista Angeloni, a Jesuit, Who resided many years in London. Translated from the Original Italian, by the Author of the Marriage Act a Novel*.

(10) 1755. *The Friend*, No. 8.

(11) 1760. *The Visitor*, No. 17.

(12) 1760–61. *The Algerine Spy*.

(13) 1766. *L'Espion Americain en Europe, ou Lettres Illinoises*.

(14) 1774. Jacob Duché, *Observations on a Variety of Subjects, Literary, Moral and Religious; in a Series of Original Letters, written by a Gentleman of Foreign Extraction, who resided some time in Philadelphia*. (Better known as "Caspipina's Letters," their supposed author being one Tamoc Caspipina, "an acrostic upon the full title of the office which Duché then

held: 'The Assistant Minister of Christ Church and St. Peter's in Philadelphia in North America.'" Tyler, *Literary History of the American Revolution*, ii. 293 note.)

(15) 1775. *An Historical Epistle, from Omiah, to the Queen of Otaheite; being his Remarks on the English Nation. With notes by the Editor.*

Books do not stand or fall by their bibliographies, however; and from even fewer cases than she has studied Miss Conant might safely have drawn the conclusions which entitle her book to consideration among the not very large number of serviceable studies in special phases of the literature of the eighteenth century.

John Dunton's
Letters from New England

EVEN though the historical literature of New England were far richer than it is in such diaries as those of Samuel Sewall and Cotton Mather and in such observations as those of Lechford and Josselyn, there would still be an honorable place for such a document as we apparently have in John Dunton's *Letters from New England*. Nothing could be more welcome than the record of a London bookseller who spent five months in Boston in the critical year 1686, whose point of view is that of a friendly outsider, whose acquaintance included not merely the clergy and the magistrates but many other types as well, whose observation comprehended Indians, adventurers, tavern-keepers, picnics, sermons, and executions, and whose portraits of people are perhaps more numerous, as they certainly are more vivid, than those of almost any other writer of that time and place. The wonder would seem to be that more extensive use has not been made of a record of which the date, contents, and point of view lead us to expect so much. Not that Dunton has been wholly neglected: many historians [10] have made use of him, and one or two [11] have praised in the highest terms the truthfulness and insight of his portraits. These portraits do, indeed, deserve our close attention. But first let us see who Dunton was and how he came to write about New England.

John Dunton [12] was born on May 4–14, 1659. His father, previously Fellow of Trinity College, Cambridge, and then rector of Graffham in Huntingdonshire, was the third John Dunton in succession to be a minister. Our John Dunton, unable to keep up this tradition, was apprenticed, when between fourteen and fifteen years old, to Thomas Parkhurst, the London bookseller, who was later to bring out Cotton Mather's *Magnalia*. Dunton's apprenticeship seems not to have been wholly industrious. When it ceased, apparently in 1681, he commenced bookseller on his own account. His first publication was entered in Michaelmas Term of 1681.[13] Many others followed, one of them a collection of funeral sermons, *The House of Weeping*, 1682, by his father. On August 3, 1682, he married Elizabeth, daughter of Samuel Annesley, D.D. For a while "prosperity and success were the common course of Providence,"[14] but presently "there came a universal damp upon Trade,"[14] and Dunton, having £500 due him in New England, decided to "ramble" thither.

In November,[15] 1685, accordingly, in the ship *Susannah and Thomas*, Captain Thomas Jenner, he set sail from the Downs for Boston. After a very long and unpleasant voyage, in the course of which he either saw or just missed seeing an amazing variety of fishes and marine animals—including an alligator[16]—Dunton reached Boston. The date of his arrival has been variously stated. Whitmore[17] puts it "within a day or two of February 10," 1686. Palfrey,[18] probably following John Nichols,[19] puts it in March. John Bowyer Nichols[20] prefers February. We have, to be sure, Dunton's own word that he was at sea "above four months."[21] But as for that, we have also Dunton's word[22] that he spent ten months in New England, although he declares that he sailed for home on July 5, 1686,[23]—an assertion wholly irreconcilable with the statement that he set sail on either November 2 or November 20, and spent four months at sea.

The true date appears as soon as we examine Sewall's *Diary*. For we know from Dunton[24] that he sailed with Captain Thomas Jenner, and we have, furthermore, a rather explicit account[25] of his arrival at Boston. "We . . . Landed near the Castle, within a mile of Boston, where we lay that Night; . . . Having refresh'd our selves the first Night at the Castle, where . . . we were very civilly treated by the Governour,[26] the next morning we bent our Course for Boston; . . . over the Ice."

Sewall's account, although it makes no mention of John Dunton, agrees in all these circumstances and also supplies the date:[27]

Wednesday, Jan[r] 27. [1686] . . . Is talk of a Ship below and some think it may be Jenner from London.

Thorsday, January 28, Mr. Jenner having lodged at Capt. Clap's last night, with Mr. Belcher and others, come near twenty together to Serj[t] Bull's over the Ice and bring the News of the Rose Frigot ready to come and bring Mr. Randolph, who is to be Deputy Governour, and Mr. Dudley Governour. . . . The Town much filled with this discourse. . . . When Mr. Jenner came in the Magistrates went all off the Bench to hear his News in the Lobby.[28]

It is entirely clear, therefore, that John Dunton arrived in Boston Harbor on the evening of January 27, 1686, and reached the city on the following day. Dunton's own chronology is so shaky that it is a satisfaction to be able to fix this date by evidence from a trustworthy source.

On February 16, 1686, Dunton was made a freeman of Boston,[29] and about the same time he opened his bookshop at Mr. Richard Wilkins's, "opposite to the Town-House," where he also lodged. He next presented various letters of introduction and began to look about him. Business did not, apparently, prevent him from making many "rambles" to neighboring towns or from cultivating the acquaintance of all who showed themselves friendly. He saw the execution of Morgan on March 11, and the arrival of Randolph on May 14. On July 5 he sailed for London, where he arrived one month later.[30]

Dunton's subsequent career may be very briefly reviewed.

He found his affairs involved in debt, was obliged to remain in hiding for ten months,[31] and then "took a trip over to Holland, Flanders, Germany, &c."[32] He returned to London on November 15, 1688,[33] and resumed business at "the sign of the Black Raven . . . opposite to the Poultry Compter."[33] There for ten years he published, compiled, and projected to his heart's content. He was temporarily saddened by the death of his wife in 1697, but remarried within a year, went to Ireland on a bookselling venture, returned, published his famous *Life and Errors* in 1705, wrote profusely and violently until 1723, and died in obscurity ten years later.

This career certainly leaves the impression of an increasingly irresponsible person. As such John Dunton seems to have been regarded by many of his contemporaries. Swift, in the *Tale of a Tub* (1704), alludes to Dunton's voluminous and indiscriminate publishing projects,[34] and in his *Publick Spirit of the Whigs* (1714) ironically praises Dunton's "famous tract entitled *Neck or Nothing*," which "must be allowed to be the shrewdest piece, and written with the most spirit, of any which has appeared from that side since the change of the ministry."[35] The Earl of Sunderland thought him "an impudent Fellow," who had "abused the greatest men in the Nation."[36] The writer of the footnote on Dunton in the *Dunciad* (ii. 144) agrees with Sunderland: "a broken[37] bookseller," the annotator calls him, "and an abusive scribbler. He wrote *Neck or Nothing*, a violent satire on some Ministers of State; a libel on the Duke of Devonshire and the Bishop of Peterborough, &c."[38] The London *Post* said of Dunton, "In spite of *native Dulness* [he] resolves to be a Wit, as he always did to be a Knave, in spite of . . . a whole volume of repentance."[39] Charges of financial untrustworthiness are also abundant,[40] though vague, and a certain R. Key seems to indicate that Dunton was known to be licentious in personal conduct.[41] Certainly there is no lack of nastiness in some of

Dunton's writings,[42] however admirable the moral tone of most of them. I fancy Dunton to have had an utterly irresponsible and fluctuating nature, in which by turns immorality, repentance, credulity, and vindictiveness directed his unceasing frenzy for publication. "Mr. John Dunton, lunatick," is the succinct characterization of him in the second number of the *Monitor* (1714),[43] and as early as 1707 Thomas Hearne records, "There is publish'd The II^d Part of the *Pulpit Fool*, by John Dunton a poor craz'd silly Fellow."[44] Certainly Dunton becomes less puzzling if we regard him, at least in his later years, as partially insane. Yet his publications contain so much that is not his own, and the evidence of others about him is so full of prejudice and obscurity, that it is a very difficult matter to decide.

The Letters from New England are eight in number, one of them apparently written from West Cowes, six from Boston, and one after the return to London.

The first, "From West-Cowes, in the Isle of Wight, Octob. 25th, 1685," is addressed to his wife and narrates the embarkation and the beginning of the voyage. It is signed "Yrs Entirely / John Dunton."

The second letter, written from Boston, dated February 17, 1685–6, and addressed "To My Only Brother Mr. Lake Dunton. Lately Return'd from Surat in the East-Indies," completes the account of the voyage. It is signed "Your truly Loving and / Affectionate Brother, / Philaret."[45]

The third letter, dated from Boston, March 25, 1686, is addressed to Mr. George Larkin, at London, and is signed "Philaret." This letter, which is one of the most important of the series, must have required a considerable sum in postage, for in Whitmore's edition it fills about ninety pages. In it, declares Dunton:

I shall observe this method:

1. Give you an Account of my Reception at Boston:
2. The Character of my Boston Landlord, his Wife and Daughter;
3. Give you an Account of my being admitted into the Freedom of this City:
4. I shall next describe the Town of Boston, it being the Metropolis of New-England; and say something of the Government, Law, and Customs thereof.
5. I shall relate the Visits I made, the Remarkable Friendships I contracted, and shall conclude with the character of Madam Brick as the Flower of Boston, and some other Ladyes, And I'll omit nothing that happened (if remarkable) during my stay here. And in all this I will not copy from others, as is usual with most Travellers, but relate my own Observations.⁴⁶

In the fourth letter, without date or place, but addressed to Dunton's cousin, John Woolhurst, at London, and signed "Philaret," we have an account of Dunton's "rambles"⁴⁷ to Charlestown, Medford, New-Town, Winnisimet,⁴⁸ Lynn, Nantascot, Wissaguset,⁴⁹ Braintree, Dorchester, and Roxbury. In the course of this letter we find short descriptions of these towns, a good deal about Indians, and an account of the apostle Eliot.

The fifth letter, undated, is to Dunton's father-in-law, Dr. Samuel Annesley, from his "Most Dutiful Son-in-Law, Philaret." It contains an account of the conversion of the Indians, for which Dunton modestly disclaims originality.⁵⁰

The sixth letter is without date, but it contains letters between Dunton and his apprentice Palmer, which in the *Life and Errors*⁵¹ are dated April 4, 1686, and April 10, 1686. It is addressed to his wife and is signed "Your ever Faithful / Philaret." It describes his ramble to Salem, whither he went alone, "save that by an Intercourse of Souls, my Dear, I had your Company."⁵²

The seventh letter, the last of those supposed to have been written from Boston, is addressed "To My Beloved Sister,

Mrs. Sarah Dunton." It contains information about various matters relating to Indians, descriptions of Wenham and Ipswich, and two portraits of people. It has no date.[53]

The final letter, "To Mr. Richard Wilkins in Boston in New England," briefly assures his former landlord of Dunton's safe arrival in London and his happy reunion with his wife.

The earliest version of Dunton's account of New England is in the *Life and Errors* (1705).[54] That account was very inadequately reprinted in 1814 in the *Massachusetts Historical Collections*.[55] In 1818 John Bowyer Nichols did much better: he not only reprinted the *Life and Errors* much more accurately and fully,[56] but also added selections from Dunton's other works, prefixed a good memoir, and appended a calendar of the Dunton MS. in the Bodleian Library.[57]

From these manuscripts a copy of the eight Letters from New England was made[58] under the supervision of Colonel Joseph L. Chester for the use of William Henry Whitmore, who first printed the *Letters from New England* in 1867 for the Prince Society. We are under great obligations to Whitmore for having made these letters accessible. One wishes very much, however, that he had reprinted the whole of the Chester MS.: to have done so would have revealed Dunton's vulgarity and his excursiveness, which, however unattractive, are important if we wish to know him. Even more does one wish that Whitmore had indicated every erasure and interpolation in the Chester MS., for these bear vitally upon the question of the date and genuineness of the Letters, questions which Whitmore hardly raised at all.

One question which Whitmore did raise, however, and which he did much to settle, is the question of Dunton's importance as an original authority. Whitmore was able to show that nearly everything that Dunton tells us about the Indians is copied almost verbatim from either Roger Williams or Cotton Mather, though Dunton often takes pains to work over the information into monologues from imaginary persons whom he met on his rambles. Whitmore further shows borrowings from Josselyn's *Two Voyages* (1674) and from J. W.'s *Letter from New England* (1682). In all, Whitmore points out about thirty cases in which, without acknowledgment, Dunton appropriates rather long passages from earlier writers. This was much more than a curious discovery, for it very importantly modified the idea of the value and purpose of the book which we might otherwise have had.

When so much has been pointed out that is not original, one is naturally moved to see if there may not be still more. It appears that there is much more.

Here, for example, is an episode of Dunton's voyage and beside it a passage from Josselyn's *Two Voyages*:

JOSSELYN	DUNTON
About 8 of the clock at night, a flame settled upon the main mast, it was about the bigness of a great Candle, and is called by our Seamen St. *Elmes* fire, it comes before a storm, and is commonly thought to be a Spirit; if two appear they prognosticate safety: These are known to the learned by the names of *Castor* and *Pollux*, to the *Italians* by St. *Nicholas* and St. *Hermes*, by the *Spaniards* called *Corpos Santos* (ed. Veazie, p. 8).	On the next Day, in the Captain's Cabin, we had hot debates about a Flame, which sometimes settles upon the main mast of a Ship . . . It is about the bigness of a good large Candle, and was call'd by the Seamen St. Ellines Fire; it usually comes before a storm, and is commonly thought to be a Spirit; and here's the conjuration of it, that tho' one is look'd upon as an ill Omen, yet if two appear, they are said to Prognosticate Safety. These are known to the Learned by the names of Castor and Pollux: to the Italians, by St. Nicholas and St. Hermes, and are by the Spaniards called Corpus Santos (*Letters*, p. 31).

One cannot help wondering, after this, if the various sailors who told Dunton so much about the different fish they had met,[59] had not managed to commit to memory large portions of some not very reliable work on natural history, the identity of which has thus far eluded our search.

In the fifth letter there is a rather distinct bit of description of the country through which Dunton rode on his trip to Natick. The letter is addressed to Dr. Annesley:

As we rid along that lovely valley I have mention'd, Sir, we saw many lovely Lakes or Ponds, well stored with Fish and Beavers: These, they tell me, are the original of all the great Rivers in the Countrey, of which there are many, besides lesser Streams, manifesting the Goodness of the Soil, which is in some places black, in others red, with clay, Gravel, Sand and Loom, and very deep in some places, as in the Valleys and Swamps, which are low grounds, and bottoms, infinitely thick set with Trees and Bushes of all sorts; others having no other Shrubs or Trees growing but Spruce, under the Shades whereof we Rambled two or three miles together, being goodly large Trees, and convenient for Masts and Sail-Yards (*Letters*, p. 216).

Josselyn had written:

Within these valleys are spacious lakes or ponds well stored with Fish and Beavers; the original of all the great Rivers in the Countrie, of which there are many with lesser streams (wherein are an infinite of fish) manifesting the goodness of the soil which is black, red-clay, gravel, sand, loom, and very deep in some places, as in the valleys and swamps, which are low grounds and bottoms infinitely thick set with Trees and Bushes of all sorts for the most part, others having no other shrub or Tree growing, but spruse, under the shades whereof you may freely walk two or three mile together; being goodly large Trees, and convenient for masts and sail-yards (*Two Voyages*, pp. 37–38).

It will be noticed that Dunton relies upon the authority of Josselyn to determine even the length of his ramble. Josselyn writes: "you may walk freely two or three mile together." Dunton echoes: "We rambled two or three miles together." No traveller ever followed his Baedeker more faithfully.

That Josselyn actually was Dunton's Baedeker appears

when we examine the short descriptions of the various towns which Dunton visited in his rambles. There are twelve of them in all,[60] and the description of each[61] is taken almost verbatim from Josselyn. The account of Nantascot is a fair example:

Josselyn	Dunton
. . . a Town called *Nantascot*, which is two Leagues from *Boston*, where Ships commonly cast Anchor.	Being come to Nantascot we took a survey of the Town, which is a Sea-Port, about two Leagues from Boston, where ships commonly cast Anchor: near which is Pullin Point, so called,
Pullin-point is so called, because the Boats are . . . haled against the Tide which is very strong, it is the usual Channel for Boats to pass into *Mattachusets-Bay*.	because the Boats are haled against the Tide, which is very strong. It is the usual Channel for Boats to pass into the Massachusetts Bay. On the South Side of the Passage there is an Island containing about Eight Acres of ground; Upon a rising Hill within this Island is mounted a Castle. Here 'twas we first Landed, when I came into the Countrey; Tho' this Castle be no stately Edifice, nor very strong, being built with Brick and Stone, yet it commands the Entrance, so that no Ship can pass by without its leave: It is kept by a Captain, under whom is a Master-Gunner, and some others.
There is an Island on the South-side of the passage containing eight Acres of ground. Upon a rising hill within this Island is mounted a Castle commanding the entrance, no stately Edifice, nor strong; built with Brick and Stone, kept by a Captain, under whom is a master-Gunner and others.	
. . . The *Bay* is large,	I then took a transient view of Pullin-Point. The Bay is large, and has Boston in view, as soon as you enter into it: It is made by many Islands, the chiefest of which is the Dear Island, which is within a flight shot of Pullin-Point: It is called Dear Island, because great store of Deer were wont to swim thither from the main Land: We then viewed Bird Island, Glass-Island, State[62]-Island, and the Governour's Garden, where the first Apple trees in the Countrey were planted, and there
made by many Islands, the chief *Deere*-Island, which is within a flight shot of *Pullin-point*, great store of *Deere* were wont to swim thither from the Main; then *Bird*-Island, *Glass*-Island, *Slate*-Island, the Governours Garden, where the first Apple-Trees in the Countrey were planted, and a vin-yard; then *Round*-Island, and *Noddles*-Island not far from *Charles*-Town:	

Josselyn	Dunton
most of these Islands lye on the North-side of the *Bay* (pp. 122–123).	also was planted a Vineyard: Then there is Round Island, so called from the figure of it, and last of all Noddles Island, not far from Charles-Town. Most of these Islands lie on the North-Side of the Bay (*Letters*, pp. 179–180).

All this does not prove that Dunton did not visit these places, for we know that he saw Boston with his own eyes, even though he avails himself of Josselyn's description of it. But it is clear that we cannot use Dunton's descriptions to show what these towns were like in 1686.

It is now time to raise the whole question of the date and genuineness[63] of these Letters. In his preface Whitmore observes:[64]

In regard to the point as to these being the letters written at the time, Mr. Chester says that he does not regard them as letters actually sent from Boston to the parties addressed. They were all written in a uniform hand, on uniform paper, and may be considered rather as a journal, kept probably during his sojourn at Boston, and intended for publication. The other theory would be that this was his letter-book, in which, according to the custom of the times, he kept copies of the letters sent.

Mr. Chester adds: "The interpolations and emendations are numerous, and some of them clearly of a later date. Sometimes entire pages were evidently after-thoughts, and occur at the end of the volume, being referred to by marks in the body of the MSS."

Further than this Whitmore did not go. We do not know, therefore, which pages were added; indeed we know hardly anything about the author's minor changes except what we can learn from the Chester MS. in the library of the New England Historic Genealogical Society. A week at the Bodleian might clear up many difficulties. Nevertheless, with the text as we have it something can be done.

On the very first page of the *Letters from New England* there is a note, which Whitmore prints as a footnote, in which Dunton refers by page to his "lately published Farewell to Dublin." The farewell to Dublin—the actual event—took place late in December of 1698, and the *Dublin Scuffle*, of which the Farewell seems to have formed a part, was not published until 1699. Again, at the very end[65] of his Letters, and also in his account of the negligence of his apprentice,[66] Dunton has passages in which he gets nearly a year ahead of the date which must be assumed for the eighth letter, if we are to suppose that the entire manuscript represents a body of letters actually sent from New England. It is therefore at least clear that we have in the Chester MS. certain passages which could not have been written from Boston in the year 1686. It remains to ask, then, whether such passages are numerous and incorporated in the letters, or whether they constitute merely a few such notes as the two just cited.

In the second letter, dated March 25, 1686, we have a reference to "Major Dudley, afterwards President."[67] Now Joseph Dudley's commission as President did not arrive until May, 1686.[68] Again, we have in the same letter, under date March 25, 1686, the following sentence: "Another Occurence that happened whilst I was here, was, the Arrival of the Rose Frigot from England with a New Charter brought over by one Rundel" [Randolph].[69] But this event did not take place until May 14, 1686.[70] However, it may be urged that Dunton should be forgiven any slight confusion of dates, provided he limits himself in these Letters to the narration of events which occurred before his departure, on July 5, 1686.

But Dunton does not by any means keep within even these rather generous limits. His account of John Eliot[71] is largely taken verbatim from Cotton Mather's *Life of Eliot*, which was not published until 1691.[72] He refers[73] to the publication of the life of Nathaniel Mather, which did not appear until

1689.[74] He quotes from Increase Mather's letter to Dr. John Leusden, which is dated July 12, 1687.[75] More curious still is a remark[76] made in connection with Cotton Mather. "Cotton Mather . . . has very lately finish'd a Church-History of New-England, which I'm going to print." Now, as every reader of Cotton Mather's *Diary* knows, the *Magnalia* was not finished until 1697.[77] Another allusion,[78] which is somewhat less obvious, carries the date still further forward. After portraying the admirable character of Comfort Wilkins, Mrs. Green, and Madam Brick, Dunton remarks, "And now Sir Daniel, I suppose you'll give some grains of Allowance to Sir John: For I believe such Females as these, wou'd set even a Gentleman of more Reformation, a longing for further Acquaintance with 'em, without making it a Crime."[79] This allusion can be to no one but Daniel Defoe, who in reply to the attacks made upon his *Reformation of Manners* (1702), published *More Reformation.* | *A* | *Satyr* | *Upon* | *Himself.* | *By the Author Of* | *The True Born English-Man.* But Defoe's *More Reformation* was not entered for publication until Michaelmas Term of 1703,[80] and bears the date 1703 upon its title-page. All of these passages, except one, throw the date forward indefinitely from 1686. The only passage which suggests two limits is the very interesting one in connection with the *Magnalia*, for it is extremely unlikely that after 1702, in which year the *Magnalia* was published by Thomas Parkhurst, Dunton would have written, even in the rough draft of these Letters, that the *Magnalia* was a work "which I'm going to print." Except for this clause, I see nothing in the Letters to show that they were not written after the *Life and Errors* (1705).[81] But without use of the MS. at the Bodleian, it is impossible to do more, though it is certainly impossible to do less, than to cast general doubt upon the date of the entire work.

We can immediately answer in the negative the question,

Is this work in its present form a body of actual letters? It is clear that the Letters as we have them have been worked over to make a book, if, indeed, they ever were actual letters. The mere fact that Dunton frequently appeals to "the reader"[82] suffices to show this, if, indeed, any further evidence were needed than the inordinate length and the general tone of the work.[83]

But although it is clear that the author intended to make a book, it is equally clear that he had not finished preparing the copy for the press. In the Chester MS., for instance, we have at one point[84] the note: "Here insert the Poem upon Punch, out of Ratcliff's Rambles."[85]

That at least a portion of the composition of these Letters was after Dunton had forgotten (if he ever knew them by experience) some of the details of his visit is suggested by these and other scattered bits of evidence. For instance, it is remarkable to find that, although Dunton assures us of the intimacy of his acquaintance with such men as Higginson, Gerrish, and Hubbard, he gets their names wrong, as well as the names of other people[86] who are incidentally mentioned. Dunton's almost complete omission of matters of public concern is another fact in point. For example, he says nothing whatever about the epidemic of small-pox, although so great was the affliction that March 25, 1686, the very date of the letter wherein so many of his characters occur, was "appointed . . . to be kept as a Day of Solemn Humiliation and Prayer throughout this Colony." The General Court had even voted to "recommend it to the Elders and Ministers of the respective Churches, to promote this work on the said day; forbidding Servile Labour to all People within this Jurisdiction, thereon."[87] All this could hardly have occurred if the Letters in their present form were based upon real letters, or upon a journal dating from the period of his actual visit.

In fact, it must be granted that Dunton is a highly unreliable person, whose narrative cannot be accepted as a record of historical fact. As an instance of this let me cite the account of the execution of Morgan.[88] Dunton assures us that after the sermon he and Cotton Mather rode to the place of execution, that a great crowd followed, and that from where he was he caught occasional glimpses of Morgan.[89] But if Dunton had been where he says he was on this occasion, he could have seen Morgan without difficulty, for we know that Cotton Mather *walked beside the criminal to the place of the execution.*[90] The close of this day of Morgan's execution was made happy for Dunton by a picnic. He tells us that he and half a dozen others got a boat and rowed to Governor's Island, had a kind of barbecue, treated the ladies, and returned in the evening.[91] Now a person who has just witnessed an execution is certainly entitled to go upon a picnic if he so desires. And yet nothing would seem to be more discouraging than certain conditions on the day of this picnic, the date of which was March 11. The winter had been very severe, and although the harbor was no longer frozen over, it had but recently begun to open.[92] Moreover, Morgan was not "turned off" until half-past five;[93] so Dunton could hardly have started on his picnic before dark; and, to make the affair seem even more dismal, we find from Sewall's *Diary* that it rained nearly all the evening.[93] All that can be said, and all that needs to be said, is that Dunton's accounts of the execution and of the picnic make a remarkable contrast, and that is probably what he was chiefly aiming at.

It remains to consider the most interesting part of the Letters,—the portraits of people.

It is more than a coincidence that in speaking of these portraits Dunton almost always employs the same word. He uses it on his title-page, he uses it in outlining the third letter (for our immediate purpose the most important of them all), and he often uses it in introducing or concluding his accounts of particular people. That word is "character," as employed in the following sentence: "And thus, Reader, I have given you the Character of another of my Female Friends in Boston."[94]

The "character" in this sense of the word, was a well-recognized, prolific, popular, and influential form in English literature of the seventeenth century.[95] We are fortunate in having several contemporary definitions of it, the most explicit and interesting of which is that in a school-book, published in 1665 by Ra[lph] Johnson, who gives not only a definition of the character but also three rules for making one. The full title of the book, of which the Harvard College Library contains a copy, is as follows:

The | Scholars Guide | From the Accidence to the | University. | Or, | Short, Plain, and Easie Rules for per-|forming all manner of Exercise in the Grammar School, viz. | Rules for Spelling, Orthography, Pointing, Construing, | Parsing, making Latine, placing Latine, Variation, Am-plifica-|tion, Allusion, Imitation, Observation, Moving-passion. | As Also | Rules for making Colloquys, Essays, Fables, Prosopo-|pæia's, Characters, Themes, Epistles, Orations, Declama-|tions of all sorts. | Together With | Rules for Translation, Variation, Imitation, | Carmen, | Epi-|grams, Dialogues, Eccho's, Epitaphs, Hymns | Anagrams, | Acrostichs, Chronostichs, &c | By Ra[lph] Johnson Schoolmaster. |[motto]| London,| Printed for Tho. Pierrepont at the Sun in St Pauls Churchyard, 1665.

The definition and rules[96] are these:

A character is a witty and facetious description of the nature and qualities of some person, or sort of people.

1. Chuse a Subject, viz. such a sort of men as will admit of variety of observation, such be, drunkards, usurers, lyars, taylors, excise-men, travellers, pedlars, merchants, tapsters, lawyers, an upstart gentleman, a young Justice, a Constable, an Alderman, and the like.

2. Express their natures, qualities, conditions, practices, tools, desires, aims, or ends, by witty Allegories, or Allusions, to things or terms in

nature, or art, of like nature and resemblance, still striving for wit and pleasantness, together with tart nipping jerks about their vices or miscarriages.

3. Conclude with some witty and neat passage, leaving them to the effect of their follies or studies.

It would be merely speculation, though not absurd speculation, to say that John Dunton himself may have had to commit this passage to memory; but it is surely not speculation to infer, merely from the presence of a definition of the "character" in a single book of this kind, that the form was generally recognized and that it was practised in schools just when that fact might easily have influenced Dunton.

That inference can be amply supported from other definitions of the character and from the existence of a very large number of books containing characters. Let us first supplement Johnson's definition from other seventeenth-century sources, and then consider some of the principal books of characters that Dunton may have known.

In 1614, just after the shameful death of Sir Thomas Overbury, there appeared a famous collection of characters by Overbury and his friends. The first edition, containing twenty-one characters, was soon followed by others with additional characters. The ninth impression,[97] 1616, has no fewer than eighty-two characters, of which one is a definition of a character, as follows:

To square out a character by our English levell it is a picture (reall or personall) quaintly drawne, in various colours, all of them heightned by one shadowing.

It is a quick and soft touch of many strings, all shutting up in one musicall close; it is wits descant on any plaine song.[98]

Although the author of this, by practising the quaintness which he preaches, may seem to have confused the subject rather than defined it, yet in one important respect he does modify the impression left by Johnson: he shows that the character may have for its subject a thing as well as a person. As a matter of fact, there are a great many impersonal characters.[99]

Another modification needs to be made in Johnson's definition—or rather in the impression left by his rules; the character is by no means necessarily adverse. Fuller's "Holy State" is more than three times as large as his "Profane State"; Hall gives us eleven "Characterisms of Virtues"; Earle has such types as a Grave Divine, a Contemplative Man, a Good Old Man; Overbury has A Wise Man, A Noble Spirit, and many others. In fact, almost every writer of characters except Samuel Butler composed many that were not adverse.

Various other character-writers[100] contribute to a definition. They show us that the character is brief,[101] witty,[102] and didactic in purpose.[103] They also show us—and this is important in considering Dunton—that the character is generic though at the same time faithful to life,[104] and that the writer of characters intentionally exaggerates[105] by making the good people better than in real life and the bad people worse.[106]

It is perhaps beginning to be clear that the character was a popular and prolific form. Bishop Hall's *Characters of Virtues and Vices* (1608) contained twenty-six separate characters; Overbury's characters, eighty-two in all, reached an eighteenth impression in 1664; Earle's *Microcosmography*, first published in 1628, contained seventy-eight characters and reached an eighth edition within sixteen years. Thomas Fuller's *The Holy and the Profane State* (1642), which contained forty-nine characters, went through at least four editions by 1663. Samuel Butler's characters, posthumously published, number no fewer than one hundred and eighty-seven. These are merely the greater names. In addition there were scores by minor or anonymous authors, and also—

particularly after the beginning of the Civil War—an immense number of pamphlets containing single characters. It would, in fact, be an entirely sober statement to say that when Dunton sailed for New England he might, had he collected character books as George Thomason did his pamphlets, have been the possessor of between three and four hundred of these volumes, containing in all considerably over a thousand separate characters.[107]

But let me not by mentioning George Thomason seem to disparage the labors of John Dunton, particularly with reference to the character. For the fact is that of the portraits in the *Letters from New England*—Mr. Heath, Dr. Bullivant, the jailer, Mrs. Green, the Widow Brick, and all the rest of them—no fewer than thirty-two are, either wholly or in part, taken almost verbatim from such books of characters as we have been discussing. The discovery of this fact, which radically modifies our estimate of the *Letters*, is the chief occasion for this paper.

To see how he does it let us place side by side Dunton's character of Mr. Heath[108] and Thomas Fuller's character of "The Good Merchant" in the *Holy and the Profane State* (1642):[109]

FULLER	DUNTON
	The next I'll mention shall be Mr. Heath—a grave and sober Merchant: And were I now to write the Character of a good Merchant, I wou'd as soon take him for the Exemplar of one, as any Man I know. This I am sure,
. . . He wrongs not the buyer in number, weight, or measure.	he never wrongs the Man that buys of him, in Number, Weight or Measure. For 'tis his Judgment that these are
These are the landmarks of all trading, which must not be removed: for such cozenage were worse than open felony. First, Because they rob a man	the Statute Laws of Trade, which, like those of the Medes and Persians, must never be remov'd; and I have heard him say that such a Cozenage is

FULLER

DUNTON

of his purse and never bid him stand. . . . Thirdly, as much as lies in their power, they endeavour to make God accessory to their cozenage, . . . For God is the principal clerk of the market: *all the weights of the bag are his work.* Prov. xvi. 11.

2. He never warrants any ware for good, but what is so indeed . . . 5. He makes no advantage of his chapman's ignorance, chiefly if referring himself to his honesty: where the seller's conscience is all the buyer's skill, who makes him both seller and judge, so that he doth not so much ask as order what he must pay.

. . . When one told old Bishop Latimer that the cutler had cozened him in making him pay twopence for a knife, not in those days worth a penny:

No, quoth Latimer, he cozened not me, but his own conscience. One the other side, St. Augustine[110] tells us of a seller, who out of ignorance asked for a book far less than it was worth; and the buyer (conceive himself to be the man if you please) of his own accord gave him the full value thereof.

worse than open Felony; because they rob a Man of 's Purse, and never bid him stand; and besides that they Endeavour to make God accessory to their cozenage by false weights: For God is the Principal Clerk of the Market: All the Weights of the Bag (as Solomon tells us, Prov. 16, 11,) being his Work. There are two things remarkable in him, (and I will instance no more.) One is, That he never warrants any Ware for good, but what is so indeed: And the other, That he makes no Advantage of his Chapman's ignorance, especially if he referrs himself to his Honesty. Where the Conscience of the Seller is all the Skill of the Buyer, the Seller is made the Judge, so that he doth not so much ask as Order what he must pay. I have read that old Bishop Latimer once bought a knife that cost him two pence (which was it seems accounted a great Price in those days), and shewing it unto his Friend, he told him, The Cutler had cozen'd him, for the knife was not worth a penny: No, replied Latimer, he cozen'd not me, but his own Conscience. So far from that was this honest Gentleman, that when a Bookseller (that shall be nameless) did out of Ignorance demand less for a Book than it was truly worth, he of his own accord gave him the full value of it. This honest Gentleman did me the favour to be my daily Visitor, and has brought me acquainted with one Mr. Gore of New York, with whom I trade, which I hope will be to my advantage.

The character of Daniel Epes[111] of Salem is worth noting,

partly because it occurs in the *Life and Errors*[112] though not in the *Letters*, and partly because in forming this portrait Dunton, instead of taking a single earlier character, as he usually does, has combined Earle's "Downright Scholar" and his "Contemplative Man,"[113] both printed in 1628:

EARLE	DUNTON
	I must also remember the great civilities I met at Salem from Mr. *Epes*, (the most eminent Schoolmaster in New-England): He hath sent many Scholars to the University in New-England. He is much of a Gentleman;
He has not humbled his meditations to the industry of complement, nor afflicted his brain in an elaborate leg. . . . He cannot kiss his hand and cry, madam, nor talk idle enough to bear her company. . . . The hermitage of his study has made him somewhat uncouth in the world, . . . He will not lose his time by being busy, or make so poor a use of the world as to hug and embrace it.	yet has not humbled his meditations to the industry of compliments, nor afflicted his brain in an elaborate leg, (he cannot kiss his hand, and cry, Madam, your humble servant, nor talk idle enough to bear her company). But though a School, and the Hermitage of his Study, has made him uncourtly, yet (which is a finer accomplishment) he is a person of solid Learning; and does not, like some Authors, lose his time by being busy about nothing, nor make so poor a use of the World, as to hug and embrace it.

A few of Dunton's minor figures, who have no names, are also copied from earlier books of characters. Such are the host at Gravesend, the jailer at Boston, and the troublesome landlord at Lynn.[114] The first of these is reprinted below in comparison with the character of "An Host" in the Overbury collection of 1614:

SIR THOMAS OVERBURY AN HOST	DUNTON
	As soon as we had look'd a little about the Town, we went into an Inn, where we found our Host a man that con-
. . . He consists of double beere and fellowship, . . .	sisted of Double (Beer)[115] and fellow-

SIR THOMAS OVERBURY
AN HOST

DUNTON

He entertaines humbly, and gives his guests power, as well of himselfe as house. He answers all mens expectations to his power, save in the reckoning: and hath gotten the tricke of greatnesse, to lay all mislikes upon his servants. His wife is the *cummin seed* of his dove-house; and to be a good guest is a warrant for her liberty. . . . In a word, hee is none of his owne: for he neither eats, drinks, or thinks, but at other mens charges and appointments (Overbury's *Works*, ed. Rimbault, p. 71).

ship; for as he was sure to supply us with Drink even without asking, so he would always thrust himself in for a snack, in helping to drink it; yet to say the truth, he was a Man of great humility, and gave us power as well over himself as his house. I observ'd him to be exceeding willing to answer all Mens Expectations to the utmost of his Power, unless it were in the Reckoning, and there he would be absolute; and had got that Trick of Court-Greatness, to lay all mistakes upon his Servants. His wife was like Cummin-seed to a Dove-house, and helpt to draw in the Customers; and to be a good Guest, was a sufficient Warrant for her Liberty. And to give you his character in few words, he is an absolute slave, for he neither eats, drinks, nor thinks, but at other mens charges and Appointments. But he sells himself at an Extravagant rate, and makes all his Customers pay dearly for the Purchase. Nor was he at all singular, for in the whole Town, there was never a Barrel better Herring (*Letters*, pp. 11–12).

It is astonishing to note the plausibility of Dunton's past tenses here and of his assurance that he himself observed the facts.

And now we must look at Comfort Wilkins, Mrs. Green, and the Flower of Boston. There are, to be sure, other women characterized in the Letters: Mrs. D——, Mrs. T——, Mrs. F——y, and three others,[116] all unfavorably delineated, are copied from earlier books of characters. But the Damsel (Comfort Wilkins), Mrs. Green, and the Widow Brick are far more elaborately portrayed than any of the other characters in the Letters. Not only does Dunton devote more space to summarizing their virtues, but he represents them as playing a considerable part in his stay here. In fact, Mrs. Green used to tell him that if Mrs. Dunton should die, "none was fit to succeed her but Madam Brick." "The Widow Brick was without doubt," says Whitmore,[117] "Joanna, daughter of Arthur Mason, who married first Robert Breck, and secondly Michael Perry. From Dunton we have the following items for identification: She was a widow, twenty-two years old in 1686, the mother of two children, and a member of Rev. James Allen's church."[118] The character certainly fulfills these requirements, and, although Dunton in his manuscript first wrote "Mrs. Birch" and then crossed it out in favor of "Mrs. Brick," I dare say Whitmore is partly right. But it is equally true that Mrs. Brick is the third section of the third part of the *Ladies Calling . . . By the Author of the Whole Duty of Man*, etc., which reached a fifth edition in 1677.[119] I reproduce the entire character with portions of the earlier character beside it.[120]

THE LADIES CALLING

1. The next state which can succeed to that of Marriage, is Widowhood.

She is a woman whose head hath been quite cut off, and yet she liveth.[121]

. . . Love is strong as death, Cant. 8. 6. and therefore when it is pure and genuine, cannot be extinguish'd by it, but

DUNTON

The Character of The Widow Brick, the very Flower of Boston; That of a Widow is the next state or change that can succeed to that of marriage. And I have chosen my Friend the Widow Brick, as an Exemplar to shew you what a Widow is: Madam Brick is a Gentlewoman whose *Head* (i. e. her Husband) has been cut off, and yet she lives and Walks: But don't be frighted, for she's Flesh and Blood still, and perhaps some of the *finest* that you ever saw. She has sufficiently evidenc'd that her Love to her late Husband is as strong as Death, because Death has not been able to Extinguish it, but it still burns

THE LADIES CALLING

DUNTON

burns like the Funeral-Lamps of old even in Vaults and Charnel-houses. The conjugal Love, transplanted into the Grave . . . improves into Piety, and laies a kind of sacred Obligation upon the Widow, to perform all offices of respect and kindness which his remains are capable of.

2. Now those Remains are of three sorts, his Body, his Memory, and his Children. The most proper expression of her love to the first, is in giving it an honorable Enterment; . . . prudently proportion'd to his Quality and Fortune, so that her Zeal to his Corps may not injure a Nobler Relic of him, his Children.

Her grief for her husband though real, is moderate, . . . our widow's sorrow is no storm, but a still rain.[122]

And this decency is a much better instance of her kindness, then all those Tragical Furies wherewith some Women seem transported towards their dead Husbands, those frantic Embraces and caresses of a Carcass, which betray a little too much the sensuality of their Love. And . . . those vehement Passions quickly exhaust themselves, and . . . seems rather to vanish then consume.

3. The more valuable Kindness therefore, is that to his Memory, endevouring to embalm that, keep it from perishing. . . .

. . . She is . . . to perfume his Memory . . . by reviving the remembrance

like the Funeral Lamps of old, even in Vaults and Charnel-Houses; But her Conjugal Love, being Transplanted into the Grave, has improv'd it self into Piety, and laid an Obligation upon her to perform all offices of Respect and Kindness to his Remains, which they are capable of.

As to his Body, she gave it a decent Enterment, suitable to his quality; or rather above it, as I have been inform'd; for Mr. Brick was Dead and Buried before I came to Boston. And that this was the Effect of that dear love she had for him, appears in this, That she wou'd not suffer the Funeral Charges to make any Abatement from the Children's Portions. Her grief for his Death was such as became her, great but moderate, not like a hasty Shower, but a still Rain: She knew nothing of those Tragical Furies wherewith some Women seem Transported towards their Dead Husbands; those frantick Embraces and Caresses of a Carcass, betray a little too much the Sensuality of their Love. Such violent Passions quickly spend themselves, and seem rather to Vanish than Consume. But Madam Brick griev'd more moderately, and more lastingly. She knew there was a better way of Expressing her Love to him, and therefore made it her Business to Embalm his Memory, and keep that from Perishing. And I always observ'd, That whenever she spoke of her Husband, it was in the most Endearing manner. Nor cou'd she ever mention him, without paying the Tribute of a Tear to his Memory. She wou'd often be reviving the remembrance

THE LADIES CALLING | DUNTON

of whatever there was praiseworthy in him, vindicating him from all Calumnies and false Accusations, and stifling (or allaying) even true ones as much as she can.

And indeed a Widow can no way better provide for her own Honor, then by this tenderness of her Husbands.

4. Yet there is another Expression of it, inferior to none of the former, and that is the setting such a value upon her relation to him, as to do nothing unworthy of it.

'Twas the dying charge of *Augustus* to his Wife *Livia, Behave thy self well, and remember our Marriage*. And she who has bin wife to a Person of Honor, must so remember it, as not to do any thing below her self, or which he (could he have foreseen it) should justly have bin ashamed of.

5. The last Tribute she can pay him, is in his Children. These he leaves as his Proxies to receive the kindness of which himself is incapable;

so that the Children of a Widow may clame a double portion of the Mothers love; one upon their Native right, as hers; the other, as a bequest in right of their dead Father.

And, indeed, since she is to supply the place of both Parents, 'tis but neces-

of some Praise-worthy Quality or other in him; and if any happen'd to say something of him not so commendable, she wou'd excuse it with a world of Sweetness, and by a frowning glance at the Relator, declare how much she was displeas'd. And tho' I cannot think it her design, yet I believe she was sensible enough that she cou'd no way better provide for her own Honour than by this Tenderness she shew'd for her Husband's. But Madam Brick shew'd a better way of expressing the Honour she had for her Husband's Memory, and that is, She set such a value on her Relation to her Husband, as to do nothing that might seem unworthy of it.

Historians inform us, That 'twas the Dying Charge of Augustus to the Empress Livia, Behave thy self well, and remember our Marriage. This Madam Brick made her Care; For having been the Wife of a Gentleman of good Quality, she so remember'd it, as not to do any thing below her self, or which Mr. Brick (cou'd he have foreseen it) might justly have been asham'd of. But Madam Brick had yet another way of Expressing the Value she had for Mr. Brick, and that is, by the kindness she show'd to the Children which he left behind him, which were only two: And this was so remarkably Eminent in her, that I have heard her say, Her Children might now claim a double Portion in her love, one on their Native Right, as being Hers; and the other on the Right of their dead Father, who had left them to her: "And truly," said she, "since I must supply the place of

THE LADIES CALLING

DUNTON

sary she should put on the Affections of both, and to the tenderness of a Mother, add the care and conduct of a Father. First, in a sedulous care of their Education: and next in a prudent managery of their Fortunes; . . .

both Parents, 'tis but necessary that I shou'd put on the Affections of both; and to the Tenderness of a Mother, add the Care and Conduct of a Father." She was as good as her Word, both in a sedulous care of their Education, and in a Prudent Management of their Fortunes. As to their Education she took care that they might have that Learning that was proper for them, and above all, that they might be furnished with ingenuous and vertuous Principles, founded on the Fear of God, which is the beginning of all true Wisdom. And as to their Fortunes, she was so far from Embeziling them, a Practice too common with some Widows, that she augmented them, while it was in the Power of her hand to do it. (For Madam Brick is but a Young Widow, tho' she is the Mother of two Children.)

. . . will furnish them with Ingenious and Vertuous Principles, such as may set them above all vile and ignoble practices.

. . . As to the . . . managing of their Fortune, there is the same rule . . . , *viz.* to do as for themselves, that is, with the same care and diligence (if not a greater) as in her own Concern. I do not say that she shall confound the property, and make it indeed her own, by applying it to her peculiar use, a thing I fear which is often don, especially by the gaier sort of widows, who to keep up their own Equipage, do sometimes incroach upon their sons peculiar.

10. I have hitherto spoke of what the widow ows to her dead husband; but there is also somewhat of peculiar Obligation in relation to herself. God who has plac'd us in this World to pursue the interests of a better, directs all the signal acts of his Providence to that end, and intends we should so interpret them . . . and a widow may more then conjecture, that when God takes away the mate of her bosom, reduces her to a solitude, he do's by it sound a retreat from the lighter jollities and gaieties of the world. And as

But Madam Brick is one that has yet more refined and Exalted Thoughts: She is highly sensible that God, who has plac'd us in this World to pursue the Interests of a better, directs all the signal Acts of his Providence to that end, and intends we shou'd so interprett them; And therefore she wisely reflected that when God took away from her the Mate of her Bosom, and so reduc'd her to a solitude, he thereby, as it were, Sounded a Retreat to her from the lighter Jollities and Gayeties of the World; and therefore in Com-

in compliance with civil custom she
. . . should put on a more retir'd temper of mind, a more strict and severe
behavior:

and that not to be cast off with her
veil, but to be the constant dress of
her widowhood.

pliance to the Divine Will, and that
she might the better Answer the Requirement of the Almighty, tho[123] put
on a more retired Temper of Mind,
and a more strict [124] . . .

Neither, did she suffer Her Pious
behaviour, to be cast off with her
Widow's Vail, but made it the constant Dress both of her Widowhood
and Life; and as a consequence hereof,
she became a Member of Mr. Allen's
Congregation; and liv'd a life of Sincere Piety: And yet was so far from
Sowrness either in her Countenance
or Conversation, that nothing was ever
more sweet or agreeable: Making it
evident that Piety did not consist in
Moroseness, nor Sincere Devotion in
a supercilious Carriage; 'twas the
Vitals of Religion that she minded,
and not Forms and Modes; and if she
found the Fower of it in her heart,
she did not think her self oblig'd to
such a *starch'dness* of Carriage as is
usual amongst the Bostonians, who
value themselves thereby so much,
that they are ready to say to all others,
Stand off, for I am holier than thou.
She did not think herself concern'd
to put on a Sorrowful Countenance,
when the Joy of the Lord was her
strength.

I had much the greater value for
Madam Brick, on the Account of a
Discourse that past between Mrs.
Green and her, which (as Mrs. Green
related it to me) was to this effect:
Mrs. Green commended her very
much, in that being a Young Widow,
in the bloom of all her Youth and
Beauty, (for she was but twenty-two)
she had given up so much of her time

There are many things which are
but the due compliances of a Wife,
which yet are great avocations, and
interruptions of a strict Devotion;
when she is manumitted from that
subjection, when she has less of *Martha's Care of serving*, she is then at
liberty to chuse *Mary's part*. Luk. 10.
42.

... Those hours which were before
her husbands right, seem now to de-
volve on God the grand proprietor of
our time: that discourse and free converse wherewith she entertain'd him,
she may now convert into colloquies
and spiritual entercourse with her
maker.

to the Exercise of Devotion, and the
Worship of God; To which she reply'd, 'She had done but what she
ought; for in her Married state she
found many things which yet are but
the due Compliances of a Wife, which
were great Avocations to a Strict Devotion; but being now manumitted
from that Subjection, and having less
of Martha's Care of Serving, it was
but reasonable she shou'd chuse Mary's
better part.' "And those hours (added
she) which were before my Husband's
Right, are now devolv'd on God, the
Great Proprietor of all my time: And
that Discourse and free Converse with
which I us'd to entertain Mr. Brick,
ought now to be in Colloquies and
heavenly Entercourses with My dear
Redeemer." Nor was her Piety and
Devotion barren, but fruitful and
abounding in the Works of *Charity*,
and she cloath'd the Naked as far as
her Ability permitted. And tho' my
self and Mr. King went thither often
(for she wou'd scarce permit a single
visit) we never found her without
some poor but honest Christian with
her, always discoursing of the things
of Heaven, and ere she went, supply-
ing her with the things of Earth.
How long she may remain a Widow,
I have not yet consulted with the
Stars to know, but that she has con-
tinu'd so two years, is evident to all
that are in Boston.

To conclude her Character, the
Beauty of her Person, the *Sweetness*
and Affability of her Temper, the
Gravity of her Carriage, and her Exalted Piety, gave me so just a value
for her, that Mrs. Green wou'd often

say, Shou'd Iris Dye (which Heaven forbid) there's none was fit to succeed her but Madam Brick: But Mrs. Green was partial, for my poor Pretences to secure vertue, wou'd ne'er have answer'd to her Towring heighths. 'Tis true, Madam Brick did me the Honour to treat me very kindly at her House, and to admit me often into her Conversation, but I am sure it was not on Love's, but on Vertue's score. For she well knows (at least as well as I do) that Iris is alive: And therefore I must justifie her Innocence on that account. And tho' some have been pleas'd to say, That were I in a single state, they do believe she wou'd not be displeas'd with my Addresses, As this is without any ground but groundless Conjectures, so I hope I shall never be in a capacity to make a Tryal of it.

But, I'm sure our Friendship was all Platonick (so Angels lov'd) and full as Innocent as that of the Philosopher who gave it the name; but if Plato was not very much wrong'd he never lov'd vertue so refinedly, as to like to court her so passionately in a foul or homely habitation as he did in those that were more Beautiful and Lovely; and this sufficiently justifies my Friendship to Madam Brick and her Spotless Innocence in accepting of it. Thus, Reader, I have given you the Character of another of my Friends of the Fair Sex in Boston; and leave you to judge whether or no she deserve the Title of *the Flower of Boston*, which at first sight I gave her (*Letters*, pp. 105–111).

So much for the Widow Brick, the Flower of Boston. And Comfort Wilkins and Mrs. Green are drawn from the same source—*The Ladies Calling*. Even the remarks which they are represented as actually having made to John Dunton or in his presence are taken almost verbatim from those earlier characters of the abstract Virgin, Wife, and Widow, as conceived by an English clergyman thirteen years before John Dunton came to Boston.

For convenience I have arranged in a table such borrowings in Dunton's Letters as have been traced to their source. The letter W indicates that Dunton's indebtedness was detected by Whitmore.

DUNTON'S SOURCE	DUNTON
	First Letter
Overbury, "Fair and Happy Milkmaid" (*Works*, ed. Rimbault, pp. 118–119).	Description of a Milkmaid (omitted by Whitmore; [125] see *Letters*, p. 11).
Overbury, "Host" (*Works*, p. 71).	The Host and his Wife (pp. 11–12).
Overbury,[126] "Almanac-maker" (*Works*, pp. 92–93).	An Astrologer (pp. 17–18).
Overbury, "A Maquerda, in plain English a Bawde" (*Works*, pp. 99–100).	A Bawd.[127]
Overbury, "A Whoore" (*Works*, pp. 82–83).	An Impudent Whore.[127]
Overbury, "A very Whore" (*Works*, pp. 83–84).	Another.[127]
	Second Letter
Overbury, "A Saylor" (*Works*, pp. 75–76).	George Monk, the Mate (p. 26).
Overbury, "A Saylor" (*Works*, pp. 75–76).	Charles King, the Gunner (p. 26).
Josselyn, p. 8.[128]	St. Elmo's Fire (p. 31).
	Third Letter
Partly from Overbury's "A Wise Man," and partly from Overbury's	Mr. Burroughs, a Merchant (pp. 59–62).

DUNTON'S SOURCE	DUNTON
"A Noble Spirit" (*Works*, pp. 60–62).	
Josselyn, pp. 124–126.	Description of Boston (pp. 66–69). W.
Josselyn, p. 139.	"There is no trading for a Sharper with them," etc., to the end of the sentence (p. 69).
J. W., *A Letter from New England*, 1682, p. 2.[129]	"As to their religion" (p. 69), etc., to the end of the paragraph. W.
Josselyn, p. 138.	"The Government, both Civil and Ecclesiastical," etc., to the end of the sentence (p. 70).
Josselyn, p. 139.	Account of the collection taken in church after the Sunday afternoon sermon (pp. 70–71).
Josselyn, pp. 137–138	"Every church (for so they call)," etc., to the end of the following sentence (p. 71).
Josselyn, pp. 134–137.	"As to their laws," and the rest of the paragraph (p. 71). W.
Partly from Josselyn, p. 137.[130]	"For being drunk" (p. 72), etc., through "and so our poor debtors" (p. 73, l. 7). W.
J. W., *A Letter from New England.*	"But for lying and cheating" (p. 73) through "fasten his Tallons first upon 'em" (p. 74). W.
Probably from Josselyn, p. 39, third paragraph, though not verbatim.	"And thus, my friend," etc., to the end of the paragraph (p. 74).
Fuller, "The Good Merchant" (*Holy and Profane State*, ed. 1840, pp. 88–91).	Mr. Willy (p. 81).
Earle, "A Modest Man" (*Microcosmography*, ed. 1811, pp. 147–150).	Mr. Mortimer (p. 86).
Fuller, "The Good Merchant."	Mr. Heath, a good merchant (pp. 88–89).
Overbury, "A Mere Pettifogger" (*Works*, pp. 129–131).	Mr. Watson, a Lawyer (pp. 89–90).
Contains one sentence from Richard Flecknoe's character "Of an extream Vitious Person."[132]	Mr. C——[131] (p. 90).
Fuller, "The Good Physician" (*Holy and Profane State*, ed. 1840, p. 42).	Dr. Oaks (p. 93).
Partly from Fuller's "The True Gentleman," partly from his "Good	Dr. Bullivant (pp. 94–96).

DUNTON'S SOURCE

DUNTON

Physician" (*Holy and Profane State*, ed. 1840, pp. 120–122, 43).

The Ladies Calling, Part ii. Sect. 1.

Comfort Wilkins, a Virgin (pp. 98–102).

The Ladies Calling, ii. Sect. 2.

Mrs. Green, the Wife (pp. 102–105).

The Ladies Calling, ii. Sect. 3. The character of Mrs. Brick also contains two sentences from Fuller's "the Good Widow" (*Holy and Profane State*, ed. 1840, p. 19).

Madam Brick, the Widow (pp. 106–111).

Fuller, "The Harlot" (*Holy and Profane State*, ed. 1840, pp. 287–290).

Mrs. Ab——l (pp. 112–113).

Flecknoe, "Of an inconstant disposition" (ed. 1673, p. 17).

Flecknoe, "Of a Proud One" (*Fifty-five Enigmatical Characters*, 1665.[134] The character "Of a Proud One," which is not mentioned in the table of contents, stands between Nos. 31 and 32). This character also contains one sentence ("Had she been with the Israelites," etc.) from Fuller's essay "Of Apparel" (*Holy and Profane State*, ed. 1840, p.133).

Doll S——der (p. 115).

Mrs. —— [133] (pp. 115–116).

Third Letter (continued) [135]

Earle, "A Prison" (*Microcosmography*, 1811, pp. 156–158).

The Prison, in Prison Lane (pp. 118–119).

Overbury, "A Jailer" (*Works*, ed. Rimbault, pp. 166–168).

The Jailer (pp. 120–121).

Cotton Mather, *The Call of the Gospel Applyed*, etc., second edition, 1687 (Sibley No. 5).[137]

Cotton Mather on the execution of Morgan (pp. 122–124).[136] W.

Joshua Moody, *An Exhortation to a Condemned Malefactor*, etc., 1687.[137]

Joshua Moody on the same [136] (pp. 125–129). W.

Increase Mather, *A Sermon, Occasioned by the Execution*, etc., second edition, 1687.[137]

Increase Mather on the same [136] (pp. 129–135). W.

Increase Mather, *A Sermon occasioned by the Execution*, etc., pp. 35–36.[137]

Morgan's last words (pp. 135–136). W.

Dunton's Source	Dunton *Fourth Letter*
	First Ramble (To Charlestown)
Josselyn, p. 126.	Description of Charlestown (pp. 149–150).
Roger Williams, *Key*, pp. 100–105.[138]	Indian Hospitality (pp. 151–153).W.
	Second Ramble (To Medford)
Roger Williams, *Key*, pp. 107–108.	Indian Hospitality, continued (p. 155). W.
	Third Ramble (To New-Town)
Josselyn, p. 127.	Description of New Town (pp. 155–156).
	Fourth Ramble (To Winnisimet)
Josselyn, p. 128.	Description of the Town (pp. 163, 167).
Roger Williams, *Key*, pp. 120–128, 132–135.	Indian Houses (pp. 163–167). W.
	Fifth Ramble (To Lynn)
Roger Williams, *Key*, pp. 158–162.	Indian Travelling (pp. 168–169).W.
Josselyn, p. 128.	Description of Lynn (p. 169).
Earle, "A bold, forward Man" (*Microcosmography*, ed. 1811, pp. 122–125).	The Troublesome Host (pp. 169–170).
Roger Williams, *Key*, pp. 207–220.	Indian Religion (pp. 171–176). W.
	Sixth Ramble (To Nantascot)
Roger Williams, *Key*, pp. 233–237.	Indian Money (pp. 177–179). W.
Josselyn, pp. 122–123.	Description of Nantascot (including the paragraph beginning, "Being come to Nantascot," and also the next paragraph).
	Seventh Ramble (To Wissaguset)
Roger Williams, *Key*, pp. 248–252.	Indian Hunting (pp. 181–182). W.
Josselyn, p. 123.	Description of the Town (p. 183).
	Eighth Ramble (To Braintree)
Roger Williams, *Key*, p. 167.	Climate of New England (pp. 184–185). W.
Josselyn, p. 123.	Description of Braintree (p. 185).

Dunton's Source	Dunton
	Ninth Ramble (To Dorchester)
Roger Williams, *Key*, pp. 196–202.	Fish of New England (pp. 186–189). W.
Roger Williams, *Key*, pp. 187–190.	Beasts of New England (pp. 189–190). W.
Josselyn, pp. 123–124.	Description of Dorchester (pp. 190–191).
	Tenth Ramble (To Roxbury)
Josselyn, p. 124.	Description of Roxbury (p. 192).
Cotton Mather, *Life of Eliot*, ed. 1691, portions of pp. 6–73; ed. 1694, pp. 6–78; *Magnalia*, ed. 1702, bk. iii. pp. 173–190.	Life and Character of Eliot (pp. 194–199). W.
Cotton Mather, *Life of Eliot*, ed. 1691, pp. 74 ff.; ed. 1694, pp. 78 ff.; *Magnalia*, ed. 1702, bk. iii. pp. 190 ff.	Conversion of the Indians (pp. 200–202). W.
	Fifth Letter
Cotton Mather, *Life of Eliot*, ed. 1691, pp. 88 ff.; ed. 1694, pp. 94 ff.; *Magnalia*, ed. 1702, bk. iii. p. 194.	Eliot's Labors among the Indians (pp. 211–212).
Josselyn, p. 127.	Description of Watertown (pp. 214–215).
Josselyn, pp. 37–38.	Brief description (about 12 lines) of the country through which he rode to Watertown (p. 216).
Cotton Mather, *Magnalia*, ed. 1702, bk. vi. p. 51.	The Indian Government (pp. 218–220, l. 8).
Roger Williams, *Key*, pp. 163–166.	Authority of the Prince's Punishments (p. 220, two paragraphs).
Cotton Mather, *Life of Eliot*, ed. 1691, pp. 80 ff.; ed. 1694, pp. 85 ff.; *Magnalia*, ed. 1702, bk. iii. pp. 192 ff.	Of the conversion of the Indians (pp. 221–224). W.
Roger Williams, *Key*, pp. 203–205.	Indian Clothing (pp. 224–225). W.
Cotton Mather, *Life of Eliot*, ed. 1691, pp. 100 ff., 104–108, 89–92; ed. 1694, pp. 106 ff., 111–116, 95–99; *Magnalia*, ed. 1702, bk. iii. pp. 197 ff., 198–199, 194.	The Converted Indians of Natick (pp. 225–233). W.

DUNTON'S SOURCE	DUNTON
John Eliot, *The Dying Speeches of Several Indians*.[139]	Dying Speeches of Indians (pp. 233–241). W.

Sixth Letter

Josselyn, p. 132.	Settlement of Salem[140] (pp. 252–253).
Overbury, "A Reverend Judge" (*Works*, ed. Rimbault, pp. 136–137).	Mr. Sewel (p. 254).
Earle, "A Grave Divine" (*Microcosmography*, ed. 1811, pp. 9–11).	Mr. Higgins(on) (pp. 254–255).

Seventh Letter

Roger Williams, *Key*, pp. 228–231.	Marriage Customs of Indians (pp. 267–269). W.
Josselyn, pp. 129–130.	Description of Wenham and the surrounding country (pp. 271–272).
Roger Williams, *Key*, p. 180.	Indian Husbandry (pp. 272–275). W.
Roger Williams, *Key*, pp. 246–247, 239–245.	Indian Trade and Money (pp. 277–279). W.
Josselyn, p. 129.	Description of Ipswich (p. 280).
Overbury, "A Good Wife" (*Works*, ed. Rimbault, pp. 72–73).	Mrs. Steward (p. 281).
Overbury, "A Noble and Retired Housekeeper" (*Works*, pp. 115–116).	Mr. Steward (pp. 281–282).
Roger Williams, *Key*, pp. 258–264.	Indian Warfare (pp. 272–275). W.
Roger Williams, *Key*, pp. 254–257.	Indian Games and Sports (pp. 286–288). W.
Roger Williams, *Key*, pp. 142–147.	Indians and News (pp. 292–293). W.
Roger Williams, *Key*, pp. 274–277.	Indian Mourning and Burial (pp. 294–295). W.

From this list it appears that there are at least eighty-four cases in which Dunton incorporated borrowed material in the *Letters*. Of these Whitmore noted thirty-three: eighteen from Roger Williams, six from Cotton Mather, three from Josselyn, two from Increase Mather, two from J. W., one from John Eliot, and one from Joshua Moody. To these we have added fifty-one passages,—twenty from Josselyn and thirty-one from various writers of characters; namely, fourteen from Overbury, seven from Fuller, four from Earle, three from Flecknoe, and three from the author of *The Ladies Calling*.

It may be suggested—indeed it has been suggested[141]—that "had this volume been issued in Dunton's life-time, he might have confessed his indebtedness." For two reasons this seems unlikely.

First, it is unlikely because of the principle which, seen in its extreme form, makes a novelist avoid footnotes. Dunton, to be sure, was not a novelist; he was not even able to achieve such approaches to the novel as were made by Addison and Defoe. Yet it seems clear that when an author, in copying such material as that which Dunton takes from Roger Williams, uses such pains as his to make the ideas appear either to be original or to have been communicated to him by persons with whom he spoke in the course of his rambles, he is manifestly trying[142] to write a kind of work in which acknowledgments of indebtedness would be out of place.

A second and more tangible objection is that to make such acknowledgments appears not to have been Dunton's custom. For in at least two works that were published in his lifetime—the *Life and Errors* (1705) and *Athenianism* (1710)—Dunton borrows freely and without acknowledgment.

In the first part of his *Athenianism* (1710) Dunton prints as his own four poems[143] which had appeared in 1685 in Samuel Wesley's *Maggots*,[144] of which Dunton had written in 1705: "I once printed a Book, I remember, under the title of 'Maggots'; but it was written by a *Dignitary* in the Church of England."[145]

In his *Life and Errors* (1705) Dunton prints, without acknowledgment, not only many of the characters that appear in his Letters, but many others as well. Comfort Wilkins, Mrs. Green, the Widow Brick, Mr. Heath, Dr. Oakes, Dr. Bullivant, and Dunton's other Boston friends appear there, sometimes more briefly sketched than in the *Letters*, but still replete with phrases taken from earlier books of characters. And in addition there are a great many characters of Dunton's English acquaintances—printers, publishers, hackwriters, and so on—in which he borrows at least a phrase or two from such writers as Hall and Earle. The character of Major Hatley, placed beside one of Hall's types, will give a fair idea of the extent of the borrowing in the more fully developed portraits.[146]

JOSEPH HALL

The Valiant Man (1608)

He is the master of himself, and subdues his passions to reason, and by this inward victory works his own peace.

. . . He lies ever close within himself, armed with wise resolution, and will not be discovered but by death or danger.

. . . and he holds it the noblest revenge, that he might hurt and doth not (Hall's *Works*, Oxford, 1837, vi. 94).

DUNTON

Major Hatley

He is the master of himself, and subdues his passions to reason; and by this inward victory, works his own peace. He is well skilled in Military Discipline; and, from being a Captain, is advanced to a Major. He lies ever close within himself, armed with wise resolution, and will not be discovered but by Death or Danger. "Piety never looks so bright as when it shines in Steel;" and Major Hatley holds it the noblest revenge that he *might hurt*, and *does not*. I dealt with this Military Stationer for six years, but left him, with flying colours, to trade with his honest Servant (*Life and Errors*, 1. 255).

Where does all this leave us? How does the discovery of these borrowings affect our knowledge of the persons characterized and our estimate of Dunton's *Letters from New England*?

It seems to me that Dunton's characters may be made to fall into three groups. First come a number of portraits in the course of which Dunton used a phrase or a sentence from some earlier writer of characters. Probably the phrase fitted as well as any original phrase would have fitted. If so the

validity of the portrait is not affected. Next come those instances in which fairly well-known persons like Mr. Epes,
Dr. Bullivant, Mr. Heath, and others, are characterized almost wholly in the words of earlier writers. In these cases it
is unsafe to apply the details of the portrait: we can be sure
merely that the character was—or that Dunton thought him
—a worthy merchant, a skilled physician, or whatever else;
that is, we can apply the title, not the details. Finally come
persons who are wholly characterized in the words of earlier
writers, and of whom nothing is known except what Dunton
tells us. Here it would seem that, in the words of Sir John
Seeley, "history fades into mere literature."

Historically considered, Dunton's *Letters from New England* have suffered a good deal in the course of this examination. Indeed, an historian might almost say that they are
not letters, that they are not from New England, and that
they are not by John Dunton. But I wish to suggest, in conclusion, that the trouble is not that the book is a bad one, but
that it has been wrongly catalogued. If we take it off the
American History shelves—where it never belonged—and
put it with English Fiction, we shall find, I think, that precisely those portions of it which were before the most absurd
and deceptive are now the most significant.

Few phases of the transition in English literature from
the seventeenth to the eighteenth century are more important or more difficult to trace than the beginnings of English
prose fiction. These beginnings have to be sought in a great
variety of documents, including fictitious voyages, histories,
and letters, imaginary adventures of animals, allegories, vi-
sions, and many other devices, which, although they often
contain fact, do not aim to be true.[147] Another matter vital to
the transition is the development from the abstract character
to the novel of character. It is well known that Addison and
Steele, in the *Tatler* and the *Spectator*, mark a half-way point

in several phases of this transition. They used fictitious letters and diaries, and in particular they made great progress in modifying the old abstract character, which they felt to be stiff, vague, and repellently didactic. Accordingly, they gave their characters names, they made them speak, they even, by becoming Mr. Nestor Ironsides or Mr. Spectator, walked right into the page themselves and spoke with their characters. They supplied descriptive backgrounds, and indeed almost everything that a novel requires, except the plot. Consequently we say truly that they greatly improved the technique of characterization in prose fiction.

Did not John Dunton, very imperfectly and probably with motives very much mixed, do many of these things? He took abstract characters, named them, made them speak, spoke with them, went on picnics with them, and, in the case of Madam Brick, almost fell in love with one of them. His mistake was not in introducing so much fiction, but rather in not casting entirely loose from fact. Our mistake has been in keeping him on our shelves beside Sewall and Josselyn, instead of beside Ned Ward and Daniel Defoe.

Nicholas Breton
Character-Writer and Quadrumaniac

THE years 1615 and 1616, in which Nicholas Breton published two little-known but not unimportant prose works, *Characters upon Essaies Morall and Divine* (1615) and *The Good And The Badde* (1616), mark an interesting point in the development of the "character." In 1608 Joseph Hall had put forth what seems to be the first book in English to consist wholly of undoubted characters. These *Characters of Virtues and Vices* were wholly delineations of persons, their aim was professedly moral, and their style—though not without an occasional flicker of sober wit—was grave and clerical. Six years later, in 1614, appeared the famous collection of characters by Sir Thomas Overbury and his friends, at whose hands the character undergoes some change. "It is," writes a contributor to the Overbury collection, in attempting "to square out a character by our English levell," . . . "a picture (reall or personall) quaintly drawne, in various colours, all of them heightned by one shadowing. It is a quick and soft touch of many strings, all shutting up in one musicall close; it is wits descant on any plaine song."[148] That is, the character may be impersonal and it should be quaintly and wittily phrased. Accordingly we are not surprised to find in the Overbury collection a character of a prison and one of the character itself, nor are we surprised that a most serious and admirable portrait, "A Worthy Commander in the Wars," should conclude with a flourish in which the "silver head" of the good soldier is made to "lean near the golden sceptre." Such was the technique of the character in 1614.

From that time until the outbreak of the Civil War, the

character was often in danger of becoming an excessively
flimsy and overstylistic affair. In 1618, for example, Geffray
Mynshul, in *Essayes and Characters of a Prison and Prisoners*,
affords an important instance of a man who wrote, in the
same volume and on the same subjects, both essays and characters, and whose method perceptibly changes when he turns
from one to the other. His essays display a greater depth and
variety of thought; his characters, a sharper and more elaborate wit. His essays show variety in point of view, fair se-
quence of thought, and an occasional mention of the writer
and of the person addressed. All these should occur naturally
enough in any kind of writing. Yet they almost never do in
Mynshul's characters, where the sentences are nearly all cast
in one mould, as can be seen from the following skeleton of
"The Character of a Prison." [149] "A prison is . . . . It is
. . . , it is . . . , it is . . . . It is . . . . It is . . . ;
it is . . . . It is . . . . It is . . . . It is . . . . It is
. . . . It is . . . . It is . . . . It is . . . . To conclude,
what is it not? In a word, it is . . . ." The blanks one
should imagine filled in with such conceitful, paradoxical,
metaphorical strokes as that the prison is "a little commonwealth, although little wealth be common there," or that the
prisoner is "an impatient patient lingering under the rough
hands of a cruell phisitian." In Mynshul's hands, the character
is clearly by way of becoming something little better than a
verbal puzzle. As compared with the essay it apparently was,
in his estimation, less subjective, meditative, and pregnant,
and more inclined to coincide with the instructions of one
Ralph Johnson, who in 1665 [150] directs his pupils in writing
characters to make "a witty and facetious description."

This conceitful tendency of the character, and the whole
matter of the relation of character and essay, could hardly be
more clearly shown than in two of Nicholas Breton's prose
works. In 1615 Breton published *Characters / Upon Essaies /*

Morall, And | Divine, | Written | For those good Spirits, | that will take them | in good part, | And | Make use of them to | good purpose.[151]

The book, as its title implies, is an application of the manner of the character to the matter of the essay. That such "charactering" of the essay was fairly well known in 1615 appears both from some of the commendatory verses prefixed to the work and from Breton's dedication of it to Bacon. A certain I. R. was kind enough to say of his friend's work:

> *Who reads this Booke with a iudicious eye,*
> *Will in true Judgement, true discretion try,*
> *Where words and matter close and sweetly coucht,*
> *Doe shew how truth, wit, art and nature toucht.*
> *What need more words these characters to praise,*
> *They are the true charactering of Essaies.*[152]

Breton himself furnishes similar evidence in his dedication of the book to Bacon:

> *To the Honorable, and my much worthy honored,*
> *truly learned, and Iudicious Knight, Sr FRANCIS BACON,*
> *his Maties Attourney Generall,*
> *Increase of honor, health, and eternall happinesse.*

Worthy Knight, I haue read of many Essaies, and a kinde of Charactering of them, by such, as when I lookt vnto the forme, or nature of their writing, I haue beene of the conceit, that they were but Imitators of your breaking the ice to their inuentions; which, how short they fall of your worth, I had rather thinke then speake, though Truth need not blush at her blame: Now, for my selfe vnworthy to touch neere the Rocke of those Diamonds, or to speake in their praise, who so farre exceede the power of my capacitie, vouchsafe me leaue yet, I beseech you, among those Apes that would counterfet the actions of men, to play the like part with learning, and as a Monkey, that would make a face like a Man, and cannot, so to write like a Scholler, and am not: and thus not daring to aduenture the Print, vnder your Patronage, without your fauorable allowance, in the deuoted seruice of my bounden duty, I leaue

these poore Trauells of my Spirit, to the perusing of your pleasing lea-
sure, with the further fruits of my humble affection, to the happie em-
ployment of your honorable pleasure.

At your seruice
in all humblenesse
NICH: BRETON

Although the extravagant tone of this address perhaps
injures the value of the first sentence as evidence of a fact in
literary history, it need not prevent us from believing that
some writers showed, and others perceived, that the "character of an essay" was a fairly well-defined variation of the
usual character. Nor need we wholly disregard Breton's suggestion that the form was influenced by the essays of Bacon,
then in their second and enlarged edition.

Breton's subjects, in his *Characters upon Essaies*, are Wisdom, Learning, Knowledge, Practice, Patience, Love, Peace,
War, Valor, Resolution, Honor, Truth, Time, Death, Faith,
and Fear. He thus helps to form the convention that, as
Ralph Johnson wrote in 1665,[153] "an Essay is a short discourse about any vertue, vice, or other commonplace."

The "charactering" of such material consists in giving it
a stylistic treatment in which mannerisms are rather tire-
somely prominent.

1. The subjects are generally personified. Wisdom, Learning, Knowledge, Practice, Patience, War, Valor, Resolution,
Truth, and Faith are feminine; Time and Death are mascu-
line; and only Love, Peace, and Honor are neuter.[154]

2. As in Mynshul, the subject of the character is also the
subject of almost every clause. The character of Peace, for
instance, may be represented by the following skeleton:
"Peace is . . . . It is . . . . It is . . . . It holds . . . .
It is . . . . It is like . . . . It needs . . . . It is . . . .
It is . . . . It fills . . . . It is . . . . It hath . . . . It
was . . . ." This is typical: rarely is the subject varied, and

very rarely does a sentence begin with anything but its subject.

3. The language is notably high-sounding and conceitful. Learning is "the nurse of nature, with that milk of reason that would make a child of grace never lie from the dug." Love is "a healthful sickness in the soul." Practice is "the patient's patience." Time "is known to be, but his being unknown, but only in his being in a being above knowledge." In this dizzy region inconsistencies necessarily abound. Indeed, Breton seems to make no effort to avoid them; his ideas are set down curiously rather than significantly and coherently. It is therefore of no particular consequence that Resolution, although "she is a rock irremovable," also "wades through the sea, and walks through the world."

4. Alliteration, both plain and crossed, is frequent, and hardly less frequent is the repetition of a prefix or suffix. The character of Truth is thus ended "in the wonder of her worth": "she is the nature of perfection in the perfection of nature, where God in Christ shows the glory of humanity." Of Practice Breton is "fearful to follow her too far in observation, lest being never able to come near the height of her commendation, I be enforced as I am to leave her wholly to admiration." In the case of Patience he makes a similar concluding flourish: "in sum, not to wade too far in her worthiness, lest I be drowned in the depth of wonder, I will thus end in her endless honour."

5. Breton's other mannerisms, however, become inconspicuous in comparison with his strange passion for arranging his ideas in sets of four. Ordinarily he does this in a perfectly parallel construction; sometimes he varies his method and achieves a sentence[155] in which, without grammatical parallelism, there are, in effect, four cadences or waves. In most of the characters in Breton's *Characters upon Essaies* every clause consists of four parts; in all, the preference for

four over any other number is overwhelming. The effect of reading Breton, when once this jingle has got into one's head, is almost inevitably to concentrate attention upon the pattern rather than upon the ideas. To illustrate I have ventured to heighten the effect of Breton's quadruplications by numbering them in his character of Truth.

TRUTH

Truth is [1] the Glory of time, and [2] the daughter of Eternity: [3] a Title of the highest Grace, and [4] a Note of a Diuine Nature: she is [1] the life of Religion, [2] the light of Loue, [3] the Grace of Wit, and [4] the crowne of Wisedome: she is [1] the Beauty of Valor, [2] the brightnesse of honor, [3] the blessing of Reason and [4] the ioy of faith: [1] her truth is pure gold, [2] her Time is right pretious, [3] her word is most gratious and [4] her will is most glorious: [1] Her Essence is in God and [2] her dwelling with His seruants, [3] her will in His wisedome and [4] her worke to His Glory: she is [1] honored in loue, and [2] graced in constancie, [3] in patience admired and [4] in charity beloued: she is [1] the Angels worshippe, [2] the Virgins fame, [3] the Saints blisse and [4] the Martirs crowne: she is [1] the Kings greatnesse and [2] his Councels goodnesse, [3] his subiects peace and [4] his Kingdomes Praise: she is [1] the life of learning and [2] the light of the Law, [3] the honor of Trade and [4] the grace of labor: she hath [1] a pure Eye, [2] a plaine hand, [3] a piercing wit and [4] a perfect heart: she is [1] wisedomes walke in [2] the way of holinesse, and [3] takes vp her rest but in [4] the resolution of goodness: [1] Her tongue neuer trippes, [2] her heart neuer faintes, [3] her hand neuer failes and [4] her faith neuer feares: [1] her Church is without schisme, [2] her City without fraude, [3] her Court without Vanity, and [4] her Kingdome without Villany: In summe, so infinite is her Excellence, in the construction of all sence, that I will thus only conclude in the wonder of her worth: she is [1] the nature of perfection, in [2] the perfection of Nature, where [3] God in Christ, shewes [4] the glory of Christianity.[156]

Of Breton's *The Good | And | The Badde, | Or, | Descriptions of the Worthies, and Unworthies | of this Age* (1616), little need be said except that, in a slightly less pronounced degree, it reveals all the mannerisms of *Characters upon Essaies*. It is, however, more like such collections of characters as Hall's, Overbury's, Stephens's, Mynshul's, and Earle's, in that its subjects are persons instead of personified things. These subjects, most of them arranged in contrasted pairs, are A Worthy King, An Unworthy King, A Worthy Queen, A Worthy Prince, An Unworthy Prince, A Worthy Privy Councillor, An Unworthy Councillor, A Nobleman, An Unnoble Man, A Worthy Bishop, An Unworthy Bishop, A Worthy Judge, An Unworthy Judge, A Worthy Knight, An Unworthy Knight, A Worthy Gentleman, An Unworthy Gentleman, A Worthy Lawyer, An Unworthy Lawyer, A Worthy Soldier, An Untrained Soldier, A Worthy Physician, An Unworthy Physician, A Worthy Merchant, An Unworthy Merchant, A Good Man, An Atheist or Most Bad Man, A Wise Man, A Fool, An Honest Man, A Knave, An Usurer, A Beggar, A Virgin, A Wanton Woman, A Quiet Woman, An Unquiet Woman, A Good Wife, An Effeminate Fool, A Parasite, A Drunkard, A Coward, An Honest Poor Man, A Just Man, A Repentant Sinner, A Reprobate, An Old Man, A Young Man, A Holy Man. It will be seen that the classification is less by ethical types, as in Hall, than by callings or ranks, as was later to be the case in Fuller's *Holy and Profane State*. Although Breton's wit is rather sharper in his adverse characters, most of the distinctive traits of his euphuistic style appear in his first character.

A WORTHY KING

A Worthy King is a figure of God, in the nature of government: he is the chiefe of men, and the Churches champion, Natures honour, and Earths maiesty: is the director of Law, and the strength of the same, the sword of Iustice, and the scepter of Mercy, the glasse of Grace, and the eye of Honour, the terror of Treason, and the life of Loyalty. His commaund is general, and his power absolute, his frowne a death, and his fauour a life, his charge is his subiects, his care their safety, his pleasure their peace, and his ioy their loue: he is not to be paraleld, because he is without equalitie, and the prerogatiue of his crowne must not be contradicted: hee is the Lords anointed, and therfore must not be touched, and the head of a publique body, and therfore must bee preserued: he is a scourge of sinne and a blessing of grace, Gods vicegerent ouer his people, and vnder Him supreme gouernour: his safety must bee his Councels care, his health, his subiects prayer, his pleasure, his peeres comfort; and his content, his kingdomes gladnesse: His presence must be reuerenced, his person attended, his court adorned, and his state maintained; his bosome must not be searched, his will not disobeyed, his wants not vnsupplied, nor his place vnregarded. In summe, he is more then a man, though not a God, and next vnder God to be honoured aboue man.[157]

It is a curious fact that quadrumania, which runs through this character and through all of *The Good And The Badde*, appears in some of Breton's other works.[158] It appears regularly in the "Necessary Notes for a Courtier" appended to *The Court and Country*, 1618. These notes consist of fifty-three questions and answers, and of the answers no fewer than forty-two are phrased in fours. The last two questions, with their answers, will probably be more than sufficient.

Q. What is the life of a Courtier?

A. The labour of pleasure, the aspiring to greatness, the ease of nature, and the command of reason.

Q. What is the fame of a Courtier?

A. A cleare conscience, and a free spirit, an innocent heart, and a bountifull hand.[159]

More curious still, perhaps, is *The Figure of Foure*, of which only the second part (1636)[160] seems to have survived. This odd little work consists of one hundred and four[161] separate observations, every one of which makes four points about something. They may be fairly enough represented by the first and the last.

1. There are foure things greatly to be taken heed of: a Flye in the

eye, a bone in the throat, a dog at the heele, and a theefe in the house.[162]

104. Foure sums are very good for a Bookseller: some wares, some customers, some money, some drink.[163]

One's first impulse is to regard such a style as suitable only for trivial matters. Many of Breton's points, to be sure, are merely quips; but very many of them are not, and when he is most serious Breton is as likely as ever to be euphuistic. One must remember that the "metaphysical" or fantastic tendency profoundly affected seventeenth-century prose as well as verse, and that, in consequence, what was considered most precious, in prose as in verse, was likely to be most ingeniously ornate. Yet undeniably the character, and English prose generally, was somewhat dangerously refined by the attentions of such men as Breton. From that danger it was rescued, in part, by the compelling nature of the subjects that began to demand treatment at the approach of the Civil War. The resulting characters of bishops and roundheads, in which the fourth and fifth decades of the century became so prolific, were not, whatever their other defects, seriously belittled by their euphuism.

Algernon Sidney
and the Motto of the Commonwealth of Massachusetts

I

AT our last meeting two interesting and difficult questions were proposed, to which another may well be added: First, did Algernon Sidney, when he wrote certain words in the Album of the University of Copenhagen, originate or quote those words? Secondly, just what did Sidney write in the album? Thirdly, how did the words *Ense petit placidam sub libertate quietem* come to be adopted as the motto of Massachusetts? To the first and second of these questions I have given little attention, although, as I have investigated the third point, certain bits of evidence have accumulated which seem to me to bear upon them.

Let me first rehearse two sets of well-known facts—those relating to the adoption of a design for the seal, and those relating to Algernon Sidney and his *Discourses concerning Government*.

Soon after the government of Massachusetts began its work of reorganization at Watertown in the summer of 1775, the need of a new seal was realized. On July 28, 1775, the Council[164] which had become the executive branch of the government ordered "That Col. Otis and Doctr. Winthrop, with such as the Honble. House shall join, be a Committee to Consider what is necessary to be done relative to a Colony Seal." On the same day the House concurred, and added to the joint committee Major Hawley, Dr. Church, and Mr. Cushing.[165]

On August 5, at the desire of the Council, the committee

was called together; and, Dr. Church and Mr. Cushing being absent, Major Bliss and Dr. Whiting were substituted.

On the same day the committee recommended to the Council that the former device should be discontinued and that "the Devise herewith be the established form of a Seal for this Colony, for the future." Although the drawing which evidently accompanied this report appears not to have survived, we can roughly conjecture what it was from the action of the Council and of the House upon the report: the Council accepted it "with this Amendment, *viz*. Instead of an Indian holding a Tomahawk and Cap of Liberty, there be an English American, holding a Sword in the Right Hand, and Magna Charta in the Left Hand, with the Words '*Magna Charta*,' imprinted on it." The House accepted the committee's report as thus amended by the Council with one important change: the House voted that "on the devise previous to the word Petit be Inserted the word Ense and subsequent to it the word placidam." That is to say, the committee seems to have recommended the motto "Petit sub libertate quietem," the Council to have accepted this motto, and the House to have inserted the two words necessary to make the motto as we know it. All this was between July 28 and August 5, 1775.[166]

It seems evident that whoever suggested the motto had in mind the line usually attributed to Algernon Sidney; but whether the suggestion originated in the committee, in the Council, in the House, or in the mind of some outsider, the record fails to tell.

II

The more scholarly leaders of the American Revolution habitually sought to fortify their cause by appealing to certain earlier writers on political theory.[167] John Adams spoke for many when he wrote in 1775:

These are what are called revolution principles. They are the principles of Aristotle and Plato, of Livy and Cicero, and Sydney, Harrington and Locke. The principles of nature and eternal reason. The principles on which the whole government over us, now stands.[168]

Among these earlier writers Algernon Sidney[169] holds an important place. His picturesque and independent career, his tragic death, and the solidity and vigor of his *Discourses concerning Government* combine to make him a very striking figure. His father was the second Earl of Leicester; his mother was the daughter of the ninth Earl of Northumberland. As a colonel—later a lieutenant-general—of horse, he fought with credit on the parliamentary side. Believing that "the king could be tried by no court,"[170] he refused to have any part in the later meetings of the court which condemned Charles I, and maintained a position in the matter which gained him the disapproval and suspicion of Cromwell. He became Councillor of State, however, in 1652; and in 1659 —having been in retirement under the Protectorate—he was made a commissioner to negotiate between the Kings of Denmark and Sweden. In the course of his visit to Denmark occurred the famous episode which gives us our motto. The version of the affair which had come to the rather choleric Earl of Leicester occasioned the following passage in a long and bitter letter to Algernon Sidney, which the Earl wrote on August 30, 1660:

It is said that the University of Copenhagen brought their album unto you, desiring you to write something therein, and that you did write in albo[171] these words:

Manus haec inimica tyrannis

and put your name to them; this cannot choose but be publicly known if it be true.[172]

On September 21, 1660, Sidney replied at length and with much patience and courage. In the matter of the line in the album, he said: "That which I am reported to have written in the book at Copenhagen is true; and having never heard, that any sort of men were so worthily objects of enmity, as those I mention, I did never in the least scruple avowing myself to be an enemy unto them."[173] It will be noted that neither in the Earl's memorandum,[172] nor in his letter, nor in Algernon Sidney's reply is there any evidence that Sidney wrote in the album more than the four words, *Manus haec inimica tyrannis*. But, excepting the text as given in Rochester's *Familiar Letters* (see p. 77), these documents were inaccessible until 1835, when they were printed by Blencowe.

After the Restoration, Sidney lived abroad, not always without danger of feeling the vengeance of Charles II, until 1677, when he was allowed to return to England. He found the events of the early 1680's too exciting to keep out of, was arrested after the failure of the Rye-House Plot, tried, condemned on very doubtful evidence, and executed December 7, 1683.

One of the three grounds on which Algernon Sidney was charged with treason was his alleged authorship of a treatise proclaiming the subjects' right of deposing kings by violence. The treatise thus used as evidence either was or strongly resembled Sidney's *Discourses concerning Government*, first published in 1698.[174]

Like the first part of the greater and more influential treatise of Locke, Sidney's *Discourses concerning Government* is a refutation, point by point, of Sir Robert Filmer's *Patriarcha, or The Natural Power of Kings Asserted*,[175] first published in 1680. In his *Patriarcha*, Filmer advances the belief that kingship is "natural" and essentially like a father's authority over his family. Earlier writers had often, though usually by way of metaphorical adornment, termed a king the father of his people: Filmer makes this metaphor the foundation-stone of his argument. Basing his treatise upon an idea somewhat more historical than the notion of a contract, and helping much to rid political philosophy of argument from biblical texts, Filmer is more important for his methods than for his results. Indeed, his results are now chiefly remembered for the attack made upon them by Locke and Sidney.

Now, without commenting upon their validity, let me briefly summarize [176] some of Sidney's principal arguments, using mainly his own words:

Our inquiry is not after that which is preferred, well knowing that no such thing is found among men; but we seek that human constitution which is attended with the least or the most pardonable inconveniences. [177]

Antiquity teaches that kings reign only by the consent of the people, in whom lay the whole source of power, for the liberty of a people is the gift of God and nature. [178] Princes as well as other magistrates are set up by the people for the public good. [179] Hence, in all controversies concerning the power of magistrates we are not to examine what conduces to their profit or glory, but what is good for the public. [180] If disagreements happen between king and people, why is it a more desperate opinion to think that the king should be subject to the censures of the people than the people subject to the will of the king? [181] That law which is not just is not a law, and that which is not law ought not to be obeyed. [182] There can be no such thing in the world as the rebellion of a nation against its own chief magistrates. The whole body of a nation cannot be tied to any other obedience than is consistent with the common good, according to their judgment; and having never been subdued or brought to terms with their chief magistrates, they cannot be said to revolt or rebel against them, to whom they owe no more than seems good to themselves, and who are nothing of or by themselves, more than other men. [183]

Laws and constitutions ought to be weighed; and whilst all due reverence is paid to such as are good, every nation may not only retain in itself a power of changing or abolishing all such as are not so, but ought to exercise that power according to the best of their understanding; and in the place of what was either at first mistaken, or afterwards corrupted, to constitute that which is most conducing to the establishment of Justice and Liberty.[184]

All nations have been, and are, more or less happy, as they or their ancestors have had vigor of spirit, integrity of manners, and wisdom to invent and establish such orders, and as have better or worse provided for this common good, which was sought by all.[185]

Perhaps I have set forth at too great length these matters relating to Sidney and his book; but it seems to me that, in trying to connect Sidney with the leaders of the American Revolution, we should think of him as they did—not primarily as the author of a striking Latin sentence, but as a martyr to liberty, and especially as the author of a work abounding in precisely the arguments that they required.

Our next step must be to ask how accessible this motto was before 1775 to the Massachusetts leaders of the American Revolution, who, as we have seen, had ample reason to study Algernon Sidney.

Curiously enough, we cannot understand this matter without some consideration of Thomas Hollis (1720–1774) and certain of his gifts and letters.[186] The Thomas Hollis in question is the third of his name, and is usually known as Thomas Hollis of Lincoln's Inn, by which title he himself requested that he should be styled. Upon the death of his father and his great-uncle, Thomas Hollis inherited their fortunes and the family interest in Harvard College. This interest soon began to show not only by gifts of money, but by gifts of certain books, which are for our purpose extremely interesting.

Hollis, as is well known, was rich, learned, eccentric, a born collector and bibliophile, and a passionate lover of liberty. He formed the habit of sending to public libraries and to private individuals copies of certain books, prints, and medals having to do with the history of republican doctrines. Upon the books especially Hollis lavished great care. To judge from those which were sent to the Harvard College Library and which escaped the fire of 1764,[187] the bindings—especially of the books that Hollis cared most for—were apt to be rich and striking.[188] Hollis had a fancy for bright shades of Russia leather, and his binder used certain dies made to Hollis's order and often representing portions of his arms. The figure of Britannia, an owl, an olive branch, a dagger, or a lion will often be found on the back or the panel of one of Hollis's books. He was, furthermore, in the habit of writing inscriptions upon the fly-leaves, in which his eager devotion to the cause of liberty found full expression.

President Holyoke and the other authorities of the College were naturally appreciative of this munificent patron and did what they could to display his gifts effectively. On July 9, 1766, President Holyoke wrote as follows to Hollis, describing the alcove in the College Library where the Hollis books were arranged:

SIR: Having reserved one of the alcoves in our Library, of which there are ten in all, for your books, we have now placed them; and a most beautiful appearance they make: we have some other alcoves that look very well, but not as the Hollis.[189] Though I look upon this as a small thing in comparison with the wise choice you have made of the subjects in them treated of, and the excellent authors among them; as they well nigh fill one alcove, we have hung therein a table, whereon is inscribed the name of Hollis, in large gilt capitals; besides which there is pasted on the inside of the cover of each of your bo[o]ks the inclosed, cut in black as to those of them we suffer to be lent out, and in red as to those we think too precious for loan, which those gentlemen who want them may consult in the library, we having all conveniences for that purpose, and the Librarian always ready to attend them.[190]

The splendors of the Hollis alcove are also sung by the unknown author of *Harvardium Restauratum* (1766):[191]

> *Harvard's new built walls contain*
> *Fairest memorials of thy* [192] *lib'ral soul.*
> *From that grand alcove, destin'd to receive*
> *The learned treasures by thy bounteous hand*
> *Presented, we behold, with wond'ring eyes,*
> *The splendid tomes, throughout the spacious room,*
> *Like orient sol diffuse their beamy glories!*

We have here, I think, a very interesting situation. At a time when the College Library—originally classical and theological for the most part—was just feeling the need of books on affairs of the state, these striking gifts of Thomas Hollis must have been for young men of the Adams, Mayhew, and Otis type one of the great formative influences of their lives.[193]

But Hollis by no means confined his generosity to Harvard College. Early in the 1750's he was attracted by the learning and vigor of the Reverend Jonathan Mayhew, whom he speedily made his most intimate New England correspondent. To Mayhew he sent such frequent and magnificent gifts that the good minister professed himself to be almost overwhelmed with Hollis's generosity. He was in the habit of sending a number of extra copies of certain books and prints and of relying upon Mayhew's discretion to place them to the best advantage.[194]

The temptation is strong to go on speaking at length about Thomas Hollis as an influence upon the formation of revolutionary sentiment; but we must leave him for the moment, to return to him later in connection with certain of his gifts.

In 1694 Robert Viscount Molesworth (1656–1725) published the first edition of *An | Acccount | Of | Denmark, | As | It was in the Year* 1692. / [motto] / *London: | Printed in the Year*

1694. / Molesworth had himself been an ambassador to Denmark in 1689, and was an ardent republican and admirer of Sidney. The introduction of his book is a vigorous plea for popular government. On page xxiii of this introduction, Molesworth writes:

> That Kingdom [*i.e.* Denmark] has often had the Misfortune to be govern'd by French Counsels. At the Time when Mr. Algernon Sidney was Ambassador at that Court, Monsieur Terlon, the French Ambassador, had the Confidence to tear out of the Book of Mottos in the King's Library, this Verse, which Mr. Sidney (according to the Liberty allowed to all noble Strangers) had written in it:
>
> > *Manus haec inimica Tyrannis*
> > *Ense petit placidam sub libertate quietem.*
>
> Though Monsieur Terlon understood not a Word of Latin, he was told by others the Meaning of that Sentence, which he considered as a Libel upon the French Government, and upon such as was then setting up in Denmark by French Assistance or Example.

Here, then, is one place where the motto might have been read. How accessible was Molesworth? There was a copy of the first edition in the library of John Adams, who also owned a copy of the sixth edition, Glasgow, 1752.[195] The Harvard College Library received in 1764 a copy of the edition of 1738, on the fly-leaf of which Thomas Hollis wrote the following inscription:

> The preface to the Acc. of Denmark, and the Translator's preface to Hottoman's Franco-gallia[196] are two of the NOBLEST in the English language.

It appears, therefore, that Molesworth in 1694 was the first to use the complete motto in connection with Algernon Sidney. Three years later, the complete motto reappears, but in a slightly different form. This is in Rochester's *Familiar Letters*, which (p. 57) contains the following version of the Copenhagen episode, with the motto in a novel form:

It is said, That the University of *Copenhagen* brought their *Album* unto you, desiring you to write something therein, and that you did *scribere in Albo* these words,

> *Manus haec inimica Tyrannis,*
> *Ense petit placida cum Libertate quietem.*[197]

More important still were the various editions of Sidney's *Discourses concerning Government.* Of these there seem to be the following:

Discourses / Concerning / Government, / By / Algernon Sidney, / Son to *Robert* Earl of *Leicester*, and Ambassador / from the Commonwealth of *England* to *Charles* / *Gustavus* King of *Sweden*. / *Published* from an *Original Manuscript of the Author*. / London, / Printed, and are to be sold by the Booksellers of / *London* and *Westminster*. MDCXCVIII. Folio.

No portrait. Copenhagen episode not given.

Discourses / Concerning / Government, / By Algernon Sidney, / Son to *Robert* Earl of *Leicester*, and / Ambassador from the Commonwealth of *Eng-/land* to *Charles Gustavus* King of *Sweden*. / The Second Edition carefully corrected. / To which is Added, / The Paper He deliver'd to the Sheriffs / immediately before his Death. / And an Alphabetical Table. / London, / Printed by *J. Darby* in Bartholomew-Close. MDCCIV. Folio.

Portrait, with motto below. Copenhagen episode not given.[198]

Discourses / Concerning / Government; / By / Algernon Sidney, / Son to Robert Earl of Leicester, / And / Ambassador from the Commonwealth of England / to Charles Gustavus King of Sweden. / Published from an Original Manuscript of the Author. / To which is added, / A Short Account of the Author's Life. / And a Copious Index. / In Two Volumes. / Vol. I. / Edinburgh: / Printed for G. Hamilton and J. Balfour. / M.DCC.L. Boston Public Library, Adams, 292.17.

No portrait, Copenhagen episode (p. xiv), with motto in full and usual form.

Discourses / Concerning / Government. / By / Algernon Sidney, Esq; / To which are added, / Memoirs of his Life, / And / An Apology for Himself, / Both Now first published, / And the latter from his Original Man-

uscript. | *The Third Edition.* | *With an Alphabetical Index of the principal* *Matters.* | [cut] | *London:* | *Printed for A. Millar, opposite Catharine's-* *street in* | *the Strand, M.DCC.LI.* Folio.

Portrait, with motto below. Copenhagen episode (p. vii), with motto in full and usual form.

Discourses Concerning Government | *By Algernon Sydney* | *With His* *Letters Trial Apology* | *And Some Memoirs Of His Life* | *London:* *Printed For A. Millar* | *MDCCLXIII* | *Or To The Tribunals Under* *Change Of Times.* 4°.

Portrait, with Molesworth version of Copenhagen episode below. The episode retold in text (p. 8) with motto in full and usual form.

The Works Of Algernon Sydney | *A New Edition* | *London, Printed* *by W Strahan Iun.* | *For T. Becket and Co. and T. Cadell,* | *In The* *Strand; T. Davies, In Russel* | *Street; And T. Evans, In King Street* | *MDCCLXXII* | [cut of liberty cap] | *"Or To The Uniust Tribunals* *Under Change Of Times."* 4°.

Same as edition of 1763, except that Copenhagen episode occurs on p. 10 of text.

Of these, the edition of 1698 does not contain the motto. The edition of 1750 was published at Edinburgh in two volumes. There is a copy in the library of John Adams (now at the Public Library of the City of Boston) which contains on the fly-leaf of the first volume the inscription "John Adams 1766." In this edition (pp. vii ff.) is "A Short Account of the Life of Algernon Sidney," which (p. xiv) contains an account of the Copenhagen episode and the complete motto. It is very important to note that John Mein's circulating library on King Street, "Second Door above the British Coffee-House," contained in 1765 a copy of the Sidney of 1750, which the compiler of Mein's catalogue regarded as deserving an analysis of its contents to the length of about twelve lines.[199]

Besides the English editions of Sidney, there are several translations in French.[200] There is in the library of the American Academy of Arts and Sciences a highly interesting copy of the French edition of 1702, published at The Hague in three duodecimo volumes:

Discours | Sur | Le Gouvernement, | Par Algernon Sidney, | Fils de Robert Comte de Leicester, | Et | Ambassadeur | De | La République D'Angleterre | Près De | Charles Gustave | Roi de Suède. | Publiez sur l'Original Manuscrit de l'Auteur. | Traduits De L'Anglois, | Par P. A. Samson. | Tome Premier. | [cut] | A La Haye, | . . . . | M.DCCII.

The first volume has a portrait of Sidney entirely different from any that I have seen in the English editions. The fourth page of the preface tells the Copenhagen incident, with the motto in the form found in Rochester's *Familiar Letters* in 1697. Each volume has the autograph of Jeremiah Gridley[201] and a bookplate showing that it was given to the Academy by the Honorable James Bowdoin, Esq.,[202] in 1790. This copy is important because it not only brings into our story James Bowdoin and Jeremiah Gridley, but—from Gridley's relation to John Adams and the other young lawyers of Adams's generation—it suggests a very considerable influence.

This leaves to be considered the four very interesting editions of 1704, 1751, 1763, and 1772. I must confess that I began this investigation supposing that, in order to come across this motto, readers of John Adams's day would have to go pretty far afield; but a glance at the portraits opposite the title-pages of these four editions will show that whoever turned to any one of them, even for a moment, could hardly help noticing the motto: in the editions of 1704 and 1751 it stands out alone and conspicuously below Sidney's portrait; in the quartos of 1763 and 1772 it is similarly placed, though imbedded in Molesworth's account of the Copenhagen episode.

Of the edition of 1704 there is at present a copy in the Boston Public Library, which was given by Mrs. W. S. Fitz, February 14, 1894. It contains the autograph of Henry Ward

Post, 1859, the bookplate of James Birch, and an almost illegible autograph (perhaps that of James Birch), below which the words "Middle Temple" can be distinguished. I have no evidence that there was a copy of this edition in Massachusetts before 1775.

Of the edition of 1751 there is an extremely interesting copy in the Harvard College Library, splendidly bound in red Russia leather, with elaborate stamping in gilt of a very special design. The volume is one of four copies printed on large paper and extra illustrated with six prints of Algernon Sidney, which are so important in their bearing upon our problem that they must be spoken of separately a little later. There is strong reason for believing that this copy of the edition of 1751, which came to the Harvard College Library from President Walker, belonged to the Reverend Jonathan Mayhew of Boston, who appears clearly to have been Hollis's most intimate friend in Massachusetts. If this was Mayhew's book, we may be perfectly sure that more than one person who was later to take a prominent part in the events of 1775 saw the book in Mayhew's study.

That there was a copy of the 1751 edition in the Harvard College Library is more than probable, though proof is almost necessarily lacking, since there is no catalogue of the College Library between 1723 and 1773. In 1723, of course, this book had not been published; in 1773 nearly the whole library had been wiped out by the fire of January 24, 1764. It will be remembered that at the time of that fire the Council was meeting in the very room which contained the folio of 1751, if the College possessed it. It is, of course, mere speculation to suggest that in that case several members of the Council would doubtless have examined a volume which in typography and binding must have been one of the handsomest in the library and which in subject-matter was of peculiar interest to Massachusetts statesmen.

Of the edition of 1763 there is a particularly interesting copy in the Harvard College Library. On the back is stamped the owl, indicating that Thomas Hollis thought that there was much wisdom in the book. On one of the fly-leaves is the following inscription:

Thomas Hollis, an Englishman, a Lover of Liberty, his Country, and its excellent Constitution, as nobly restored at the happy Revolution, is desirous of having the honour to deposite this book in the public library of Harvard College, at Cambridge in New England.

Pall Mall, ap. 14, 1763.

On the next leaf, below the printed figure of Britannia, Hollis wrote:

Felicity is freedom, and freedom is magnanimity!

THUCYD.

I need not emphasize the accessibility of a motto opposite the title-page of a book thus bound and inscribed, placed in the Hollis alcove of the Harvard College Library.

It is certain that Jonathan Mayhew also received a copy of this same edition of Sidney, although he had probably received previously the folio of 1751; for on November 21, 1763, Mayhew wrote to Hollis as follows:

I received, together with your last another Box of Books.

Indeed, Sir, you so confound me with your repeated favors of this Sort, that I know not what to say by way of Acknowledgement; I shall therefore leave you to conjecture with what sentiments of gratitude I receive them. Tho' I have of late been much engaged, I have read most of the Books & Publications which you last sent me excepting two or three which I had before met with.

After mentioning several other books sent by Hollis, Mayhew says of the Sidney:

By the *Spirit* of the Notes on the New Edition of the admirable *Sydney*, I am so well satisfied *who* added them, as not to desire *any Information on that* head.

[81]

Late in the same letter Mayhew assures Hollis that "Duplicates of Books sent, are distributed agreeably to your Directions, and my best Discretion."[203] It is probable, therefore, that some of these duplicates were copies of Sidney and that Mayhew gave them to two or three other Massachusetts men.

After Mayhew's death in 1766, Andrew Eliot[204] became Thomas Hollis's chief correspondent in New England, although no one could quite fill Mayhew's place in Hollis's affection. That Hollis sent Andrew Eliot a copy of Sidney in November of 1767 is clear from Eliot's letter to Hollis of December 10, 1767.[205]

The remaining edition, that of 1772, is in the Harvard College Library, though there is no evidence that it was in Massachusetts before 1775.[206] There is a copy of the book in the John Adams library, though the absence of his autograph makes it not perfectly certain that he owned the book before 1775.[207]

Another source of local but real interest is a "set of prints" from Thomas Hollis, sent to the Harvard College Library. The volume is a handsome thin folio, characteristically bound at Hollis's order, and with his initials on the side. Within, he has written on the fly-leaf:

Thomas Hollis, an Englishman, a Lover of Liberty, Citizen of the World, is desirous of having the honour to present this set of prints to Harvard College at Cambridge in New England.

Pall Mall, sept. 14, 1764.

The book contains thirteen handsome prints all engraved at Hollis's order. Of these the seventh in order is Sidney's, with the motto below, approximately as in the frontispiece to the editions of 1763 and 1772.

Although no actual proof can be attached to it, a word ought to be said here about the very interesting set of prints[208] bound up with the large paper copy of the 1751 edition of

Sidney, which is now in the Harvard College Library and which was originally, I think, presented to Jonathan Mayhew. These six prints are in different states, but in each case the motto appears very conspicuously.

Another interesting gift of Thomas Hollis to the Harvard College Library was a fine copy of Lucan[209] in the quarto edition printed at Leyden in 1728. From the binding, and the "Floreat Libertas" which Hollis has written into the text at one point,[210] it is clear that he considered the gift an important addition to his republican propaganda. On the fly-leaf at the end of the book Hollis has written

> *Manus haec inimica Tyrannis*
> *Ense petit placidam sub libertate quietem.*
> A. SIDNEY.

Not less striking than any of the books thus far discussed is a copy of John Locke's *Letters concerning Toleration*, London, 1765, for the gift of which to the Harvard College Library we are again indebted to Thomas Hollis, who wrote on the fly-leaf:

> Thomas Hollis, an Englishman, Citizen of the World, is desirous of having the honor to present this Book to the Library of Harvard College, at Cambridge in N. England.

> Pall Mall, jan. 1, 1765.

The profound influence of Locke upon the leaders of the American Revolution is well known. "Locke, in particular, was the authority to whom the Patriots paid greatest deference. . . . Almost every writer seems to have been influenced by him, many quoted his words, and the argument of others shows the unmistakable imprint of his philosophy."[211] It is safe to assume, therefore, that many readers before 1775 handled the Hollis copy of Locke's *Letters concerning Toleration* in the Harvard College Library. As they did so, they inevitably came across the last four words of the motto, for on the back cover these words are stamped as below:

———PLACIDAM SVB LIBERTATE QVIETEM

It would seem, therefore, that those who between 1751 and 1772 knew the Harvard College Library, or enjoyed the friendship of Thomas Hollis or of his most intimate New England correspondents, could hardly have failed to have the Sidney motto impressed upon their memory as a striking summary of his doctrines.

In the case of a few prominent Massachusetts men, we fortunately have real evidence that they knew their Sidney. Josiah Quincy, Jr., in his will, which is dated February 28, 1774, wrote: "I give to my son, when he shall arrive at the age of fifteen years, Algernon Sidney's Works, John Locke's Works, Lord Bacon's Works, Gordon's Tacitus & Cato's Letters." "May the spirit of liberty rest upon him."[212] On May 13, 1767, Andrew Eliot writes to Thomas Hollis to say that he is pleased with a certain treatise which "justly gives the author a place among the most noble writers on government." "I could have wished, however," he adds, "that when the editor mentioned him as inferior *only* to *Milton*, he had also inserted *Sydney*, 'that,' as you justly style him, 'Martyr to Civil Liberty.' I am perhaps prejudiced in favor of that great man, because he was the first who taught me to form any just sentiments on government."

On Friday, May 17, 1766, the Reverend Jonathan Mayhew preached a Thanksgiving sermon which was afterwards published under the title of *The Snare Broken*.[213] On page 35 of this sermon he wrote:

Having been initiated, in youth, in the doctrines of civil liberty, as they were taught by such men as Plato, Demosthenes, Cicero, and other renowned persons among the ancients; and such men as Sidney and Milton, Locke and Hoadley, among the moderns; I liked them;

they seemed rational. . . . As I advanced towards, and into, manhood; I would not, I cannot now, tho' past middle age, relinquish the fair object of my youthful affections, LIBERTY; whose charms, instead of decaying with time in my eyes, have daily captivated me more and more.

But Mayhew and Andrew Eliot, interesting as they are, yield to John Adams, who stands forth conspicuously among those who may well have been responsible for bringing about the adoption of our motto.

On September 17, 1823, John Adams wrote to Jefferson:

I have lately undertaken to read Algernon Sidney on government. There is a great difference in reading a book at four-and-twenty and at eighty-eight. As often as I have read it and fumbled it over, it now excites fresh admiration that this work has excited so little interest in the literary world. As splendid an edition of it as the art of printing can produce, as well for the intrinsic merits of the work, as for the proof it brings of the bitter sufferings of the advocates of liberty from that time to this, and to show the slow progress of moral, philosophical, political illumination in the world, ought to be now published in America.[214]

This letter seems to show that John Adams first became acquainted with Sidney's *Discourses concerning Government* in the year 1759, although—as we have seen—it was not until 1766, apparently, that he possessed a copy. In his *Defense of the Constitutions of Government of the United States of America*, 1778,[215] the fifth chapter consists of extracts from various writers on government. Of these, three pages are from Sidney. Later, in the same work[216] Adams names certain writers on government—Sidney first of all—and then remarks: "Americans should make collections of all these speculations, to be preserved as the most precious relics of antiquity, both for curiosity and for use." Most interesting of all, however, is a passage in the final paragraph—the peroration itself—of John Adams's speech in defence of Captain Preston in 1770. No one here needs to be told that, by defending the officer who was thought to have ordered the firing which began the Boston massacre, Adams was taking a very serious step. It is inconceivable that he did not prepare his speech with the greatest care. When, therefore, we find him, at the peroration of this speech, appealing to the authority of Sidney, that fact has great weight in settling the question of Sidney's place in the thought of the period. But notice the words with which John Adams introduces his quotation from Sidney's *Discourses*: "To use the words of a great and worthy man, a patriot and a hero, an enlightened friend to mankind, and a martyr to liberty—I mean Algernon Sidney—who, from his earliest infancy *sought a tranquil retirement under the shadow of the tree of liberty, with* his tongue, his pen, and *his sword*,"[217]—and then follows the quotation. Here we have, five years before the motto was officially adopted, at least one bit of clear evidence that it was known. Had Adams been in Watertown instead of in Philadelphia from July 27 to August 5, 1775, one might easily imagine that he suggested the motto.

But John Adams was in Philadelphia at this time; Andrew Eliot had gone to Connecticut;[218] Jonathan Mayhew had died in 1766 and Josiah Quincy, Jr., in April of 1775. Others were left on the scene, to be sure, who knew their Sidney well enough to have suggested the motto, and doubtless many such persons have eluded my search; but so far as the immediate suggestion of the motto between July 27 and August 5 is concerned, it seems to me that—unless led by positive evidence—we are not very safe in going outside of the committee, the members of which were, it will be remembered, Colonel Otis, Dr. Winthrop, Major Hawley, Major Bliss, and Dr. Whiting.[219] Perhaps it is because I know so little about the last three; but at any rate I am strongly impressed by the eligibility of Dr. Winthrop to fill the missing place. Dr. Winthrop is, of course, Professor John

Winthrop (1714–1779)[220] who graduated from Harvard in 1732, was appointed to the Hollis Professorship of Mathematics and Natural and Experimental Philosophy in 1738, and received the degree of LL.D. from the University of Edinburgh in 1771 and from Harvard in 1773.[221] Professor Winthrop was twice offered the presidency of the College, and was generally regarded as its most eminent professor. His eminence, furthermore, extended beyond the field of science: not only was he internationally famous for his discoveries in regard to comets, but he impressed the Reverend Charles Chauncy as knowing "a vast deal in every part of literature,"[222] and is regarded by President Quincy as "perhaps better entitled to the character of a universal scholar than any individual of his time, in this country."[223] Winthrop would not have been afraid of a Latin motto, for he himself wrote Latin prose and perhaps Latin verse;[224] and the fact that he held the Hollis Professorship from 1738 to 1779 guarantees his special interest in the benefactions of the Hollis family. If anyone feels that even Winthrop might easily miss seeing the Hollis books, let him remember that the library consisted of only five thousand volumes, that it was all in one room, that the Hollis books were much the most conspicuous part of it, and that John Winthrop's son, James Winthrop (1752–1821), was librarian from 1772 to 1787,[225] and so would almost inevitably have called each of the Hollis books to his father's attention as fast as it came. In fact, so long as we are obliged to be content with mere probabilities, is not the claim of John Winthrop to have made the immediate suggestion of the motto strong enough to stand until it is overthrown by positive proof in favor of someone else?

I end, as I began, with three unsolved questions. It would have been delightful to run down that Latin quotation. It would be pleasant to know whether Sidney wrote in the album one line or two, and, if two, precisely what form he gave to the second line. It would be still more worth while to discover positive evidence in regard to the identity of the person who first suggested the motto in or to the committee. But to me this problem is most interesting not as a threefold puzzle in such details, but as a broader study in the development of one very important formative influence upon our people from 1750 to 1775. When it is so considered, it seems to me that the dominating figure is, ultimately, not Mayhew or Adams, but our republican benefactor, Thomas Hollis of Lincoln's Inn—the man who in 1766 wrote to Jonathan Mayhew:

More books, especially on government, are going to New England. Should those go safe, it is hoped that no principal books on that FIRST subject will be wanting in Harvard College, from the days of Moses to these times. Men of New England, brethren, use them for yourselves, and for others; and God bless you!

On the Authorship of
Singing of Psalms a Gospel Ordinance

AMONG the treasures of the collection recently given to the Harvard College Library by the widow of the late Frederick L. Gay is a unique copy of the first edition of a work usually ascribed to John Cotton:

Singing / Of / Psalmes / A Gospel-Ordinance / Or / A Treatise, / Wherein are handled these foure Particulars. / 1. *Touching the Duty it selfe.* / 2. *Touching the Matter to be Sung.* / 3. *Touching the Singers.* / 4. *Touching the Manner of Singing.* / By John Cotton, Teacher of the / Church at *Boston* in *New-England.* / London; / Printed by M. S. for *Hannah Allen*, at the *Crowne* / in *Popes-Head-*Alley: and *John Rothwell* at the / *Sunne* and *Fountaine* in *Pauls-*Church-yard. / 1647.

On the reverse of the title-page, in the handwriting of John Cotton, is a list of "Faults in ye Printing corrected" as follows:

Faults in ye Printing corrected.

Pag. 4. lin. 16.	not ædifyed	reade	is not ædefyed.
lin. 32.	Prov. 9, 10.	reade	2 Chron. 35:21, 22.
Pag. 24. lin. 4.	Instruments	reade	Instructions.
lin. 16.	as	reade	but as.
Pag. 26. lin. 21.	Donology	reade	Doxology.
Pag. 35. lin. 13.	have	reade	not have.
Pag. 47. lin. 22.	to	reade	so.
Pag. 49. lin. 17.	to ye Golden Calf	reade	to ye making of ye Golden Calf.
lin. 32.	left in	reade	left it to.
Pag. 51. lin. 7.	Partition of wall	reade	Partition wall.
Pag. 52. lin. 6.	cleane	reade	uncleane.
lin. 28.	and	blot out	
lin. 31.	in singing forth ye Praises of ye Lord, Adde, yet neither were their Psalmes types of ours but one & ye same: neither was their singing with voyces a type of ours: but both of them a Performance of one & ye same morall Duety, the singing of ye Praises of ye Lord, so		

Pag. 53. lin. 7. so   reade yet.
Pag. 64. lin. 5. Art   reade Act.
Pag. 65. lin. 3. As   blot out
Pag. 70. lin. 11. to Abuse   reade to Prævent
     lin. 25. Idoll   reade Idiot

Below this list of errata[226] is a rather surprising memorandum, apparently in the handwriting of the younger Thomas Shepard (1635–1677), who graduated from Harvard College in 1653, and in 1659 was ordained teacher of the Church at Charlestown, where he remained until his death. Shepard writes:

Mr. Edward Bulkley pastor of ye Ch of X^t in Concord told me Sept. 20. 1674 that w^n he boarded at m^r Cotton's house at ye 1st coming forth of this book of singing of psalmes, m^r Cotton told him that my Father Shepard had the chief hand in ye composing of it, & y^{r}fore, m^r Cotton said, I am troubled that my bro: Shepard's name is not praefixed to it.

The title-page of the Gay copy is also interesting. At the top, apparently inked over an older inscription, appears the autograph of Thomas Shepard, with the date 1655. Below that we find "Wm Brattle's book March 23 170^4/$_5$." Just above the words "By John Cotton" we find, apparently in the hand of the third Thomas Shepard (1658–1685), the words "my H[onore]d Grandfather Mr. Thomas Shepard pastor of Camb: as my Father told me Mr. Cotton acknowledged w[he]n it came forth."

To decide from internal evidence whether John Cotton or Thomas Shepard is more likely to have written the *Singing of Psalms a Gospel Ordinance* is a task quite beyond my powers. I should suppose that the similarity of the two men in learning and in style would, in fact, make extremely difficult the work of anyone who should attempt to settle the matter on such grounds. I propose merely to record the existence of this odd bit of testimony to Shepard's authorship,[227] and then to attempt a partial answer to the question which one naturally asks,—namely, Why did not John Cotton take measures to see that Shepard's name was prefixed to the work?

That this question suggests itself indicates that we naturally assume the seventeenth-century author to have had the same control over his work as that enjoyed in our own time, —that is, we assume that he could make sure that title-page, front matter, and text were all as he wished them to be. Let me cite a few instances to show that the seventeenth-century author was to a surprising degree at the mercy of the publisher.

George Wither's *Scholar's Purgatory*, undated, but published about 1625, contains a very interesting character sketch of a good stationer and another of a bad stationer.[228] It must of course be remembered that Wither's quarrels with the publishers somewhat injure the value of his very spicy testimony. Of the mere stationer Wither says that he

will not stick to bely his author's intentions, or to publish secretly that there is somewhat in his new imprinted books against the state, or some Honourable personages; that so, they being questioned, his ware may have the quicker sale. He makes no scruple to put out the right author's name, and insert another in the second edition of a book; and when the impression of some pamphlet lies upon his hands, to imprint new Titles for it (and so take men's moneys twice or thrice for the same matter under diverse names) is no injury in his opinion.

If he gett any written Coppy into his powre, likely to be vendible, whether the Author be willing or no, he will publish it; And it shall be contrived and named alsoe, according to his owne pleasure: which is the reason, so many good Bookes come forth imperfect, and with foolish titles. Nay, he oftentymes gives bookes such names as in his opinion will make them saleable, when there is litle or nothing in the whole volume sutable to such a Tytle.[229]

It was probably somewhat more than forty years later that

Samuel Butler wrote his character of A Stationer, concerning whom he finds nothing good to say:

When a book lies upon his hand and will not sell, notwithstanding all his lies and forgeries of known mens approbation, his last remedy is to print a new title-page, and give it a new name, (as mercers do by their old rotten stuffs) and if that will not do it is past cure, and falls away to waste paper. He makes the same use of mens names as forgers do, and will rob the living and the dead of their reputation by setting their hands to the frauds and impostures of false and counterfeit scriblers, to abuse the world, and cheat men of their money and understanding.[230]

These passages, of course, are written by satirists who were almost required by the rules to exaggerate the foibles of humanity. There are a number of cases in which the evidence is somewhat less open to doubt.

In 1646 *The Perfect Diurnal*, No. 185, which is dated February 8–15, contains (p. 1486) a note that "such hath bin the malice of some ignorant Anonymous" as to write a pamphlet "to scandalize and vilifie the army under his Excellency Sir *Tho. Fairfax*," in which pamphlet he gives a false account of a murder "for the better vending of his pamphlet."

Three years later the same periodical gives us another instance:

This is desired to be inserted; That Whereas there was lately printed, and put to publike sale a book called *A discription of the Country and People of Scotland*; That consisted of some invectives against that Nation which was entituled to Mr. *James Howell*, I do hereby declare and attest that *He* was not the Author thereof, nor had any thing to doe with it, and that there was use made of his name, not out of any designe to prejudice so well known and worthy a Gentleman, but to further only the vending of the thing; Therefore with all due respectfullnesse, I do hereby crave his pardon, and desire the world to take notice hereof.

London this 6 of July: 1649   *per me I. Stephens.*[231]

In 1649 *The Perfect Diurnall* for July 30–August 6, No.

314, contains on the last page the notice that "there is an excellent peece come forth entituled An hue and cry after *Vox Populi*, written by that learned and judicious Minister, Mr. *John Collins* in Norwich." But a month later, in No. 319 (p. 2513), the editor found it necessary to retract, which he did as follows:

About a moneth since at the request of a Bookseller of Norwich, was incerted in the *Diurnall* that Master Collins MInister [*sic*, for Minister] of Norwich, had published a book intituled a hew and cry after Vox populi, the said Mr. Collins desires you to take notice, that he did not write or compose the said book, but utterly disclaims it.

On September 22, 1655, Lord Tweeddale wrote to Cromwell from Edinburgh, declaring that in a late pamphlet called *A Short Discovery of his Highness the Lord Protector's Intentions touching the Anabaptists in the Army*, etc., his *"name is used to a Forgery."*[232]

In 1659 Edward Reynolds found it necessary to declare that he did not write a certain book advertised as his. He inserted his disavowal as an advertisement in the *Publick Intelligencer*, No. 2, p. 380 (April 18–25, 1659):

Advertisement:

Whereas in a Catalogue of Books Printed and sold by Henry Marsh *at the Princes Arms in Chancery-lane near Fleetstreet, annexed to a Book of* Edw. Leigh *Esq; entituled,* England *Described, there is mention of a Book called,* A Word of Caution to the present Times, in relation to the Atheists and Errorists thereof. By *Edward Reynolds* D. D. *The said* Edward Reynolds *doth hereby declare, That he never was either the Author or Publisher of any such Book, but hath been herein wronged by the Compiler and Publisher of that Catalogue.*

Although many other cases might be cited,[233] perhaps one more will suffice; and this is a colloquy which appears in the course of John Tutchin's trial for a libel (1704) entitled *The Observator:*

Mr. Mountague. The question I would ask you, is; do you, when you have a copy, strictly keep to the letter of the copy? Or do you, as you think convenient, alter it?

How. I have altered it oftentimes to make it safe.

Mr. Mountague. Then you do take it on you to alter?

How. To strike out a line, never to alter his sense.

Mr. Mountague. Do you not insert any thing?

How. Yes, frequently a word.

Mr. Mountague. Do you not take upon you to insert several words, and leave out several?

How. Yes.[234]

As may readily be imagined, New England authors were not less imposed upon than their English brethren by these conditions of publication. In the preface to *A Disputation Concerning Church-Members and Their Children*, London, 1659, the writer gives us, particularly in his last sentence, some astonishing light upon this situation:

And this is the rather said, because perhaps the Reader may have been deceived in some other Treatises, which have gone abroad, and generally been look't upon, as the compilement of the Elders in New-England; whereas they had but one private person for their Author. So it is indeed in the 32 Questions, the Answerer whereof was Mr. Richard Mather, and not any other Elder or Elders in New England, who likewise is the Author of the discourse concerning Church-Covenant printed therewith, which latter he wrote for his private use in his own Study, never intending, nor indeed consenting to its publication, nor so much as knowing unto this day how the copy of it came abroad into those hands by whom it was made publick, save that he conjectures some procured a copy of it from Mr. Cotton, to whom (such was their intimacy in his lifetime) he communicated it, as he writes in a late Letter to a Son of his now in England who it seems had enquired of him concerning those Treatises; and much less is there any truth in that which is said in the Title page prefixed to the Discourse of Church-Covenant, as if it were sent over to Mr. Barnard Anno 1639; Mr. Mather having neither acquaintance nor any intercourse by Letters with Mr. Barnard.

The case of Edward Johnson's *Wonder-Working Providence of Sions Saviour in New England* is sufficiently well known.[235] It will be remembered that Nathaniel Brooke, who brought out in 1653, under date of 1654, the first edition of Johnson's book, inserted the unsold copies as the third part of *America Painted to the Life*, 1659, and asserted that the whole was "written by Sir Ferdinando Gorges Knight." Against this fraud the younger Gorges (grandson of the alleged author) protested in the following advertisement, which appeared in the *Mercurius Politicus* for September 13, 1660:

I, Ferdinando Gorges, the entituled Author of a late Book, called *America Painted to the Life*, am injured in that additional Part, called Sion's Saviour in New England (as written by Sir Ferdinando Gorges:) that being none of his, and formerly printed in another name, the true owner.

Both Shepard and Cotton had suffered from this kind of vexation. Of his *Sincere Convert* Shepard is reputed[236] to have written to Giles Firmin:

It was a collection of such notes in a dark town in England, which one procuring of me, published them without my will, or my privity. I scarce know what it contains, nor do I like to see it; considering the many Σφαλματα typographica, most absurd; and the confession of him that published it, that it comes out much altered from what was first written.

"And this," exclaims Albro,[237] "was said in October, 1647, a year after the English publisher, in his fourth edition, declared that the book had been 'corrected and much amended by the author.'"

Of John Cotton his grandson wrote that "few of John Cotton's works were printed with his own *knowledge* or *consent.* . . . his printed works, whereof there are many, that *praise him in the gates*, though few of them were printed with his own *knowledge* or *consent.*"[238] And of Cotton's sermon on the Seven Vials, Lechford says: "Mr. Humfrey had gotten the notes from some who had took them by characters, and printed them in London without Cotton's consent."[239]

Some further light is thrown upon this question when we consider the printer of *The Singing of Psalms*. M. S., who printed the edition of 1647, is presumably Matthew Simmons.[240]

Of John Cotton's works the following were printed by M. S. or by Matthew Simmons: in 1644, *The Keyes of the Kingdom of Heaven* was "printed by M. Simmons for Henry Overton"; in 1645, *The Covenant of Gods free Grace* was "printed M. S. for Iohn Hancock"; in 1645, *The Way of the Churches of Christ in New England* was "printed by Matthew Simmons"; in 1647, *The Bloudy Tenent Washed* was "printed by Matthew Symmons for Hannah Allen"; and in 1648, *The Way of the Congregational Churches Cleared* was "printed by Matthew Simmons for John Bellamie."

With Thomas Shepard's works the case is similar: in 1641, *The Sincere Convert* was "Printed by T. P. and M. S. for Humphrey Blunden"; in 1646, *The Sincere Convert* was again "printed by Matthew Simmons"; in 1648, *Certain Select Cases Resolved* was "printed by M. Simmons for J. Rothwell"; in 1648, *The First Principles of the Oracles of God* was "printed by M. Simmons."

Whether Simmons did or did not print the second edition (1650) of *The Singing of Psalms* cannot be told from the title-page, the imprint on which runs thus: "London, Printed for J. R. at the Sunne and Fountaine in Pauls-Church-yard; and H. A. at the Crowne in Popes-Head-Alley. 1650." Since J. R. and H. A. are presumably John Rothwell and Hannah Allen, the stationers for whom Simmons printed the edition of 1647, it is not unlikely that Simmons also printed for them the edition of 1650.

Whether Simmons printed the edition of 1650 or not, the fact that he occasionally printed works by Cotton and by

Shepard after 1647 may suggest, though of course it does not prove, that these authors had no reason to be seriously annoyed at anything that occurred in connection with the publication of *The Singing of Psalms* in 1647.

It thus seems fairly evident that we should hesitate to give way to the impression that John Cotton was at fault for having failed to make sure that Thomas Shepard, if he was the principal author of the discourse on *The Singing of Psalms*, received credit therefor upon the title-page.

John Dunton Again

SEVEN years ago, in a paper read before this Society [the Colonial Society of Massachusetts], I tried to vindicate John Dunton from the charge of attempting to write history. I now offer a short supplement to that earlier paper.

Dunton, it will be remembered, was a London bookseller, publisher, and miscellaneous writer, who at the age of twenty-seven came to Boston in January, 1686, and remained there or thereabouts until the following July. In 1705, as a part of his *Life and Errors*, he published a short account of his trip. In 1867 the Prince Society published a very much more extended account of Dunton's visit drawn from manuscripts in the Bodleian Library,—the so-called *Letters from New England*. Of these letters, eight in all, six purport to be written from New England and were formerly regarded by some as "unique sketches of New England life, honestly drawn, and defective rather than erroneous."[241] Unique they not improbably are; but they come so far short of being honestly drawn or free from error that they cannot safely be used by anyone who fails to realize Dunton's extraordinary propensity for borrowing material. His accounts of people and of places are particularly untrustworthy, since for the latter he relies upon Josselyn and for the former upon various seventeenth-century writers of "characters," from whom he copies almost verbatim, though he takes considerable pains to make his work seem original.

The second of Dunton's eight letters, supposedly written to his brother from Boston,[242] and dated February 17, 1685–6, is an account of the voyage. In the course of this voyage Dunton either saw or just missed seeing a most remarkable variety of sea animals,—a whale, flying-fish, shark, tortoise, dolphin, musculus, torpedo, sea-calf, sea-horse, swordfish, thresher, sunfish, porpoise, and alligator. Each of these he describes, usually to the length of about half a page.

In these descriptions there are several suspicious features. When, for example, we find Dunton writing of the captured whales, "When the victory is got over 'em, and the mighty victim lies at their Conquering Feet, they fearless then survey his huge and massy Body, and tell all his goodly Fins, which like so many Oars in a great Gally do serve to row his Carcase through the Seas at his own pleasure," [243] we feel that the style is obviously unlike Dunton's. Then there are expressions which suggest either an earlier date than 1686 or a different kind of book from his: "equalizeth," for instance, in the sense of "is equal to," "chaps," for "jaws," and such forms as "swimmeth," "hath," "writeth," "saith," "massy," and such expressions as "in this his large dominion" and "except they be afrighted with the sound of Drums and Trumpets." Nor is one's confidence in Dunton increased by his references to DuBartas and Munster, for with him such apparent ingenuousness usually means not that he has used the originals, but that he has been reading someone who cites them. Moreover, the descriptions of the musculus, dolphin, flying-fish, sunfish, and sea-horse conclude with moral applications which suggest not only an earlier date than Dunton's, but also a more clerical point of view. [244] On the musculus, for instance, which swims before the whale as a guide, Dunton moralizes thus: "Which office of that little Fish, may serve as a fit Emblem to teach Great Ones that they ought not to contemn their Inferiours: There may come a time when the meanest Person may do a Man some good." Then too the descriptions follow one another rather in the formal order of a treatise than in the casual manner to be expected in an epistolary account of a voyage. Again, the inclusion of the alligator in the fauna of the North Atlantic in January gives considerable ground for skepticism about the whole account; while the conclusion of Dunton's description of the Tortoise—"it is observable that if any of these Sea-Fowl be taken on the land, . . . they will never give over sighing, sobbing, and weeping, . . .; yea, even Tears will trickle from their Eyes in great abundance"—certainly looks like one of those statements which caused Joseph Addison mildly to observe of Ferdinand Mendez Pinto that he was "a person of infinite adventure, and unbounded imagination."

Altogether, there seemed justification enough for suggesting, as, without conclusive proof, I did seven years ago, that the various sailors who told Dunton so much about the fish that they had met had managed to commit to memory large portions of some not very reliable work on natural history.

At any rate, such now appears to be the fact, and my confidence in Dunton was not in the least misplaced. In fact, I underestimated his powers, for he has woven together passages almost literally copied from three books.

The first of these books is a volume of travels, not to New England, but to the East Indies, containing the "familiar letters" concerning his travels which Pietro della Valle wrote to his friend Mario Schipano. They were published in folio at London in 1665, translated by one G. Havers.[245] To them is appended an account of Sir Thomas Roe's voyage to the East Indies, and it is from this part of the book that Dunton borrows.[246]

The second of Dunton's sources is a curious work called *Speculum Mundi*, by one John Swan.[247]

The third and principal source of Dunton's borrowings is a most extraordinary work by Daniel Pell, which may be called for short *An Improvement of the Sea*.[248]

The extent of these borrowings and the curious way in which passages from different authors are often combined make it seem worth while to reproduce in full Dunton's fourteen descriptions of sea animals and his sources, arranged in parallel columns. These follow.

THE FLYING FISH

DUNTON'S SOURCE

DUNTON

Here we saw great quantities of Sea-fowl flying, which seem'd strange to me so far off of Land, tho' not quite out of sight of it. But the Mariners told me, that was very ordinary, even when out of sight of Land; for that these Fowls live generally upon Fishes, and indeed they wou'd be often-times popping at 'em: While we were thus observing the Flying Fowles, one of the Seamen affirm'd that he had seen Flying Fishes, and that they had wings like a Rere-Mouse, but of a silver-colour; and that under the Tropick of Capricorn they fly in shoals like stares. Nature has given this fish Wings (as he affirm'd) for the preservation of its Life, for being often pursued by the Beneto, Porpoise, and other ravenous Fish, with the same Eagerness as the hungry Hound pursues the timorous Hare, it is oftentimes forced to save it self by flying. It is observed by the Mariners, That this fish will rather chuse to fly into a Ship or Boat, if any be near, than be taken by its Enemies; tho' this only makes good the Proverb, Out of the Frying-Pan into the Fire (Dunton, p. 24).

It hath wings like Reere-mice, but of a silver hue; they are much persecuted of the other fishes, and for to escape they flie in flockes, like Stares, or Sparrowes (A Treatise of Brasill, in *Purchas his Pilgrims*, Glasgow, 1906, xvi. 487).

. . . the *Flying-fish*, whom God out of wisdom has given wings unto, (like a foul) for the preservation of its life in the great waters. This poor creature is often hunted, chased, and pursued, by the *Boneto*, *Porpise*, and other ravenous fish, which follow it with as much violence as the hungry hound does the poor silly and shelterless *Hare*. Insomuch that it is forced one while to fly, and another while to swim; . . . It is observed by the Mariners, that this fish rather than it will bee taken by its enemies in the waters, it will many times betake it self in its flight into ships, or boats. And alas this makes the Proverb good, *Out of the frying-pan into the fire* (Pell, p. 199).

CHESTER NOYES GREENOUGH

THE SEA–HOG

DUNTON'S SOURCE

DUNTON

The weather being a little clear, several Fishes were seen playing above-water, not far from our Ship, which made me do my utmost with the assistance of Palmer and another of the Passengers, to get above deck again; and indeed I did not lose my labour, for I saw a vast number of Fishes called Sea-hogs, or Porpoises. They were headed much like a Hog, and tooth'd and tusk'd much like a Boar; These Sea-hogs take such delight in one anothers Company, that they swim together in great Numbers, exceeding the largest herd of Swine I ever saw by Land, for those by Land are far inferior for multitude, to those that are in the Seas. These Porpoises, or Hog-fish, are very swift in their motion (as if they came of the race of the Gadaren swine that ran violently into the sea) —and are like a company marching in rank and file; they leap or mount very nimbly over the waves and so down and up again, makeing a melancholy noyse when they are above the water: when they appear they are certain presagers of foul weather. There is one thing very remarkable about this Fish, and that is, That if one of them happen to be wounded, either by shott or Harping Iron; the whole Herd pursue him with the greatest fury and violence that may be, seeming to contend who shou'd fall upon him first, and have their Teeth deepest in his Carcase (Dunton, p. 32).

The Sea-hog, or Swine. This creature is headed like an Hog, toothed, and tusked like a Boar, . . . These beasts take such delight in one anothers company, that they are to be seen in greater troops and herds, than the greatest land-herds of Swine that ever were seen, for they are not comparable unto the multitudes that bee of them, and are in the Seas (Pell, p. 222).

The *Porpisces* or *Hogfish* . . . are (as if they came of the race of the *Gadaren* Swine, that ran violently into the Sea) very swift in their motion, and like a company marching in rank and file; They leap or mount very nimbly over the waves, and so down and up again, making a melancholy noise, when they are above the water. These are usually, when they thus appear, certain presagers of very foul weather (Roe, p. 329).

I have observed, that when this fish hath been wounded by shot or Harping-iron, that hee is no sooner peirced, and mortally wounded, but every one of the same kinde will follow him with the greatest violence that can bee, striving and contending who should beat him first, and have their teeth and mouthes the deepest, and fastest in his carkass (Pell, p. 223).

THE SHARK

DUNTON'S SOURCE	DUNTON

DUNTON

My constant indisposition would not suffer me to stay long upon the Deck at a time, and therefore having view'd those Sea-Hogs, I was forc'd to retire again into my Cabin: but Palmer afterwards brought me word that they had seen a Fish called Shark, a very dangerous and ravenous Fish, as the Mariners told me, of whom they are more afraid than of all the Fishes in the Sea beside; for if he chance to meet with any of them in the Water, he seldom suffers them to Escape without the loss of a Limb at least and many times devours the Whole Body; so great a Lover is this Fish of Humane Flesh; insomuch that some have observ'd that they have endeavour'd to clamber up the sides of the Ship, out of a greedy desire of Preying on the Sailors: This Fish, it seems, is of a very great Bulk, with a double or treble set of Teeth, as sharp as Needles: But Nature has so order'd it, that as an allay to his Devouring Nature, he is forc'd to turn himself upon his Back, before he can take his prey, by which means many escape him which else would fall into his Clutches. It is, my Brother, from the Devouring Nature of this Fish, that we call those Men Sharks, who having nothing of their own, make it their business to live upon other Men, and devour their Substance (Dunton, p. 33).

They have in the Salt-water a frequent aspect of the ravenous, feral, and preying sort of fish called a *Shark*, of whom the Mariner is more afraid than of all the fish in the Sea besides. This *Pickroon*, if hee can but take any of them bathing themselves . . . hee will tear them limb from limb, so great a lover hee is of the flesh of man. Some have observed of this fish, that they have not stuck to clammer up upon their ship sides, out of a greediness to feed upon the Sailors. . . . To describe you this creature, I must tell you, that he is of very great bulk, and of a double or treble set . . . of teeth, which are as sharp as needles, but God out of his infinite wisdom considering the fierceness, and violence of the creature, has so ordered him, that hee is forced to turn himself upon his back, before hee can have any power over his prey, or otherwise nothing would escape him (Pell, p. 206).

THE SUN-FISH

DUNTON'S SOURCE	DUNTON

DUNTON

Being a little better, I got upon the Deck again, and the weather being

[103]

DUNTON'S SOURCE

. . . whose usual property is to come out of the depths in the sweetest and calmest weathers, to lye sleeping and beaking [*sic*] of himself upon the Surface of the Seas, . . . Mariners sometimes will hoyse out their boats and take them up.

It brought into my mind, that it is a very perilous thing for a Christian to bee found asleep (by that mortal and deadly enemy Satan) when and whilst hee is standing Sentinel upon his guard. The Devil is of an indefatigable spirit, ὁ πειράξων, in the present tense, which reports him not to bee lazy but busy, not a loyterer but a stickler, and a stirrer in his pernicious work; . . . (Pell, p. 202).

DUNTON

pretty clear, the mariners discovered a Fish called the Sun-fish, of a lovely bright and shining colour, whose property it is in Calm weather to come out of the Depths, and lie sleeping and basking itself upon the Surface of the Waters, by which means often-times the Mariners have an opportunity of taking them. This, my Brother, made me reflect how dangerous a thing it is for any one to sleep unguarded in the midst of Enemies, especially so industrious and indefatigable an Enemy as the Scripture represents the Great Enemy of our Souls to be, who goes about continually like a roaring Lion, seeking whom he may devour (Dunton, p. 34).

THE ALLIGATOR

DUNTON'S SOURCE

They have a frequent aspect of that wonderful and impenetrable sort of Beasts which the *Mariners* call an *Alligator*. . . . This Beast is of a vast longitude and magnitude (some say many yards in length) in colour, hee is of a dark brown, which makes him the more invisible, and indiscernable when hee lyes his *Trapan* in the waters. . . . Of such strength is this beast, that no creature is able to make his escape from him, if hee get but his chaps fastened in them. . . . This beast hath his three tyer of teeth in his chaps, and so firmly scaled and armed with coat of Male, that you may as well shoot, or strike upon or at a Rock and Iron, as offer to wound him (Pell, pp. 228–229).

DUNTON

Being laid down upon the Bed one Day to repose my self, Palmer comes down to me, and tells me, I had lost the sight of a very great and strange Creature, which our Captain call'd an Alligator; this Creature is of a vast length and breadth, (some say many yards in length:) in colour he is of a dark brown, which makes him the more imperceptable when he lies as a Trapan in the Waters. He is of so vast a strength that no Creature is able to make his Escape from him, if he gets but his Chaps fastened in them; for he has three Tere of Teeth in his Chaps and so firmly sealed [*sic*] and armed with Coat of Male, that you may as well shoot at a Rock, or strike against Bars of Iron, as offer to wound him (Dunton, p. 35).

THE DOLPHIN

They oftentimes have a frequent sight of that sociable & companionable Sea-fish, called the *Dolphin*. *Naturalists* tell us that these creatures do take great delight to accompany the swift-sailing ships that come through the Seas. . . . I have seen them accompanying of us for a long time together, . . . some swimming on head, some on stern, some on the *Starbord*-side of us, and othersome on the *Larbord*, like so many Sea-pages, or Harbingers runing before our wooden horses, as if they were resolved by the best language that fish could give us, to welcome us into and through the waters, and telling us that they would go along with us (Pell, p. 203).

. . . not so much I think for the love they bear unto man, (as some write,) as to feed themselves with what they find cast overboard: whence it comes to pass, that many times they feed us; for when they swim close to our ships, we often strike them with a broad instrument, full of barbs, called an Harping-iron, . . . This Dolphin may be a fit Emblem of an ill race of people, who under sweet countenances, carry sharp tongues (Roe, pp. 328–329).

I must acquaint you, That whilst I thus lay musing in my Cabin, one of the Seamen came, and told me that they had had a Dolphin swiming a pretty while by the Ship side, as if it did intend to vye with them in sailing: I made what haste I cou'd upon the deck, but came too late to see it, for the sociable Fish had now withdrawn himself: But the account I had of it from them that saw it, was, This Fish takes great Delight in sailing along by those Ships that pass through the Seas; and one of the mariners affirm'd that in some voyages he had seen several of them accompanying their ship, for a long time together; some swimming a head, and some a stern, some on the Starboard, and others on the Larboard side, like so many Sea-Pages attending them, seeming to tell us we were welcome into their Territories; or as if they were resolved to be our safe-conduct thorow 'em. But this is not so much, I think, for the love they bear unto man, (as some write,) as to feed themselves with what they find cast overboard,[249] whence it comes to pass, that many times they feed us, for when they swim close to our ships we often strike them with a broad instrument, full of barbs, called an Harping-iron. The Dolphin may be a fit emblem of an ill race of people who under sweet countenances carry sharp tongues. As to their being generally represented as a Crooked Fish, I enquir'd about it, and am inform'd it is only a vulgar errour of the Painters,[250] for 'tis a straight a Fish as any swims the Ocean: If I am in an Errour,

CHESTER NOTES GREENOUGH

DUNTON'S SOURCE

Plinie hath written much of this fish, . . . affirming that he is not onely sociable and desirous of mans company, but delighted also in sweet and sense-charming musick.

Amongst the fishes that did swiftly throng
To dance the measures of his mournfull song,
There was a Dolphin did the best afford
His nimble motions to the trembling chord.

But whether that in the storie of *Arion* be true, I am not able to say. . . . Howbeit this scruple may not take away the love of the Dolphin towards man. For besides those things related in *Plinie*, of a boy feeding a Dolphin, and carried on his back over the waters to school, . . . others also have in a manner written to the same purpose. And amongst the rest, *Ælian* tells a storie of a Dolphin and a boy: this boy being very fair, used with his companions to play by the sea side, and to wash with them in the water, practising likewise to swimme: which being perceived by a Dolphin frequenting that coast, the Dolphin fell into a great liking with this boy above the rest, and used very familiarly to swimme by him side by side: . . . sometimes the boy would get upon the Dolphins back, and ride through the waterie territories of Neptunes kingdome, as upon some proud pransing horse, and the Dolphin at all times would bring him safely to the shore again. . . . At last it chanced that the boy, not care-

DUNTON

Brother, I hope you'll rectifie me, for I am sure you must have seen of 'em in your Voyage to Suratt: Dubartas records of this Fish, that he's a great Delighter in Musick: on which he has these Verses:

Among the Fishes that did swiftly throng
To dance the measures of his Mournful Song,
There was a Dolphin that did best afford
His Nimble Motions to the Trembling Chord:

But whether that in the Story of Arion be true I cannot say:—However, very remarkable is the Story related by Pliny, of a Boy feeding a Dolphin, and carried on his back over the Waters to School: They did swim sometimes side by side, and at last, grew so familiar, that sometimes the Boy would get upon the Dolphin's Back, and ride in Triumph through Neptunes Wat'ry Kingdom, as upon some proud Prancing Horse: At last, it so unhappily fell out, that the Boy careless how he sat upon the Fishes Back, was by his Sharp and brisly Fins wounded to Death: which the commiserating Dolphin straight perceiving swam to the Land, and there laid down his wounded Burden, and for very sorrow Died. In memory whereof, a Poet writes,

The Fish would Live, but that the Boy must Dye,
The Dying Boy, the Living Fish Torments:
The Fish tormented hath no time to cry,

DUNTON'S SOURCE

full how he sat upon the fishes back, but unadvisedly laying his belly too close, was by the sharp pricks growing there, wounded to death. And now the Dolphin perceiving by the weight of his bodie, and by the bloud which stained the waters, that the boy was dead, speedily swimmeth with all his force to the land, and there laying him down, for very sorrow died by him. In memorie whereof, let these few lines be added,

The fish would live, but that the boy
must die:
The dying boy the living fish torments.
The fish tormented hath no time to crie;
But with his grief his life he sadly vents.

(Swan, pp. 372–373.)

DUNTON

But with his Grief, his Life he sadly vents.

(Dunton, pp. 37–39.)

THE SWORD–FISH AND THE THRESHER

DUNTON'S SOURCE

They have many times a frequent sight of that pleasurable, and most delightful fish-combat that is betwixt the *Sword-fish*, the *Whale*, and the *Thresher* . . . the *Sword-fish* is so weaponed, and well armed to encounter his enemy, that hee has upon his head a fish-bone that is as long, and as like to a two-edged sword, as any two things in the world resemble one an-

DUNTON

The Mariners discover'd two Fishes of a different sort and size, which they inform'd us were the Sword-fish and the Thresher: and told us they believ'd the Whale was not far off; and when I ask'd what reason they had to suppose so, they told me, That those two Fishes were always at a Truce between themselves, but always at open Wars with the Leviathan: And that nothing was more pleasant, than to see the combat between the Three, i.e. The Sword-fish and the Thresher upon one side, and the Whale on the other. For this Sword-fish is so well weapon'd, and arm'd for an Incounter with its mighty Enemy, that he has upon his Head a Fish-Bone, that's both as long and as like to a two-edged sword, as

DUNTON'S SOURCE

other, save onely that there bee amany of sharp spikes . . . upon either edge of it, and the property of this Fish is to get underneath the *Whale*, and there to riple him, and rake him all over the belly, which will cause him to roar, and exclaim upon the *Theeves* that beset him, as if there were a dart in the heart of him, and the *Thresher* playes his part above table, for when his partner forces him upwards, hee layes on to purpose upon the *Whales* back, insomuch that his blows are audible two, or three miles in distance, and their rage and fury is so great against the *Whale*, that one would think they would cut him, and thrash him to peeces (Pell, pp. 221–222).

DUNTON

any two things can resemble one another, save only that there are a great many sharp spikes on either edge of it: Nature has it seems instructed this Fish what use to make of it; for being thus arm'd the property of this Fish is to get underneath the Whale, and with his Two-edg'd Sword to rake and riple him all over's Belly, which causes him to roar and bellow at such a prodigious rate, as if a Thousand Darts were sticking in his heart, and then the Thresher, (when by the bellowing of the Whale he understands the Sword-fish is assaulting him below) straight get a top of him and there plays his part, assaulting him with such thick and massy blows, as may be plainly heard at two or three miles distance; and this rage and fury is so great against the Whale, that one wou'd think they'd cut and thrash him all to pieces (Dunton, pp. 39–40).

THE WHALE

DUNTON'S SOURCE

DUNTON

Whilst we all were walking up and down, it was my hap to fix my Eye on something I knew not what, which unto me seem'd like a moving Rock; and shewing of it to a Seaman, we soon discover'd it to be one of those floating Mountains of the Sea, the Whale: As we came nearer him, I saw his very Breath put all the Water round in such a ferment, as made the very sea boyl like a Pot. I do confess I had a very great desire to take a more particular view of him, because GOD gives him such an Elaborate and accu-

Verse 32. *Hee makes a path to shine after him, one would think the deep to bee hoary.* . . . The *Whale* puts as

DUNTON'S SOURCE

admirable a beauty upon that part of the Sea his body swims in, as the *Sun* does upon the *Rainbow*, by gilding of it with its golden, and irradiating beams (Pell, p. 219).

I have seen . . . them . . . sending forth such strange, and prodigious smoaks and fumes, as if there were some Town or Village of smoking chimneys in the Seas (Pell, p. 217).

Now may they take a view of his head, in which are eyes as large as some pewter dishes, and room enough in his mouth for many people to sit in. Now may they look upon his terrible teeth, and handle his great and *tree*-like tongue, which is upwards of two yards in breadth, and in length longer and thicker than the tallest man that is upon the earth. Out of which part the Marines extract above an Hogshead of Oyle (Pell, p. 216).

This creature is of such an incredible . . . strength . . . that in *Greenland* (that great *Whale*-slaughtering place of the world) when they come once to dart an Harping-Iron into him, hee will so rage, rend, and tear, that if there were an hundred . . . *shallops* neare unto him, hee would make them fly in a thousand shivers into the skyes (Pell, p. 214).

When the victory is got over the Whale, then they may go round about

DUNTON

rate Description in the 41st of Job: And this I particularly observ'd, That the Sun shining upon him, cast a very orient Reflection upon the Water; which is also confirm'd by the Description given of him, Job 41:32. He maketh a path to shine after him, one wou'd think the Deep to be hoary: Another thing I observ'd was, That there was so great a smoak where he was, that it seem'd to me as if there had been a Town full of Smoaking Chimneys in the midst of the Sea. I do confess I never saw so large and formidable Creature in my Life. He appear'd to me as big as either of the Holmes's, two little Islands that lie at the mouth of the Severn, near Bristol in England. It was impossible for me to take the True Dimensions of him: His Eyes are as large as two great Pewter-Dishes, and there's room enough in his Mouth for many People to sit round in, as those that have been at the Taking of them affirm. His teeth are terrible, and his Tongue is above two yards in breadth, and in length exceeds the tallest man on Earth, out of which they extract above a Hogshead of Oyl. Ex pede Hercules. I have been told that the Whale is of such incredible strength, that in Greenland (where most of them are taken) when they come once to dart an Harping-iron into 'em, they rage and rend at so extravagant a rate, that if there were an hundred Shallops near him, he'd make 'em fly into a thousand shivers, and send 'em up into the Skies. When the victory is got over 'em, and the mighty victim lies at their Conquering Feet, they

DUNTON'S SOURCE

him, and tell all his goodly fins, which are as so many *Oars* upon his sides, to row his great and corpulent carkass to and again in the Seas at his pleasure, which are reckoned to bee three hundered and upwards, and by these hee goes at what rate hee pleases in the waters, as violently as an arrow out of a bow, or a bullet out of a peece of Ordnance (Pell, p. 216).

In smooth water, warm, and calm weather, they are now and then to bee seen sporting . . . of themselves, and shewing their great and massy bodies above the waters, unto the aspect of the ships that sail hard by them in the Seas. One while rising up, and another while falling down, one while appearing, and by and by disappearing (Pell, p. 217).

. . . Some Whales . . . in calm weather often arise and shew themselves on the top of the water, where they appear like unto great Rocks, in their rise spouting up into the Air with noise, a great quantity of water, which falls down again about them like a showre. The Whale may well challenge the Principality of the Sea, yet I suppose that he hath many enemies in this his large Dominion; for instance, a little long Fish called a Thresher, often encounters with him; who by his agility vexeth him as much in the Sea, as a little Bee in Summer, doth a great Beast on the shore (Roe, p. 327.)

Munster writeth, that near unto Ireland there be great whales whose bigness equalizeth the hills and mightie mountains, . . . and these (saith he)

DUNTON

fearless then survey his huge and massy Body, and tell all his goodly Fins, which like so many Oars in a great Gally do serve to row his Carcase through the Seas at his own pleasure: and they are reckoned by the most curious Anatomists of him to be above three hundred, and by these he can go, if he pleases, with that swiftness and violence, as Arrows scarce fly swifter from a Bow, nor Bullet from a piece of Ordnance. The Seamen tell me, That in smooth Water and calm weather, they are often seen sporting of themselves, and shewing their great and massy Bodies upon the Surface of the Waters, easily discernible by Ships that sail hard by 'em in the Seas, one while rising up, and in a little time fall down again and disappear. Some whales in calm weather often arise and shew themselves on the top of the water, where they appear like unto great Rocks, in their rise, spouting up into the Ayr with noyse, a great quantity of water which falls down again about them like a showr. The Whale may well challenge the Principalitie of the Sea, yet I suppose that he hath many enemies in this his large Dominion; for instance, a little long Fish called a Thresher often encounters with him, who by his agilitie vexeth him as much in the Sea, as a little Bee in Summer, doth a great Beast on the shore. Munster writeth, That near unto Ireland, there be great Whales whose Bigness equalizeth the Hills and mighty Mountains; and these, saith he, will drown and overthrow the greatest ships, except they be afrighted

DUNTON'S SOURCE

will drown and overthrow ships except they be affrighted with the sound
of trumpets and drummes . . . (Swan,
p. 360).

DUNTON

with the sound of Drums and Trumpets (Dunton, pp. 42–44).

THE MUSCULUS

DUNTON'S SOURCE

Plinie writeth of a little fish called
Musculus, which is a great friend to the
whale: for the whale being big would
many times endanger her self between
rocks and narrow straits, were it not
for this little fish, which swimmeth as
a guide before her. Whereupon *Du
Bartas* descants thus,

A little fish that swimming still before
Directs him safe from rock, from shelf
and shore:
Much like a child that loving leads
about
His aged father when his eyes be out;
Still wafting him through ev'ry way so
right,
That reft of eyes he seems not reft of
sight.

Which office of that little fish, may
serve as a fit embleme to teach great
ones and superiours, that they ought
not to contemne their inferiours; for
they are not alwayes able so to subsist
of themselves, that they never stand
in need of their helps who are but
mean and base in the eyes of greatnesse: there may come a time when
the meanest person may do some good,
and therefore there is no time wherein
we ought to scorn such a one, how
mean soever he be (Swan, p. 362).

DUNTON

Pliny writes of a little Fish called
Musculus, which is a great Friend to
the Whale; for the Whale being big,
wou'd many times endanger her self
between Rocks and narrow straits,
were it not for this little Fish which
swimmeth as a Guide before her.
Whereupon Dubartus descants thus:

A little Fish, that swimming still be-
fore,
Directs him safe, from Rock, from
Shelf, from Shore:
Much like a Child, that living Leads
about
His Aged Father when his eyes are out:
Still wafting him through every way
so right,
That reft of Eyes, he seems not reft of
sight.

Which office of that little Fish, may
serve as a fit Emblem to teach Great
Ones that they ought not to contemn
their Inferiours: There may come a
time when the meanest Person may
do a Man some good; and therefore
there is no time wherein we ought to
scorn such a one. To conclude, my
Brother, and sum up all I have to say
of him in one word, That what the
Spirit of God says of Behemoth, I
may say of the Leviathan, as to the
Sea at least, He is the Chief of the
Ways of God (Dunton, p. 44).

THE CALAMORIE

Dunton's Source	Dunton

The *Calamarie* is sometimes called the *Sea-clerk*, having as it were a knife and a pen. Some call him the *Ink-horn-fish*, because he hath a black skinne like ink, which serveth him in stead of bloud. And of these fishes there be more kinds than one: for the *Cuttle* hath also an inkie juice in stead of bloud. . . . *Plinie*, . . . affirmeth that both male and female, when they find themselves so farre forth discovered, that if they cannot be hid they must be taken, do then cast this their ink into the water; and so by colouring it, they obscure and darken it: and the water being darkened, they escape.

About this time we discover'd another Sea-Wonder, to wit, a Fish called a Calamorie; which some call the Ink-horn-Fish, because he hath a black Skin like Ink, which Serveth him instead of Blood; When they are like to be taken, they then cast their Ink into the Water, and so by colouring it, they obscure and darken it, and the Water being darken'd, they escape.

For through the clouds of this black
   inkie night,
They dazling passe the greedie fishers
   sight.
(Swan, pp. 378–379.)

For through the Clouds of this dark
   Inky Night,
They dazling pass the greedy Fishers
   Sight.
(Dunton, pp. 45–46.)

THE TORPEDO

Dunton's Source	Dunton

The Torpedo, or the *Cramp-fish*, . . . is indued with a very prodigious & clandestine quality, if it be but touched, or handled, the body is presently stunned, and benummed, as an hand or leg that is dead, and without all feeling. I have known some that have taken of this kinde at unawares . . . They have been for some hours in a very desponding estate, whether they should ever recover their pristine constitution, and health again, or no?
(Pell, p. 226.)

During the time that we were lolling and rowling thus upon the restless Ocean, our Mariners discover'd that admirable Wonder of the Torpedo, or Cramfish, a Fish much better to behold than handle, for it has this prodigious, yet clandestine quality, that if it be but touch'd or handled, the person touching it is presently benummed, as a Hand or Leg, that is Dead, and without feeling: In which condition they sometimes continue for two or three Days together; and with difficulty obtaining the use of their Limbs again
(Dunton, p. 46).

COLLECTED STUDIES

THE SEA–HORSE

But that which brought us the first Dawning of Hope, with respect to the Discovery of Land, was the Discovery which one of the Seamen made, of three or four great Fishes, which he call'd Sea-Horses; and not without reason, for their fore-parts were the perfect figure of a Horse, but their hinder parts perfect Fish; when the rest of the Seamen saw these Creatures, they all rejoyc'd, and said we were not far from Land; the reason of which was, That these Sea-Horses were Creatures that took a great delight in sleeping on the Shore, and therefore were never seen but near the Shore: This was but a collateral Comfort, for tho' these Sea-Horses delight in Sleeping on the Shore, yet they might swim two or three hundred Leagues into the Sea for all that: But we that look'd upon our selves in a perishing Condition, were willing to lay hold on any little Twigg of Hope, to keep our Spirits up. One of the Seamen that had formerly made a Greenland Voyage for Whale-Fishing, told us that in that Country he had seen very great Troops of those Sea-Horses ranging upon Land, sometimes three or four hundred in a Troop: Their great desire, he says, is to roost themselves on Land in the Warm Sun; and Whilst they sleep, they appoint one to stand Centinel, and watch a certain time; and when that time's expir'd, another takes his place of Watching, and the first Centinel goes to sleep, &c. observing the strict Discipline, as a Body of Well-regulated Troops. And

In their voyages to *Greenland* . . . they have . . . hot disputes and skirmishes with the great and warlike *Horses* of the Seas, which . . . range upon the land, in great, and (almost) innumerable Troops. Sometimes by three or four hundred in a flock; sometimes more, and sometimes less. Their great desire is to roost themselves on land in the warm Sun; and whilst they adventure to fall asleep, by their appointment, they give orders out to one of the company to stand sentinel his hour, or such a certain time, and upon the expiration of it, another takes his turn upon the watch whilst the rest sleep, during such time till it goes round amongst them. And provided any enemy approach them, the Sentinel will neigh, beat, kick, and strike upon their bodies, and never leave till hee hath rowsed them up out of their snorting slumbers to shift for themselves, and betake themselves to the Seas. But *Sailors* being too cunning for them, get betwixt them and the Sea, and fall a beating out the brains of the first that comes to hand . . . and . . . many . . . have averred that they have killed of them whilst they have been no longer able for want of breath and strength. And the reason why they kill so many of these creatures is, because their teeth is of great worth and value, and very vendable in the Southern parts of the world.

From this Creature I have learned to apply thus much unto my self in particular, That it is a very dangerous thing for a man to bee out of his general and particular Calling (Pell, p. 209).

if it happen that at any time an Enemy approach, the Centinel will neigh, and beat, and kick, and strike upon their Bodies, and never leave till he has wak'd 'em; and then they run together into the Seas for shelter. But for all this Caution, the Sailors are, it seems too cunning for them; and get between them and the Sea, and beat out the Brains of the first that comes to hand; and so have done, till they have kill'd so long, that they have wanted strength to kill another; and that which moves the Seamen to this cruelty, is, because their Teeth are of great worth and value, and are a very vendible Commodity in the Southern parts of the World. And since it is the Shore on which these Creatures meet with this Destruction; and that if they had kept at Sea, they had been safe: I cou'd not but reflect, That those who leave their settled stations, whether out of Principles of Profit or of Pleasure, and will be trying New Experiments, and putting of New Projects on the Tenters, do often times make very poor Returns; and are convinc'd it had been better for 'em to have kept that station which Providence at first had put 'em in (Dunton, pp. 47–48).

THE SEA–CALF

They are not without a frequent sight of that admirable fish called the *Sea-calf*, which is both headed and haired like a Calf, swiming oftentimes with his head above water. There be

The next day after our Codfishing was over, and they were all gone out of sight, I know not whither, we discover'd a Fish call'd the Sea-calf, whose Head and Hair's exactly like a Calf's: This Creature's an amphibious

DUNTON'S SOURCE

very many of this kinde, in, and about the several *Islands* in *Scotland* . . ., at night they will come on shore to sleep and rest themselves, and early in the the morning, they will betake themselves to the Sea, not daring to stay on land for fear of surprizals (Pell, p. 224).

DUNTON

Animal, living sometimes at Sea, and sometimes on Land: I am told there are several of this kind of Creatures in the Islands about Scotland, (but more of that in my rambles thither,) and that at night they will come on Shore to sleep and rest themselves; and early in the morning return to Sea, not daring to stay on Land, for fear of surprisals. This Fish was a further Inducement to our Sea-men to believe that we were upon the Coast of America, and very neer Land: And these distant Hopes we Emprov'd for our support the best we cou'd (Dunton, p. 48).

THE TORTOISE

DUNTON'S SOURCE

They are not destitute of a frequent aspect of that wonderful, and Jehovah-extolling-creature called the *Sea-Turtle*, or the *Tortoise*. This Bird-fish at the time of the year constantly leaves the Sea, and betakes her self to the shore, where shee will shoot an infinite number of Eggs, and cover them in the sand, and as soon as ever she hath done, shee departs the place, and makes for the Sea again, not daring to stay and brood them, as other birds will do, because shee hath no wings to flye withall, and to help her self, if in case shee should bee set at. And when her young ones are once hatched (which come to that maturity by reason of that warmth that is in the sand) they will go as directly towards the Sea, as if they had been in it many a time before they had their being, and although the Sea bee a mile or two from

DUNTON

This morning we saw a Sea-Turtle, or Tortoise, (which it seems are frequent on the New-England Coast:) And its flesh is a very delicious Food. It is the property of this Creature at one time in the year constantly to leave the Seas, and betake her self to the Shore, where she will lay an infinite number of Eggs, and cover them in the Sand; and as soon as she has done, she leaves them, and goes to Sea again, not daring to sit and hatch them, as other Birds will do, because she has no wings to fly away, in case of an attack. And when her young ones by the Heat of the Sun are hatch'd they'll all go as directly to the Sea, as if they had been there before, or that they had been bred in't; yea, tho' sometimes the old one leaves her eggs a mile or two from Sea, and quite out of sight on't; such is the mighty Power

DUNTON'S SOURCE:
the place, the old one left her Eggs in, out of a natural instinct they will finde the Sea, although it bee out of sight.

It is observable, that if any of these Sea-fowl bee taken on land (as oftentimes they are by Sea-men) that they will never give over sighing, sobbing, weeping, and bewayling of their Captivity as long as life is in them, tears will drill, and trickle from their Eyes as from children, in great abundance (Pell, pp. 224–225).

DUNTON:
of Natural Instinct. It is observable, that if any of these Sea-fowl be taken on the Land, as oftentimes they are by Sea-Men, that they will never give over sighing, sobbing, and weeping, as long as Life is in them; yea, even Tears will trickle from their Eyes in great abundance (Dunton, p. 52).

These borrowings amount in all to twenty-one,—one from Purchas, three from Roe, four from Swan, and thirteen from Pell. If to these we add the eighty-four cases previously indicated,[251] John Dunton's total score of passages incorporating borrowed material reaches the not inconsiderable figure of one hundred and five. The relative proportions of original and borrowed matter in the passages referred to in this article are approximately as follows: of matter borrowed from Roe, seven per cent; from Swan, fourteen per cent; from Pell, fifty-eight per cent; and of matter apparently original, twenty-one per cent.[252]

The way in which these sources came to my notice prompts me to make two observations that may perhaps be of interest to those engaged in similar investigations. After having spent many hours in fruitless efforts to find these authors by turning over such books of voyages as I could think of, and after having with similar lack of success pursued the search from the point of view of zoölogy,[253] I at length remembered that Dunton is a person who copies not merely ideas but also words. I accordingly made a short list of unusual words used by Dunton in these descriptions. Two of these words were "harping-iron" (*i.e.*, harpoon) and "calamorie." Looking up the first of these in the invaluable *Oxford Dictionary*, I found, ascribed to Pietro della Valle, a sentence which I remembered in Dunton; and similarly the article on "calamorie" in the *Oxford Dictionary* led me to John Swan. To those, therefore, who deal with authors that are in the habit of borrowing without much change of phrasing, I recommend the *Oxford Dictionary*.

Pell was much harder to find. Indeed I should probably have missed Pell altogether if it had not been for the late Daniel Butler Fearing. There could hardly be a severer test of the range of Mr. Fearing's great collection of books on angling than to search in it for such a book as Pell's. Fortunately, the officials of the Harvard College Library, to which Mr. Fearing's collection came in 1915,[254] have arranged in chronological order some of the older angling books. As a result I found Pell within an hour after the notion of looking through the Fearing Collection first occurred to me. This seems to me a striking illustration of the help that a great collection of "dead" books may give to workers in fields apparently remote from that of their collector.

These passages about the sea-animals in John Dunton—particularly since the more misleading parts of his letters have been cleared up—were perhaps not so likely to mislead historians of New England as to justify the labor of discovering their sources. Nor has any zoölogist, so far as I know, ever been tempted to cite Dunton as evidence that alligators formerly abounded in the North Atlantic. But to trace Dunton's sources is at least an amusing pastime, and it throws some additional light on his methods. These methods are so extraordinary that I have long since ceased to be astonished at anything he does. Yet I do confess to some surprise, in view of these revelations concerning Dunton, at one sentence in his account of the whale: he was particularly glad to see a whale, he says, "because GOD gives him such an Elaborate and accurate Description in the 41st of Job." I must say that when Dunton ventures to comment on the accuracy of God, he seems to me to be going pretty strong, even for him.

Barrett Wendell

FIRST as an assistant, then as a colleague, and always as a pupil and friend, I knew Barrett Wendell from 1899 until his death. Our work together was chiefly in American literature, a subject which engaged much of his attention and exhibited his character and skill as a teacher with singular attractiveness. For his knowledge on all subjects was derived nearly as much from travel and conversation as from study, and the fullness with which he thus understood earlier New England, not to mention other phases of American literature, was to me a constant lesson in the insufficiency of knowledge derived merely from books.

When our acquaintance began, Mr. Wendell's position at Harvard was distinguished and in some respects unique. He had been an instructor in English from 1880 to 1888, then for ten years an assistant professor, and in 1898 he had been made a full professor. In 1891 had appeared his *English Composition*, which even we undergraduates felt had minimized the unattractiveness of that subject, though we did not realize how long it was destined to survive, in spite of the vast number of its rivals, on account of its apt and memorable analysis and its uncommon virtue of exemplifying the qualities which it recommends. In the same year, 1891, Mr. Wendell had very skilfully contrived to humanize Cotton Mather—a particularly difficult task at that time because the Mather diaries still had to be used in manuscript. Two years later, in 1893, had come *Stelligeri and Other Essays concerning America*. Not a few of us were attracted by the highly characteristic title essay of this volume, and thus came to a dim realization of what his older friends knew to be one of the deepest passions of Barrett Wendell's life—his curious and beautiful piety toward the Harvard of the past.

When in 1898 Mr. Wendell began to offer his course in American literature, he was, I believe, the first to present that subject systematically at Harvard. It at once obtained a well-deserved popularity, and occupied him more and more until, in 1900, he published his *Literary History of America*. Criticism of that book for its preoccupation with the writers of New England has never been lacking and is no doubt deserved; yet it treated many of them—even the greatest—with what their admirers thought scant courtesy and, partly on account of its very faults of proportion and of judgment, aroused some very useful counter-blasts and greatly advanced the prestige of its subject in American colleges.

Mr. Wendell tried only once—and then not quite successfully[255]—to write the history of a period. The history of a literary genre he never essayed: that was a kind of research in which he often expressed disbelief. Nor did the allurements of "classicism" and "romanticism" at all attract him. What he liked was personality in literature—particularly distinguished personality—and he sought it with less and less preference each year for any particular century or country. Herein lies one of several resemblances between him and his master, James Russell Lowell.

It was characteristic of Mr. Wendell to be intensely interested in subjects for a time. He would improve his lectures each year until he felt that he could not much better them; then he would usually publish them; and after that he did not much care about teaching that particular thing again. His gradual loss of faith in the teaching of English composition began not long after he had published his admirable book on that subject, and had become complete long before his death. Similarly he had, in 1896, taken the lead in devising a series of courses in which English literature from 1557 to 1892 was treated in units of about a half-century. These courses were largely taken and did a great deal of good. In 1906, however, Mr. Wendell, sharing with a few other members of the Department certain doubts about the success of these courses, took the lead in abolishing them.

In spite of his widespread and often very detailed knowledge, Mr. Wendell had little sympathy with the usual programme of studies leading to the degree of Doctor of Philosophy; could not use German; cared nothing for sources; was never thoroughly familiar with the periodical literature of his subject; and rarely investigated minute points. In a prefatory note written for a book by his intimate friend, Professor John Hays Gardiner, Mr. Wendell spoke of his own "impatience of detail"; but this phrase (curiously echoing the almost identical words of James Russell Lowell) does not explain his antipathy to all that German scholarship holds dear. For Barrett Wendell could take great pains with whatever he thought worth while. He deeply admired the best of the French theses for the *Doctorat ès lettres* and often expressed the wish that he could do work like that of his friends Beljame and Legouis.

Though Mr. Wendell took little note of the needs of graduate students, he was eagerly interested in getting undergraduates to take a better Bachelor's degree, and his efforts to persuade men to try for distinction by the simultaneous study of history and literature were fruitful, and, in fact, did much to hasten the adoption of the present requirement at Harvard of a general examination for the Bachelor's degree.

His manner in the classroom, his ingenious and often deliberately eccentric diction, and the whole air and presence of the man, endeared him to many, though they excited the speechless rage of some. He was never commonplace: on that point his best friends agreed with his harshest critic. No book or lecture from him, no speech, even of the shortest, in Faculty or committee, but was marked by the full impress of an extraordinarily interesting and suggestive mind—a mind which detested the mysteries of the augur as it did the vulgarity of the barbarian.

Although the teacher whom I have thus endeavored imperfectly to summarize owed most of all to himself, he was deeply indebted to James Russell Lowell, with whom he had studied Dante and Old French. In a sense, Mr. Wendell may be said to have carried on some portion of the priceless tradition which is suggested by the names of Lowell and of Charles Eliot Norton. It is perhaps not inappropriate, therefore, particularly since I cannot find words of my own at all fit to define the feeling of his pupils toward him, to close with some sentences (from *Stelligeri*) in which Mr. Wendell summarized his impression of Lowell as a teacher.

Here was a man who . . . found in literature not something gravely mysterious, but only the best record that human beings have made of human life; who found, too, in human life—old and new—not something to be disdained with the serene contempt of smug scholarship, but the everlasting material from which literature and art are made. Here was a man, you grew to feel, who knew literature, and knew the world, and knew you, too; ready and willing, in a friendly way, to speak the word of cordial introduction. There came . . . a certain feeling of personal affection for him, very rare in any student's experience of even the most faithful teacher.

The "Character"
As a Source of Information for
the Historian

WHAT is the "character"? How did it develop in England? What material does it offer to the historian? Where can this material be found? Are there any special precautions to be employed in using it? These are questions which, if fully answered, would necessitate a book; but perhaps brief suggestions will be better than nothing.

The character is a special type of essay much resorted to by English writers of the seventeenth century and by no means uncommon in later times. It may best be defined by quoting a contemporary definition and adding an example. The definition is that given by an English schoolmaster named Ralph Johnson, and is taken from a text-book called *The Scholars Guide from the Accidence to the University*, London, 1665. Johnson gives not only the definition of a character, but also three rules for making characters. The definition and rules are these:

A character is a witty and facetious description of the nature and qualities of some person, or sort of people.

1. Chuse a Subject, viz. such a sort of men as will admit of variety of observation, such be, drunkards, usurers, lyars, taylors, excise-men, travellers, pedlars, merchants, tapsters, lawyers, an upstart gentleman, a young Justice, a Constable, an Alderman, and the like.

2. Express their natures, qualities, conditions, practices, tools, desires, aims, or ends, by witty Allegories, or Allusions, to things or terms in nature, or art, of like nature and resemblance, still striving for wit and pleasantness, together with tart nipping jerks about their vices or miscarriages.

3. Conclude with some witty and neat passage, leaving them to the effect of their follies or studies.[256]

From this definition it is clear that the character is a sort of composite photograph which, although it lacks the vividness of individual portraiture, has a certain generic significance that does not attach to portraits of individuals. The examination of a large number of seventeenth-century English characters shows:

(1) that, in spite of Johnson's definition, many English writers discriminated between the delineation of an individual and the delineation of a class of persons: the former, they called the "portrait"; the latter, the "character";

(2) that the character may be written about an inanimate object, such as a tavern, a prison,[257] or a tennis-court. As a matter of fact, the number of such characters is extremely large, and the light thrown by them upon contemporary conditions is fairly important;[258]

(3) that though the character is usually adverse, it need not necessarily be so; perhaps one character in every four or five is favorable.

As an example to make the preceding points somewhat clearer Overbury's character (1614) of "A Puritan" will serve as well as any:

A PURITAN

Is a diseased piece of apocalypse: bind him to the Bible, and he corrupts the whole text. Ignorance and fat feed are his founders; his nurses, railing, rabies, and round breeches. His life is but a borrowed blast of wind: for between two religions, as between two doors, he is ever whistling. Truly, whose child he is is yet unknown; for, willingly, his faith allows no father: only thus far his pedigree is found, Bragger and he flourished about a time first. His fiery zeal keeps him continually costive, which withers him into his own translation; and till he eat a schoolman he is hide-bound. He ever prays against non-residents, but is himself the greatest discontinuer, for he never keeps near his text. Anything that the law allows, but marriage and March beer, he murmurs at; what it disallows and holds dangerous, makes him a discipline. Where the gate stands open, he is ever seeking a stile; and where his learning ought to climb, he creeps through. Give him advice, you run into traditions; and urge a modest course, he cries out counsel. His greatest care is to contemn obedience; his last care to serve God handsomely and cleanly. He is now become so cross a kind of teaching, that should the Church enjoin clean shirts, he were lousy. More sense than single prayers is not his; nor more in those than still the same petitions: from which he either fears a learned faith, or doubts God understands not at first hearing. Show him a ring, he runs back like a bear; and hates square dealing as allied to caps. A pair of organs blow him out of the parish, and are the only glyster-pipes to cool him. Where the meat is best, there he confutes most, for his arguing is but the efficacy of his eating: good bits he holds breed positions, and the Pope he best concludes against in plum-broth. He is often drunk, not but as we are, temporally; nor can his sleep then cure him, for the fumes of his ambition make his very soul reel, and that small beer should allay him (silence) keeps him more surfeited, and makes his heat break out in private houses. Women and lawyers are his best disciples; the one, next fruit, longs for forbidden doctrine, the other to maintain forbidden titles, both which he sows amongst them. Honest he dare not be, for that loves order; yet, if he can be brought to ceremony and made but master of it, he is converted.[259]

How did the character develop in England? So far as we know, the character begins with Theophrastus, a Greek writer of the period of Alexander the Great, whose thirty essays, all adverse, are almost precisely like the work of the seventeenth-century English writers.[260] There is some evidence that characters of Theophrastus have always been more or less used by rhetoricians as school exercises.[261] Besides coming into England directly from Theophrastus or by way of the rhetoricians, the character may have been built up in part as the result of a group of less formal influences, among which are the satire of estates, vagabond books, satire of fools, grobian satires, and the like.[262]

The sum of all these influences, and perhaps others, results in a very close approximation to the character from the hand of Ben Jonson in his *Cynthia's Revels* (1601).

It seems not to have been until 1608, however, that any book appeared consisting wholly of characters or containing the word "character" in its title. This was Joseph Hall's *Characters of Vertues and Vices*. From the year 1608 until about the year 1642 we have a rather distinct period of character-writing, in which scores of books appeared, containing several hundred separate characters. The great character-writers of this period in addition to Bishop Hall are Sir Thomas Overbury and his friends (1614) and John Earle (1628). During this period the character comes nearer to literature than it did until Addison modified it to his use in 1709 and 1711. It is full of vivid side-lights on the habits, speech, costume, and manners of the period, especially the seamy side of it, and is for the historian an admirable supplement to the evidence afforded by the drama. One of the greatest dangers of the character in this period is its tendency to become flimsy through excess of attention to style; but the best of these characters, notably those by Earle, seem destined to last indefinitely as a valuable part of English literature.[263]

With the outbreak of the Civil War, the second period in the history of the character opens, and lasts roughly until 1688. In this second period the pamphlet-character rather than the essay-character is the usual thing. These pamphlet-characters are more likely to appear separately than in large collections; their style is usually less painstaking; their length, instead of being a matter of a few hundred words, as is commonly the case between 1608 and 1642, is often a half dozen or even a score of quarto pages. In their subject matter, above all, the pamphlet-characters, as written from 1642 to 1688, differ from their predecessors. Instead of selecting people distinguished by foibles and commenting lightly and wittily upon them, the writer of the pamphlet-character pounces upon one of the many discordant elements in church or state, such as a Bishop, an Independent, or a Fifth Monarchy Man, and summarizes the beliefs of the group thus personified in one. In other words, during this period the almost innumerable pamphlets which fly back and forth[264] include scores[265] whose writers, fully aware of the popularity which Overbury, Earle, and their like had given to the character, borrowed that name and a few of the tricks that went with it in order to make their controversial efforts more effective. Yet, as Thomas Fuller's *Holy and Profane State* (1642) and Samuel Butler's immense collection of characters[266] may serve to remind us, such essay-characters as were the usual thing from 1608 to 1642 are by no means unknown between 1642 and 1688.

The year 1688 may conveniently form another landmark in the history of the character, because in that year there appeared at Paris the first edition of La Bruyère's *Les Caractères ou les Mœurs de ce Siècle*. La Bruyère was translated into English in 1699, and was doubtless much read by Englishmen in the original French. His influence was in the direction of vivifying the character by decreasing its length, and especially by bringing in more background and environment. Instead of isolating people like botanical specimens, La Bruyère gets his effects by considering them in motion, in conversation, and in contact with other persons. There is Theodectus, for example, who "is heard in the ante-chamber; as he comes on he raises his voice; he enters, he laughs, every body stops their ears at his vociferations." There is Hermagoras, who knows not who is King of Hungary, and stares at naming the King of Bohemia. Speak not to him of the wars in Holland, or Flanders, or at least you must excuse him from answering the questions you ask concerning them: he knows not when they began or ended; battles and sieges are all new to him; but he is very well read in the *Giants' Wars*, he can relate them to the least circumstances; he discourses with the same fluency on the horrid convulsions of the Babylonian and Assyrian monarchies; he is acquainted with the original of the Egyptians and their dynasties. He never saw Versailles, or ever will; but the Tower of Babel he has seen, and counted the steps; he has found out how many architects were employed about that building, and even has their names at his fingers' ends.

And there are scores of others.

Among the English works which belong in the same general category with La Bruyère, two may be mentioned— Edward Ward's *The London Spy*, 1698–1700, and Addison's and Steele's *Tatler*, 1709, and *Spectator*, 1711.

Ward's *London Spy*, a highly readable though at times indecent book, narrates a fictitious trip through the London of 1700 set down in the form of a "*Journal*, intended to expose the *Vanities* and *Vices* of the *Town*." It abounds with vivid characters, many of them pretty low down in the underworld. Yet it may be doubted whether a historian can afford to neglect such material as the following character of a "Projector," which helps one to understand what kind of people took stock in the South Sea Bubble and how some of the earlier pages in the *Transactions* of the Royal Society gave the wits wicked hints for exaggeration into such caricatures as this:

When we had each of us stuck in our Mouths a Pipe of *Sotweed*, we began to look about us: Do you mind (says my Friend) yonder *old Sophister* with an *Indian* Pipe between his meagre Jaws, who sits staring at the Candle with as much Stedfastness as a Country *Passenger* at *Bow-Steeple*, or a Child at a *Raree-Show*? That's a strange whimsy-headed Humorist; observe his Posture, he looks like the Picture of *Aesculapius* behind an *Apothecary's* Counter: And has as many Maggots in his Noodle, as there are Mice in an old Barn, or Nits in a *Mumper's* Doublet. He has a wonderful projecting Head, and has lately contrived one of the prettiest Pocket-Engines for the speedy blanching of *Hasle-Nuts* and *Filbert-Kernels*, that ever was invented; he'll crack and skin two for a Squirrel's one; and in a few Years, by a little Alter-ation, will improve it to the use of *Walnuts*. I'll asure you he's a Member of the *Royal Society*, and had as great a Hand for many Years together in bringing the *Weather-Glass* to Perfection as any of them. He puts great Faith in the *Philosophers-Stone*, and believes he shall one Time or other be as rich as *Croesus*, though he has almost beggar'd himself in the search of it; and has as large a Pair of *Bellows* in his *Labo-ratory*, as ever an *Alcymist* in Town. He try'd a notable Experiment the other Day, in setting Fire to a large Hay-stack he had in the Country, and order'd the Ashes to be brought to Town, from whence he propos'd to prepare a Medicine, call'd *Sal Graminis*, which should infallibly cure all Distempers in *Horses*, and be the rarest Medicine for *Cows*, *Sheep*, or *Oxen*, and all sorts of Creatures that feed upon *Grass*, that any *Grazier* or *Farrier* can use in any Distemper. But sending it up in an ill Season, the Ashes got wet in their Carriage, and quite lost their Virtue, that he was forc'd to sell them to a West-Country *Barge-man* in order to dung Land.

The *Tatler* and the *Spectator* are also full of characters, in various stages of development,[267] most of which contribute to our knowledge of life in the period of Queen Anne. As a mere handful of portraits chosen from this immense gallery, we have the tradesman so interested in foreign politics that he cannot manage his business or support his family (*Tatler*, No. 155); the Pedant (*Tatler*, No. 158); The Very Minor Poet (*Tatler*, No. 163); the Tory Country Squire (Sir Roger de Coverley) and the Whig City Merchant (Sir Andrew Free-port) (*Spectator*, No. 2); a Younger Son (*Spectator*, No. 108); and Tom Puzzle, whose "knowledge is sufficient to raise doubts, but not to clear them" (*Spectator*, No. 476). It would be a bold historian who, after reading these seven bits of por-traiture, could say that he knew the period sufficiently without going further among the characters to be found in these two most engaging of English periodicals.

Such delineations of character did not, however, monopolize the field: in the period after 1688 collections of essay-characters survived in fair numbers,[268] and the pamphlet-character survived in large numbers.[269]

Where may this material be found? There is no very full bibliography of the Character, though Professor E. C. Baldwin, in the *Publications of the Modern Language Association of America*, for June, 1904, prints a list of about one hundred and fifty characters. Professor H. V. Routh's chapters (Vol. iv, chap. xvi, and Vol. vii, chap. xvi) in the *Cambridge History of English Literature* add a few more. Philip Bliss, in his admirable edition of Earle's *Microcosmographie*, London, 1811, has an extremely valuable list of other character books, which list is greatly extended in a copy of Bliss's edition, enriched by Bliss's own manuscript notes, to be found in the Bodleian Library, Oxford. Such well-known collections of seventeenth-century pamphlets as the *Harleian Miscellany* and the *Somers Tracts* contain many characters, and there is a useful volume compiled by Henry Morley called *Character Writings of the Seventeenth Century*, London, 1891. One should of course consult the entries under the word "character" in the catalogue of the British Museum and other large libraries.

Are there any special precautions to be observed by the historian in using the character? Without question there are.

In the first place, the character confessedly exaggerates, or, as Richard Flecknoe put it in his *Fifty-five Enigmatical Characters*, 1665, "It extols to *Heaven*, or depresses into *Hell*; having no mid-place for *Purgatory* left." In other words, the character-writer follows the example of the good Bishop Joseph Hall, who, in 1608, thus introduced his well-known collection of *Characters of Vertues and Vices*:

More might be said, I deny not, of euery Vertue, of euery Vice; I desired not to say all, but enough. If thou doe but read or like these, I haue spent good houres ill; but if thou shalt hence abiure those Vices, which before thou thoughtest not ill-fauored, or fall in loue with any of these goodly phases of Vertue; or shalt hence finde where thou hast any little wish of these euils, to cleare thy selfe, or where any defect in these graces to supply it, neither of us shall need to repent of our labour.

Like Hall, the average character-writer exaggerated each of his types in the direction of its dominant quality: he made the selfish man more selfish than he really was in order that the odiousness of his vice might be the more apparent, and also, no doubt, in order to gratify himself. For the satirist's cross-grained genius is after all a form of art. Therefore, characters have in most cases to be handled with the same caution that would have to be used in letting the drawings of Hogarth illustrate the eighteenth century. Those drawings might very properly confirm other evidence, and even establish a strong presumption when they were unsupported; but manifestly one could not safely argue merely from Hogarth's "Election Series" that political elections in the eighteenth century were quite as corrupt and disorderly as they are there represented.

In the second place, the character, particularly between 1614 and 1640, was markedly stylistic in its traditions. Many character-writers, notably Breton, Mynshul, and Lupton, were so euphuistic that a very considerable allowance must be made by the historian for their exaggerations in the interest of style. A striking instance of this is to be found in the work of Nicholas Breton, who, in the year 1616, published a collection of characters called *The Good And The Badde*. That book contained a character of "A Worthy King," which runs in part as follows:

He is [1] the Lords anointed, [2] and therefore must not be touched, [3] and the head of a public body, [4] and therefore must be preserved. He is [1] a scourge of sin and [2] a blessing of grace, [3] God's vicegerent over His people, and [4] under Him supreme governor. [1] His safety must be his councils care, [2] his health his subjects prayer, [3] his pleasure his peers' comfort, and [4] his content his Kingdom's gladness. [1] His presence must be reverenced, [2] his person attended, [3] his court adorned, and [4] his state maintained. [1] His bosom must not be searched, [2] his will not disobeyed, [3] his wants not unsupplied, nor [4] his place not unregarded.270

It is perfectly clear that Breton is here more or less obsessed by a mania for arranging his ideas in sets of four, and, to bring out that fact, I have taken the liberty, in printing the passage just quoted, of numbering his ideas in fours. This is an extreme instance, but by no means unique. Breton was only one of several writers who were quite capable, after saying three things that they really meant, of adding a fourth point which they did not particularly mean in order to round out the pattern. For this tendency, and for similar exaggerations in the interest of decoration, a somewhat liberal allowance must be made. It is a tendency, however, which vitiates the work of only a relatively small number of character-writers, and the student can very easily tell whether or not he has to do with a euphuist like Breton or with a writer whose style is not such as to tempt him into exaggeration.

Third, there is the fact that certain minor character-writers copy from each other without the slightest scruple. By this is meant far more than that their work bears a strong resemblance to that of their predecessors. Such a resemblance is to be expected, since both, in a general way, drew from the same models, and since the later men accepted most of the conventions which the earlier men had given to the character. The sort of copying that the historian must be aware of in order to know how to interpret a character-writer is perhaps best known to those who have dogged the footsteps of that extraordinary succession of minor character-writers who mercilessly took toll of the excellent Bishop Earle. The purloiners in question are Louis Du Moulin (*Charactères*, 1654),

Thomas Ford (*The Times Anatomiz'd in severall Characters*, 1647), J. Dymock (*Le Vice ridiculé et la vertue louée*, 1671), Samuel Vincent (*The Young Gallant's Academy*, 1674), Richard Head (*Proteus Redivivus*, 1675), the anonymous authors of *The Character of a Whig, under several Denominations*, 1700, and *Hickelty-Pickelty: or, a Medley of Characters*, 1708, and especially the notorious John Dunton, whose *Letters from New England* borrow liberally from Earle and others.[271] When he deals with these people the historian must be on his guard: he will certainly be deceived if he accepts them at their face value; yet he may be misled in a different direction if he fails to remember that what they say, though not original, may have been repeated because it was still true.

What, then, does the character offer to the historian? It enlarges his knowledge of the resorts most frequented by the fashionable London world. It throws valuable light upon the state of English prisons. It tells us a good deal about university life. It yields some exceedingly valuable generalizations about various foreign nations. And, although in the great majority of cases the character is the work of adverse critics, it occasionally, as in John Geree's *Old English Puritan* (1646), offers a peculiarly valuable portrait from the favorable side. Speaking more generally, the character—especially between 1608 and 1642—contains a great deal of material about costume and manner of life in England and about all the vulnerable points of every considerable group—social, political, or religious—from James I down to the Georges. Indeed it is probably not too much to say that as a generalized representation of what the seventeenth- and eighteenth-century wits meant by the vices and virtues—especially the vices—characters are not less valuable than plays or novels.

A Letter relating to the Publication of
Cotton Mather's *Magnalia*

EVERY reader of Cotton Mather's diary knows how deep and constant was his concern for the fate of the precious manuscript of the *Magnalia*. From the summer of 1700 when he sent it to England until the autumn of 1702 when he first saw the great folio in actual print, its welfare was a matter of anxiety which prayers and vigils controlled, perhaps, but could not banish. Forgetting how momentous was, for him, the outcome of an undertaking which both in bulk and in significance overtopped all the other publications of his busy life, the modern reader is probably disposed to wish that he had more sparingly recorded his concern for the manuscript.

However that may be, we are certainly not too fully informed about the vicissitudes of the book after it reached London. Hence the importance of a letter—apparently unpublished—which the Reverend John Quick wrote to Cotton Mather from London on March 19, 1702.[272]

Before turning to the letter it will perhaps be worth while to recapitulate the story as we get it from Cotton Mather himself.

Even before the book was wholly written, Mather had announced the scheme of it in his *Johannes in Eremo* (1695).[273] Some two years later, when the work was approaching completion, the *Diary*[274] records his pleasure at receiving a book which not only quotes from his writings and, though written by a conformist, much magnifies the names and lives of nonconformists, but also advertises the *Magnalia*. The book is *A Compleat History of the Most Remarkable Providences, . . . Which have Hapned in this Present Age. . . . London: John*

Dunton. . . . MDCXCVII., a folio written by William Turner (1653–1701). At the end are advertised *"Books now in the Press, and designed for it. Printed for* John Dunton." Among these is the *Magnalia*, which is announced as follows:

> The Church-History of New England, is now almost finished, including the Lives of the most eminent *Divines* of that Country from the first planting of it, down to this present Year, 1696. 'Tis written by Mr. *Cotton Mather*, Pastor of a Church in *Boston*, from whom I shall receive the *Manuscript Copy* as soon as compleated;[275] and being a large Work, 'twill be Printed in *Folio*, by way of Subscription.

Thus, even before the manuscript of the *Magnalia* was sent to London, it had been advertised not less than twice, and at least one London publisher—if not a very trustworthy one—awaited it.

From 1700 on the entries become more frequent; hence it will be convenient to omit those which merely record Mather's anxiety and to abstract the others, chronologically, with the reference to the *Diary* in each case.

June 8, 1700:	Mather sends the *Magnalia*, with "Directions about the publishing of it," to England (i. 353).
December 12, 1700:	Receives "Letters from *England*, full of Encouragement, concerning the hopeful Circumstances" of the *Magnalia* (i. 375).
May 10, 1701:	Speaks of "my *Church-History*, now in *London*" (i. 399).
June 13, 1701:	Although his "*Church History*, is a bulky thing, of about 250 sheets," which "will cost about 600 *lb*" to publish, although "The Booksellers in *London* are cold about it" and "The Proposals for *Subscriptions*, are of an uncertain and a tedious Event," nevertheless "behold, what my Friend Mr. *Bromfield*, writes me from *London*, March 28, 1701: 'There is one Mr. *Robert Hackshaw*, a very serious and Godly man, who proposes to print the *Ecclesiastical History of*

N. E. . . . AT HIS OWN CHARGE. . . . He declared He did it not with any Expectation of Gain to himself, but for the Glory of God' "[276] (i. 400).

September 27, 1701: The publication of the *Magnalia* is "unhappily clog'd by some Dispositions of the Gentleman, to whom I first sent it" (i. 404).

February 10, 1702: The *Magnalia* "runs great Hazards of Miscarrying" (i. 411).

May 1, 1702: Receives important news: "My *Church-History* has been in extreme Hazard of Miscarrying. The Delay, given by the nice Hummours [*sic*] of my Friend [277] in whose Hands it was left, unto the kind Offers and Motions of the Gentleman, that would have published it a Year ago,[278] exposed it unto the Hazard of never being published at all. God continued the Opportunities and Inclinations of that Gentleman to go on with the Undertaking. When they began to fail, God stirr'd up a very eminent Bookseller,[279] to come in, with obliging Tenders of his Assistance. Letters to Advise me of this, were dated as long ago as the twentieth of last *November*, . . . At last, on this Day, after so long a Delay, comes in the Ship that had these Letters; which also tell me, that they hoped the Work would be finished, by the Month of *March*, which is now past" (i. 427).

Anyone who has tried to launch a book into an indifferent world, even in these days of cables and quick mails, will hardly fail to realize some of Cotton Mather's distress at the delayed appearance of the work which, we must always remember, was not only one of the beloved children of its author's busy brain but also—as he verily believed—an important piece of the Lord's business.

Meanwhile what was going on in London? It has already appeared that as early as March, 1701, Robert Hackshaw had made an offer, that someone—perhaps Bromfield—had endangered the enterprise by asking for terms too unfavorable to the booksellers, and that somehow Thomas Parkhurst had at last taken over the work. But the relation of Parkhurst, Hackshaw, and Bromfield to each other and to the business in hand is far from clear.

To make it somewhat clearer we shall now present Quick's letter, after having given a brief account of his life.

John Quick (1636–1706) was a Devonshire man, born at Plymouth; an Oxford graduate, with Puritan inclinations, fostered at Exeter, which under the severe but able leadership of Conant was then a large, strong college. He graduated B.A. in 1657. Quick held several livings in Devonshire, did not conform at the Restoration, and consequently was arrested and imprisoned more than once. Settling in London, he became the head of a congregation in Bartholomew Close, Smithfield. There he died in 1706, known as a serious scholar and preacher.

Besides the usual minor publications of a Puritan minister of the period, Quick wrote two much larger works. His *Synodicon in Gallia Reformata*, in two folio volumes, was published at London in 1692 by T. Parkhurst and J. Robinson.[280] As this work amply shows, Quick was profoundly interested in the welfare of the Protestant churches in France, and laborious in gathering the documents to illustrate their history. His other large work never got into print. This was another great collection, but this time of biographies rather than documents: his *Icones Sacrae* is said to contain the biographies of seventy divines, French and English.[281] Calamy acknowledges his debt to it, and—as Quick's letter to Cotton Mather will presently show—a sketch of John Flavell had been made from it by a process of abridgment so violent as greatly to distress the author. Otherwise the work seems to have remained unused. It is now—three folio volumes—in Dr. Williams's Library, London.[282]

Finally, let it be noted that in forwarding the publication of Cotton Mather's book, John Quick was not only doing a service for a fellow Puritan whose father had preached in Quick's own pulpit[283] at Bartholomew Close, but was returning in kind a favor which he had but two years earlier received from the younger Mather. For in 1700, Cotton Mather records[284] that to one of his own works which was then being published he did "adjoin a savoury little Discourse, of Mr. *Quick*, a Reverend *Presbyterian* in *London*, about *A Claim to the Sacrament*, as well to confute our pretended *Presbyterians*, as to promote practical Godliness."

And now at last we come to the letter:

Reverend S^r

Octob^r the 10. at Euening in ye yeare of our Lord 1701—I received this order (the Originall of wch I communicated as I haue also of ye following Receipts to your worthy Brother m^r Sam.[285] the last week) from m^r Hackshaws man "m^r John Quick, Reverend S^r, Herewith I "send you m^r Cotton mather his Letter to your self, & doe desire that "according to his Order you will be pleased to deliver ye Copy of his "Treatise called magnalia christi Americana to this Bearer, w^o will giue "you my Receipt for it, & thereby you will obliege, S^r, your friend & "seruant R. Hackshaw.[286]

Haueing perused this script, I told m^r Hackshaws serv^t, "Friend, I "dont know you, I shall not deliver ye mscr. to any but into your mas-"ter's own hands, & I desire He would come in person & receiue it.

The next day about 5. in ye afternoon m^r Hackshaw came to my hou[se] & demanding your mnscr. History of me, I tendred him this Acquittance to be signed by him for my discharge.

"London, Octob^r 11, 1701. I doe acknowledg to haue received of "m^r John Quick min^r of ye Gospell by order of ye R. m^r Cotton mather "Pastor of ye Nor[th] Church in Boston of New England ye manuscript "Copy of his magnalia christi Americana in seven Books, The wch "manuscript I promise to pu[t] into ye presse very speedily, & that m^r

"Quick shall haue yᵉ correcting of yᵉ sheets, as they are wrought off
"from yᵉ presse, that so it may not be prejudiced through yᵉ negligence
"of yᵉ Printer, witness my hand yᵉ day & yeare above : written.

mʳ Hackshaw haueing read it scrupled yᵉ signing it, excepting
again[st] theise clauses "*The wᶜʰ manuscr. I promise to put into yᵉ presse*
"*ver[y] speedily, & yᵗ mʳ Quick shall haue yᵉ correcting of yᵉ sheets as they*
"*are wrought off from yᵉ press &c.* I demanded yᵉ reason of his Refuseall.
To wch He replyed in theise words, "Sʳ, I will not ingage [my] self one
"way or other about yᵉ printing of it, onely I will be accountable to mʳ
"Cotton mather for yᵉ manuscr. But, Sʳ, said I, showing him y[our]
Letter to me, yᵗ mʳ mather desires it may be printed with all conve-
[nient] expedition, & yᵗ I should oversee yᵉ correction of yᵉ presse. He
answer[ed:]

"Sr, I haue read it, but I shall engage for nothing, nor will I be con-
"cernde at all about it's impression, but another shall. Sʳ, said I, pr[ay]
"wº is it? mʳ Hackshaw replys, *I haue treated with mʳ Parkhurst, who*
"*will buy yᵉ paper of me, & print it, provided I will take off an hundred*
"*books, wch I intend to send to N. E. & yᵉ Caribbee Islands, there to be*
"*disposed of. And Parkhurst will present mʳ Mather with some books*
"*as he thinks fitting, I suppose about Ten.*²⁸⁷

I wondred I confesse yᵗ I heard no news this morning (Octobʳ 11.)
of m[y] Booksellers, wº had promised to be with me, & to strike up a
bargain wi[th] me for yᵉ Coppy, & I had certainly sent you either a
fair Bill of some scores of Guineas, or at least an Hundred Books wellbound for your Copy. But what you shall now haue for all your pains
& Labour I know not. I cant blame Parkhurst for saueing his coppy-
money, nor mʳ Robert Hacksh[aw] for selling off a warehouse of Paper,
yᵗ had long layen on his hands. nor would I haue you to blame me if
there be any failures in your Book when printed; for thô I endeavourd
to doe you all yᵉ right & service I could & that your History might be
published with all advantage to your self & reputation, yet you see how
I am excluded from all intermeddling with it. I am full of fears for
your Labour, least there should be any Interpolations or detruncations
from it. I haue bin dealt with all very unfairly by Parkhurst, for me [?]
to gratify his extreame importunity, I let him haue my manscr. I con of
mʳ fflavells Life to be prefixt to yᵉ late Impression of all his works in 2.

voll. in folio,[288] He took it, & got it abridged, but so horribly mained & wounded, that yᵉ poor man in yᵉ Almanack[289] has not more arrows shaking in all yᵉ members of his body, than that Icon of mine has wounds & maimes. And yet it must passe in yᵉ world as if it were my own Composure; when as Sʳ, it's no more mine, than if you should chop off my hands, arms, & leggs, & [binding?] pieces of wood to those parts, you should say, this is whole Mʳ Quick. when I expostulated with him for this durty useage, & demanded of him wᵒ did it, He answered me as the Cyclops did Neptune, it was one mʳ Outis,[290] he did not know whom. Sʳ, one thing more I will adde, for I am concernde for you. Tis well you liue 3000. miles off London, or else Burre rediviue[291] would cry to you as he did to Sʳ Walter Rawleigh, "*I am undone* "*by* yᵉ *printing of your history, & you cannot* doe *lesse than take off 500.* "*books or more to help reimburse me of my dammages.* And yet yᵉ man got an estate by Sʳ Walter's History, thô yᵉ world was really damnified by yᵉ losse of yᵉ two remaining Vollumes, wᶜʰ Sʳ Walter in a passion, because he would haue no more undone by Him, cast into yᵉ fire. But let me returne from my Digression. I urgde mʳ Hackshaw againe twice or thrice, yᵗ I might have yᵉ oversight of yᵉ sheets as they came from yᵉ Presse, & prefix a short Dedicatory Epistle of an half sheet to yᵉ King. Unto wᶜʰ he answered, "I haue left all to Parkhurst, wᵒ will take a "fourtnights time to peruse it, & then He will tell me, whether He "will print it or no. However I will be accountable to mʳ Mather for "his Copy. whereupon in complyance with your order, wᶜʰ he gave me, I resigned to him your Entire manuscr. together with yᵉ Additionall prints[292] you sent me to be inserted in their proper place, takeing from Him this Receipt, yᵉ Originall I keep by me for my own Indemnity. "London, Octobʳ 11. 1701. I doe acknowledg to haue received of mʳ "John Quick minʳ of yᵉ Gospell by order of yᵉ R. mʳ Cotton Mather "Pastor of yᵉ N. Ch. at Boston in New Engˡ the mnscr. Copy of his "magnalia christi Americana in 7. Books, for yᵉ wᶜʰ mnscr. I will be "responsible unto mʳ Mather aforesaid, witnesse my hand yᵉ day & "year aboue-written, R. Hackshaw."

you should haue received this account sooner, would my health haue permitted me. N.B. Governour Dudley[293] desired that he might read over (wᶜʰ He did in my Library) his ffather's Life, & altered one or two words, wch as I remember were theise, "*not a servant* but uncle or "Guardian to ye Earle of Lincolne. He approved of your performance. I had proposed theise Articles to my Booksellers, w^o should haue purchased your Mnscr. of me. 1. 100. Guineas or so many Books wellbound. 2. Six of ye larger Paper 294 richly bound for your Patrons. 3. To be put into ye Presse immediately. 4. Every sheet to be brought to me hot from ye Presse to be revised & corrected.295 5. The Paper & character to be ye same with my printed Proposalls.296 6. not one to be sold off till all your Books were first delivered to me. 7. The best chart of New Engl. The best Topographicall Delineation of Boston, & your effigies' in mezzotinto to be præfixed to ye whole work. But all theise fair designes, hopes, & endeauors of mine for you are now vanished into smoak. Most of all am I grieued for ye Paper & character, wch compareing with ye specimens herewith sent you will certainly affect & afflict you, for they doe me very much. And how to remedy any other miscarriages about ye Impression I am utterly at a losse. The delays in publishing my Icons was no detriment, but in truth a furtherance to your work. For I wûd haue procured you all my subscribers. But I dônt owe ye Booksellers that suit & service. It hath pleased ye Lord to continue his heavy hand upon now full 20. Monthes, & this Week hath bin a racking torture to me. Dear S^r, haue me recommended to your R. Father, & to all our Brethren with you. The R. R. m^r How,297 m^r Hammond, m^r Alsop, m^r Griffyth, m^r Bragge, & my poor self can not be long on this side ye Graue, we are hastening homeward apa[ce]. O! Lift up a petition for me, That I may finish my course with joy, & obtaine ye end of my ffaith, ye salvation of my soul. I am waiting for y^t blessed hope, ye glorious appearance of ye great God, & our Saviour ye Lord Jesus Christ. Come Lord Jesu! even so come quickly! I thank you for your pious & usefull meditations, wch have much refreshed me. Had my ffast sermons about 3. years agoe upon ye 5. of Jer. 12. upon ye 64. Esay. 1. & upon 25. Jer. 29, & 11. Psal. 3. bin compared with those excellent ones of your Honoured ffather on Ezek. 9. 3. together with his Epistle to ye Reader, you would ha[ve] said, I had borrowed all my notions from Him, thô I never saw them, till your Brother presented them to me this munday.298 But ye same holy spirit suggested to us both ye same thoughts, ye very self same holy matter. O! y^t they wᵒ haue ears would heare what yᵉ spirit saith unto yᵉ churches! Forgiue me the tedium of this epistle. I shall never trouble you at this rate any more. Grace be with your spirit! So prayeth, Dear Sʳ,

Your most affectionate thô unworthy fellow servᵗ

JOHN QUICK

London, March. 19.

1701/2.

postscript, what & if yᵉ minʳˢ of N. E. did address her majesty Qu. Anne, congratulateing her happy succession to yᵉ throne? Engrosse it in parchmin, subscribe it with as many hands as you can, of Pastors of churches, & send it over here to be presented by some wᵒ you can intrust. I am confident it will be kindly taken, & turne to good Account for you. What you doe, doe quickly. Let your Address be short but cordiall & melting.

This letter certainly does something toward filling the gaps in the story of the *Magnalia*. It makes quite clear the relation of Hackshaw and Parkhurst; it shows how persistent, though vain, was Quick's endeavor to secure the opportunity to examine the proof-sheets before publication; and it opens a tantalizing prospect of mezzotint portraits, patrons, and various other worldly considerations which the "Chief of Sinners" in his far-away Boston study must have found it hard to renounce.

Why was this devout, unwieldy book called the *Magnalia*? We know that Cotton Mather had a fondness for beginning his titles with a word or phrase from the Hebrew, Greek, or Latin.[299] And it is a matter of record that the word "magnalia" occurs several times in Latin,[300] notably in the Vulgate version of Acts ii. 11, where the Greek τὰ μεγαλεῖα τοῦ Θεοῦ becomes "magnalia Dei," which in the King James Version is "the wonderful works of God." It can, therefore, be asserted with confidence that to every Puritan of anything like Cotton Mather's learning "magnalia" was familiar, had a Biblical connotation, and would probably have been rendered into English about as it is rendered by King James's translators.

[142]

Of less importance are the cases—the *Oxford Dictionary* gives three—where seventeenth-century writers use "magnalia" in English prose.[301]

At least four times before Cotton Mather used it, the word "magnalia" had formed a part of the title of an English book, and one of these titles is so similar to our New England *Magnalia* as to suggest a source. These four titles are:

1. *Magnalia Dei. A Relation Of some of the many Remarkable Passages in Cheshire Before the Siege of Namptwich, during the Continuance of it: And at the happy raising of it by the victorious Gentlemen Sir Tho. Fairfax and Sir William Brereton. Together With the Deliverance and Victory by the Garrison at Nottingham: certified in a Letter to a worthy Member of the House of Commons. Published by Authority and entred according to order. Psal. 31. 23, 24. . . . London: Printed for Robert Bostock dwelling at the Signe of the Kings head in Pauls Church-yard.* 1644. 4°. [2 leaves and] pp. 1–22.[302]

2. *Magnalia Dei ab Aquilone; Set Forth, In A Sermon Preached Before The Right Honourable the Lords and Commons, at St Margarets Westminster, upon Thursday Iuly 18, 1644. being the day of publike Thanksgiving for the great Victory obtained against Prince Rupert and the Earle of Newcastles Forces neere Yorke. By Richard Vines, Minister of Gods Word at Weddington in the County of Warwick, and a Member of the Assembly of Divines. Published by Order of both Houses. London, Printed by G. M. for Abel Roper at the signe of the Sunne over against St Dunstans Church in Fleet-street.* 1644. 4°. [2 leaves and] pp. 1–21 [and 1 leaf].[303]

3. *Magnalia Naturae: Or, The Philosophers-Stone, lately exposed to publick Sight and Sale. Being a true and exact Account of the Manner how Wenceslaus Seilerus, the late famous Projection-Maker, at the Emperor's Court at Vienna, came by, and made away with a very great Quantity of Powder of Projection . . . for some Years past. Published at the Request, and for the Satisfaction of several Curious, especially of Mr. Boyle, &c. By John Joachim Becker. . . . London. . . .* 1680. 4°. 38 pages. (This curious pamphlet is reprinted in the *Harleian Miscellany*.)[304]

4. The fourth example seems much more significant. It bears the title: *Magnalia Dei Anglicana. Or, Englands Parliamentary-Chronicle. Containing a full and faithfull Series, and Exact Narration of all the most memorable Parliamentary-Mercies, and mighty (if not miraculous) Deliverances, great and glorious Victories, and admirable Successes, of the Counsels and Armies of this present Parliament, both by Sea and by Land, over the whole Kingdom of England, in the most just defence and Vindication of her Religion, Laws, and Liberties, from the yeer, 1640. to this present yeer, 1646. . . . Collected cheifly for the high Honour of our Wonderworking God; And for the unexpressible Comfort of all Cordiall English Parliamentarians. By the most unworthy Admirer of Them, John Vicars. . . . Imprinted at London, for J. Rothwell, at the Sun & Fountain, in Pauls Church-yard, and Tho. Underhill, at the Bible in Woodstreet. 1646.*[305]

Part I of Vicars has a very long separate title-page which may be shortened to: *Jehovah-Jireh. God in the Mount. . . . 1644.* (Pages 1–434 and Index.) Although the pagination is continuous and (in the Harvard copy at least) Part II has no separate title-page,[306] Part I may be said to end with page 87: "But here, good Reader, I have thought fit to shut up the sluce and flood-gates of this most fluent River; to put a period to the first part of this our famous and most memorable *Parliamentarie Chronicle*," etc.

Part III has another very long separate title-page: *Gods Arke Overtopping the Worlds Waves, Or The Third Part of the Parliamentary Chronicle. . . . 1646.* The paging runs to 304; then follows an index, or "Table."

Part IV is called: *The Burning-Bush not Consumed. Or, The Fourth and Last Part Of The Parliamentarie-Chronicle. . . . 1646.* This has 476 pages of text, followed by a table.

To say nothing about the similarity of their titles for subdivisions, the likeness is as close as it could be between John Vicars' *Magnalia Dei Anglicana* of 1646 and Cotton Mather's *Magnalia Christi Americana* of fifty years later. There is apparently no evidence[307] to show that Cotton Mather ever owned a copy of Vicars. But he may well have had one, or at least have heard of its title. And to make just that slight change in Vicars' title would have been exactly in Cotton Mather's manner.[308]

Let us conclude, as John Quick did, with a postscript about Queen Anne. It is surely interesting to find this London Puritan urging upon a Boston minister the importance of a certain diplomatic gesture. Did Cotton Mather respond to the suggestion?

The date of Quick's letter, it will be remembered, was March 19. King William had died on March 8. On April 23 occurred the coronation of Queen Anne. Well might Quick urge speed, for before his letter could reach Boston, addresses to the Queen began to pour in from her loyal subjects the two great universities, from the various dioceses, boroughs, and the like.[309]

On June 16, 1702, in spite of his wife's extreme illness, Cotton Mather was able to note in his diary: "Several Addresses of some Consequence, especially one to the Queen, did I draw up, about this Time."[310]

In the *London Gazette*, No. 3829 (July 20–23, 1702), we find these items:

Boston *in* New-England, June 8.

On the 28th of May *last we received Advice of the Death of His late Majesty, and of Her present Majesty's happy Succession to the Throne: The Council and the General Assembly were then sitting, and the Members of the Council immediately took the Oath of Allegiance to her Majesty. The next day the Council, attended by the Representatives in the General Assembly, the Ministers, Justices of the Peace, Gentlemen, Merchants, and other Inhabitants, Proclaimed Her Majesty, the Troop of Guards and the Regiment of Militia being in Arms, who, when the Proclamation was ended, fired three Volleys, which was followed with Huzza's, and loud Acclamations of* God save Queen Anne, *and the Cannon of the Castle and Forts, and of Her Majesty's Ship the* Gosport, *and the Merchant*

Ships then in our Port, was discharged. In the Evening the Company was entertained at the Town-House, and other Places, and all other Demonstrations of Joy were given suitable to the Occasion. The 31st, the Representatives took the Oath of Allegiance. The 4th Instant, the Members of the Council and other Gentlemen of the Town went into Mourning for the Death of His late Majesty. The Bells were tolled from 8 till 10 in the morning, and from 2 till 4 in the afternoon; Funeral Sermons were preached in all the Churches, and the Guns of the Castle and Forts, and of the Ships in our Port, were all discharged.

Windsor, July 19. The following Address was presented to Her Majesty by Constantine Phipps *Esq; introduced by the Rt. Hon. the Earl of* Nottingham, *Her Majesty's Principal Secretary of State.*

To Her most Excellent Majesty *Anne*, by the Grace of God, of *England, Scotland, France* and *Ireland*, Queen, Defender of the Faith, &c.

The humble Address of the Council and Representatives of Your Majesty's Province of the Massachusetts-Bay *in* New-England, *in General Court assembled.*

Most Gracious Sovereign.

The Surprizing Intelligence of the Awful Stroke of Divine Providence, in the Death of our late Sovereign Lord King William III. *of ever Glorious Memory, filled us with no little Consternation, and very sensibly affects us with a deep Sorrow for so unspeakable a Loss; which we humbly crave leave to Condole with Your Majesty and our Nation; and at the same time most heartily to Congratulate Your Majesty's happy Accession to the Throne, whereby our Grief is alleviated, in that Your Majesty's known Zeal for, and firm Adherence to, the Protestant Religion, gives us Assurance of enjoying Prosperity under Your Majesty's auspicious Reign, which God grant may be long and prosperous.*

Humbly beseeching Your Majesty, That the benign Influences of Your Royal Goodness and Protection may be extended to Your Majesty's good Subjects in this Province, at so great distance from the Royal Seat.

That Almighty God would afford Your Majesty the Assistance of all Divine Grace, is and shall be the hearty and fervent Prayer of Your Majesty's most Dutiful, Loyal, and Obedient Subjects.

Boston, *June* 6. 1702.

Then follows an address from Barbadoes. "Which Addresses Her Majesty received very graciously."

This address, to be sure, is not quite what Quick suggested: it is an address from the Legislature, not from the clergy. But the date is very close to the date when Mather notes that "about this Time" he wrote an address to the Queen. Moreover it does not appear that any other of the American colonies sent addresses. There seems, therefore, rather more than a possibility that it was Quick's suggestion that prompted Cotton Mather, and Cotton Mather's pen that wrote the address.

Defoe in Boston

O N March 13, 1721, the *Boston Gazette* advertised as "just published" and "to be sold by Benjamin Gray Bookseller" a small eight-page pamphlet called "*News from the Moon. A Review of the State of the British Nation*, Vol. 7, Numb. 14. Page 53. Tuesday, May 2, 1710." At the January meeting, 1910, of this Society [the Colonial Society of Massachusetts], our late associate Andrew McFarland Davis submitted this pamphlet to a very careful examination, but felt that there remained "several questions for future settlement by the bibliographers engaged in the study of Defoe's works."

The main questions proposed by Mr. Davis were: (1) the possibility of an Edinburgh edition of the seventh volume of Defoe's *Review* and its relation to the London issues of that volume; (2) the identity of the printer of *News from the Moon*, conjecturally supposed to be James Franklin; (3) the relation of *News from the Moon* to certain other writings and certain events of that period. Let us, in that order, consider these three topics.

I

Following the specifications on the first page of *News from the Moon*, Mr. Davis asked the authorities of the British Museum to send him a copy of Volume VII, No. 14, of Defoe's *Review*, and indicated the nature of the subject-matter which he naturally expected to find in that number. He was told that the number which he required was not No. 14, dated Tuesday, May 2, 1710, and paged 53–56, but No. 15, dated Saturday, April 29, 1710, and paged 57–60. Mr. Davis was naturally puzzled at these discrepancies. However, with the assistance of our associate Albert Matthews, and with the aid of an incomplete run of the seventh volume of the *Review* owned by the American Antiquarian Society, Mr. Davis made what was, in view of the inaccessibility of much of the material involved, a brilliant conjecture. That there was an Edinburgh edition of the sixth volume of Defoe's *Review* had long been known.[311] Mr. Davis and Mr. Matthews thought, though they were unable to prove, that there might have been an Edinburgh edition of the seventh volume, or of a portion of that volume, and that such a volume might contain a number that would correspond in subject-matter, date, numbering, and pagination with *News from the Moon*.

The conjecture was correct: the first thirty-five numbers, at least, of the seventh volume of the *Review* exist in an issue which in respect to numbering, pagination, and dates, and to a certain extent in subject-matter and typography, are unlike the London issue. One of these numbers corresponds exactly (except for minute details in phrasing) with *News from the Moon*. Let us call these thirty-five numbers the Edinburgh issue of the *Review*, though probably it was printed in London. The Library of the University of Texas, which has these Edinburgh issues, very kindly supplied a photostat of the number that was reprinted in *News from the Moon* and a few essential facts concerning the other thirty-four numbers. Although this discovery is not of startling importance, it is perhaps better that, since the question was raised by a member of this Society, the answer should not be made by an outsider.

Careful examination would almost certainly reveal some marked differences between the relation of the London to the Edinburgh issues of Volume vi and the relation of the London to the Edinburgh issues of the first thirty-five numbers of Volume vii.

We know that Defoe was in Scotland during much, if not all, of the latter part of the period (from the end of March,

1709, to the end of February, 1710) covered by Volume VI. He was in Scotland by September 13, 1709.[312] He was in northern Scotland when he wrote the Edinburgh issue of *Review*, No. 73 (September 22). In No. 84 (Edinburgh, October 18) he says (p. 33, last sentence): "I am writing this paper in Scotland, where I could look out of my Window, and see the Fields standing full of the Shocks of Corn." He was in Scotland when he wrote the Edinburgh issue of No. 95 (November 12). At the end of December (London No. 115) a parcel of *Reviews* from Edinburgh missed the Wednesday post and did not arrive until Friday, December 30; therefore there was no London issue of Thursday, December 29. On January 28, 1710, the *Review* (Edinburgh No. 128) announced that the author was "leaving Scotland for a time."

Thus Defoe probably remained in Scotland from early September, 1709, until almost the end of January, 1710—the period, roughly, from No. 70 to No. 128 of the Edinburgh issue. In March, 1710, Defoe was apparently in London: the material of his Edinburgh No. 142 (March 2) had been published in London on February 25; on March 8, he wrote to Stanhope offering to appear at any time as a witness against Sacheverell.[313] The late appearance of the Edinburgh Nos. 147, 148, and 149 was explained in the paper as due to the fact that the letters "which bring the printed copies from England" had gone astray. The notice spoke of the author as one "who lives so remote."

In the early days of the seventh volume, that is, between April 1 and June 20, 1710, Defoe seems to have been in London. There are letters from Defoe dated from London on April 7 and on June 17; and passages in the *Review* of April 13, June 1, and June 8 imply, to say the least, that he was then in the city or near at hand.

Of these thirty-five numbers it would seem that London No. 6 corresponds to nothing in the Edinburgh series and that Edinburgh No. 35 corresponds to nothing in the London series. With these two exceptions, the contents seem to be substantially the same. Nos. 1–5 of the two issues correspond in subject-matter. London Nos. 7–35 correspond to Edinburgh Nos. 6–34. And after No. 35 the Edinburgh issues seem not to exist.

So far as the text may be regarded as conclusive, one could not confidently say whether the Boston printer of *News from the Moon* followed the London or the Edinburgh issue. Disregarding punctuation, italics, and the like (as the Boston printer obviously did), there are thirty-three variations between the Boston reprint and the two other versions. In thirty-one of these, both the London and the Edinburgh issue differ from the Boston reprint, though not from each other. In one instance the Boston reprint follows the Edinburgh issue, which differs from the London issue. And in one instance the Boston reprint follows the London issue, which differs from the Edinburgh issue. In each of these last two cases the Boston reprint avoids a trifling typographical error (*Gases* for *Cases*, *trangress* for *transgress*) which either the London or the Edinburgh printer had committed.[314]

But since the Boston reprint agrees with the Edinburgh issue in date, number, and pagination, and thus differs from the London issue in each of those points, we may confidently say that the Boston printer followed the Edinburgh issue.

II

Who printed *News from the Moon*? Its date of publication seems approximately fixed by the advertisement which, on March 13, 1721, declares it to have been then "just published." The place of publication is assumed to have been Boston because it was advertised there, it was to be had of a Boston bookseller, and it seems to concern Massachusetts affairs. The printer is often assumed to have been James

Franklin. The Brinley *Catalogue*, No. 1441, attributes the work, questioningly, to him.[315] Charles Evans (*American Bibliography*, 1. 302) describes the pamphlet as "[Boston: Printed by J. Franklin. 1721.]" The form of the entry would seem to indicate certainty about all three of the facts recorded. Mr. Ford definitely declares James Franklin to have been the printer.[316] But none of these give their evidence. Mr. Davis suggests[317] that "the specific attribution to the press of J. Franklin may have been the result of a careful examination of the font of type and the various ornaments used in the pamphlet." Feeling that judgment on the basis of type was too technical for me to indulge in, I have wholly ignored that phase of the subject. It is greatly to be desired that some expert should tell us, if he can, who printed the pamphlets that, like *News from the Moon*, bear no printer's name but obviously concern Massachusetts affairs at a time when disputes were warm and the press was sharply watched.

I have, however, collected a little evidence based on the printer's ornaments that appear on the first page—except for that there is no title-page—of *News from the Moon*; and I present that evidence briefly, for whatever it may be worth to some later investigator more learned in the details of printing.

The ornaments in question were used in books and pamphlets printed at London from 1711 on. *The Critical Specimen*, which is a satirical little pamphlet aimed at John Dennis, has them on its title-page. But unfortunately the printer's name is not given: "London: printed in the Year, 1711" is all that the title-page tells us. In 1714, there were two editions, both bearing these ornaments, of Churchill's *Annals*, both "printed for S[arah] Popping at the Black Raven in Pater-Noster-Row; and sold by the Booksellers of London and Westminster." The work leans strongly to the Whig side, praising Marlborough's "Glorious Actions both in the Field

[152]

and Cabinet." In the same year (1714) John Dennis published *Whigg Loyalty*, which was "Printed by T. Warner near Ludgate," and which uses the ornaments. And in 1716 we have them in Samuel Rosewell's *The Protestant Dissenters Hopes from the Present Government. Freely Declar'd. And the Grounds that support them. . . . London: Printed and sold by* J. Roberts *in* Warwick-Lane, J. Harrison *at the* Royal Exchange, S. Boulter *at* Charing Cross, *and* T. Fox *in* Westminster Hall.[318]

Of works printed in Boston which make use of these ornaments and which bear the imprint of James Franklin, I find:

1718. Increase Mather and others, *Sermon, Charge, etc., at Thomas Prince's Ordination*. Boston: printed by J. Franklin for S. Gerrish. HCL.

1719. Richard Bernard, *The Isle of Man*. Boston: reprinted by J. Franklin for B. Eliot. Harvard-Andover.

1720. *A Letter from One in the Country*. Boston: J. Franklin for D. Henchman. MHS.[319]

(Date doubtful). Nathan Bailey, *Preliminary Exercises on the Most Easy and Fundamental Rules of Syntaxis, English and Latin*. Boston: printed by J. Franklin for D. Henchman. HCL (imperfect).

Of works printed in Boston which made use of these ornaments and which bear the names of other printers than James Franklin, there are, at least, the following:

1718. Increase Mather, *A Sermon Preached at Roxbury, October 29, 1718. When Mr. Thomas Walter Was Ordained*. Boston: printed by S. Kneeland for J. Edwards. HCL.

1719. *An Addition to the Present Melancholy Circumstances of the Province Considered*. Boston: printed by S. Kneeland for B. Gray and J. Edwards. MHS.[320]

1720. [Oliver Noyes?],[321] *A Letter from a Gentleman, containing some remarks upon the several answers given unto Mr. Colman's entituled, The Distressed State of the Town of Boston*. Boston: printed by S. Kneeland for Nicholas Boone, Benjamin Gray, and John Edwards. BPL.[322]

1720. *A Vindication of the Remarks of one in the country upon The Distressed State of Boston, from some exceptions made against 'em in a letter to Mr. Colman.* Boston: printed by S. Kneeland for D. Hench-man. BPL.[323]

1721. [Cotton Mather], *The World Alarm'd.* Boston: printed by B. Green for S. Gerrish. MHS.

1721. Cotton Mather, *The Accomplish'd Singer.* Boston: printed by B. Green for S. Gerrish. HCL.

1724. Thomas Foxcroft, *God's Face Set against an Incorrigible People.* Boston: printed by B. Green for John Eliot. HCL.

1726. Thomas Foxcroft, *Ministers, Spiritual Parents. A sermon preach'd at the ordination of the Rev. Mr. John Lowell.* Boston: printed by B. Green for Samuel Gerrish. HCL.

Of works printed (or supposed to have been printed) in Boston which make use of these ornaments and which bear the name of no printer, there are, at least, the following:

1720. *Some Proposals to Benefit the Province.* Boston: printed for and sold by Benj. Eliot. AAS.[324]

1721. [John Wise?], *A Friendly Check, from a Kind Relation, to the Chief Cannoneer, founded on a late information,* dated N.E. Castle-William, 1720,21. MHS.[325]

1721. [John Wise], *A Word of Comfort to A Melancholy Country; or the bank of credit fairly defended.* By Amicus Patriae. Boston. HCL.

1722. [Cotton Mather], *The Minister.* Boston. HCL.

1724. [Edward Wigglesworth], *Sober Remarks on A Modest Proof of the Order and Government Settled by Christ and his Apostles in the Church.* 2nd ed. Boston. Printed for Samuel Gerrish. HCL.

1725/6. *The Explanatory Charter Granted to the Province of the Massachusetts Bay Anno 1725.* MHS.

(N.d.) *A Letter from the Author of the Postscript of the defence of a book, entituled, A Modest Proof of Church Government, &c. to Jonathan Dickinson, author of the remarks on that postscript.* HCL.

From these few titles—four by James Franklin, four by Samuel Kneeland, four by Bartholomew Green, and seven by unknown printers—no positive conclusion can be drawn. As matters stand, the assumption that James Franklin printed

News from the Moon, in so far as that assumption is based on the use of certain printer's ornaments, seems unsafe.

The Boston Athenæum has a copy of the Edinburgh issue of Defoe's *Review*, Vol. vi, which bears upon its half-title the autograph of "J. Franklin," as well as the inscription "Andrew Craigies Book 1756."[326] The "J. Franklin" of the Athenæum volume may be James Franklin, or his father Josiah,[327] or his brother John, who was postmaster of Boston when he died. No authentic autograph of James Franklin seems to be known. The Athenæum signature bears a fairly close resemblance—especially in the flourish at the end—to the autograph of John Franklin that is reproduced in Winsor's *Memorial History of Boston* (ii. 271). Furthermore, Andrew Craigie seems to mean by his inscription that he acquired the book in 1756. It was on Friday, January 30, 1756, that John Franklin died.[328] In its issues of August 5 and August 12, 1756, the *Boston News-Letter* advertises for sale on August 12 "A large and valuable Collection of BOOKS belonging to the Estate of Mr. John Franklin, late of Boston, Gentleman, deceased." These facts seem to take us rather far toward establishing John Franklin's ownership for some period ending in 1756.[329] It is possible that John Franklin acquired the book from James Franklin, who died in February, 1735,[330] and still more likely that James may have had the use, if not the ownership, of it. One would very much like to know if John Franklin's books included any of those mentioned in the notice of the *Courant's* "office library" in 1722. To whatever extent he did possess such books, there might seem to be a fair chance that this Athenæum copy of the *Review* was in the possession of James Franklin before passing through John Franklin's hands to those of Andrew Craigie. Certainly, if this book did belong, as early as 1721, to James Franklin or his brother John, there would seem to be some possibility that that person also possessed other numbers of the *Review* and that the chances of James Franklin's having printed *News from the Moon* had thereby been somewhat strengthened.

But the present state of the evidence does not seem to permit any settlement of that interesting question.

III

Perhaps the most difficult question that Mr. Davis asked, or at least the one that takes longest to answer, was that concerning the relation of *News from the Moon* to the controversies of 1720–1721 in Massachusetts. ". . . It has been supposed to have had some connection with the legislative controversies of that time," says Mr. Davis.[331] The Brinley *Catalogue*, No. 1441, calls it "a satire aimed, apparently, at the House of Representatives, for their proceedings against the publisher and printer of 'New News from Robinson Cruso's Island.'" Evans[332] calls it "a burlesque on the prosecution of Benjamin Gray for ordering the printing of 'A Letter to an Eminent Clergy-man.'" Mr. Ford[333] regards it as "a burlesque on the trial of a fellow printer." Mr. Davis found that *News from the Moon* "does not deal with the currency."[334] He amended the explanation in the Brinley *Catalogue* because he did not find that there were any proceedings in the matter of *New News from Robinson Cruso's Island*.[335] And at the end of his article (p. 15) he wrote: "The question, How could a reprint of an article by Defoe be of value in the polemics of that day? remains still a mystery." And again: "How then could it be possible that the general public could appreciate the application of Defoe's satire to a new situation sufficiently to justify its republication?"

Before we attempt to answer these questions, the reader must be warned not to expect too much: we are not at all likely to find that *News from the Moon* fits into the Boston situation of 1721 in the way that the final piece of a picture puzzle fits, completing an interdependent series of fragments that cry out for the final piece and leave no place for any additional fragment or for any fragment of another shape. For such an exact fit is hardly to be found in the original *Review*, though in that case the whole was the work of a single writer. It is hardly to be found in the case of the *Spectator*, where, though there were several contributors, the editorship was wholly in the hands of a single man. Certainly it could not be expected in the case of a very considerable body of books, pamphlets, and periodical essays, by various authors, representing a warfare that was waged on several fronts at once.

Moreover, we must always remember that *News from the Moon* was not written to apply to the Boston situation of 1721: it was a reprint of a pamphlet intended to apply to the English situation of 1710. And it was virtually a literal reprint of that pamphlet. The detail of "114" men, for example, which in the original *Review* seems to have had a definite significance, the details of "Lord A——" and "Mr. H——d" and "a Lord Bishop" and so on, which could have had specific personal application in England, are reprinted in the Boston pamphlet, though they could have had no specific American application. If the notion of substituting local hits in place of such details as these ever crossed the mind of the Boston printer, he doubtless rejected the idea because he thought that it might prove convenient to be able to point out certain details in *News from the Moon* which, he might plausibly say, could not by any stretch of the imagination be interpreted in terms of Massachusetts dignitaries.

It will be enough, therefore, if in answer to Mr. Davis's questions we can discern some purpose that may make reasonable, in a general way, the action of the person—let us call him the printer—who, about March, 1721, introduced Defoe's pamphlet to his Boston readers.

Just what does *News from the Moon*[336] contain? It is the story of a tailor (*i.e.*, an author) who is put on trial for making a coat (*i.e.*, a piece of writing which takes the measure of a certain man or group of men) that is thought by certain persons to fit them and not to represent them correctly. This coat is called, in the language of the world in the moon, "a *Thocacterraca*, in *English*, a *Representer* or a Character Coat."

For convenience, let us in the remainder of our short summary of *News from the Moon* use the words "author" and "character" instead of "tailor" and "character coat." The author, then, is questioned by the authorities about his purpose in writing a certain "character." In his defense he alleges that a "character" made for one man may fit, or seem to fit, another, and sometimes a great many. This is partly because the kind of people who are liable to satirical representation are, at least in the country of the moon, very much alike. And it is especially true because there are some men who, when they read a "character," cannot help trying to make it fit them, whether it will or no. They even go so far as to distort the natural meaning of the "character" to see if they can make it fit them. Thus, in the case of Defoe's *Review*, when the author happened "to be Pointing out the Character of a State Mountebank, a City Hero, a Coward to his Cause, a Fool, a Knave, and a Deserter of his Friends . . . One said, . . . *that's at me*; another, *that's at me*; and the like; . . . when far was it from the Thoughts of that poor Author, to do any of these Gentlemen so much Honour."

All this, pleads Defoe, is very hard on the poor author, because a "character" is "made to represent him that it represents." The writer's design is not to fit an individual, but simply to write a "character"; if it fits many individuals, the writer cannot help that.

Having completed his bold defense, which is much more vivid and effective than can be shown by any summary, the tailor, far from showing any desire to mend his ways, "threw the Coat down in the middle of the Hall," and the pamphlet ends there.

The key-word in this account of *News from the Moon* is the word "character." But, before we attempt to define the "character" and outline its history in England up to the year 1721, it will be well to inquire into Defoe's purpose in writing for his *Review* a paper on this subject.

The paper in question (*Review*, VII, No. 14 in the Edinburgh issue) appeared late in April, 1710.[337] In the preface to his seventh volume, Defoe, who was of course an ardent supporter of a free press, writes as follows about the imminent tax upon periodicals:

If such a Design goes on, it will soon appear whether it be a Proposal to raise Money, or a Design to crush and suppress the Papers themselves; if it be the first, it may really answer the End, there being as I have Calculated it, above two Hundred Thousand single Papers publish'd every Week in this Nation, and a light Tax would raise a considerable Summ, and yet not check the Thing; but if it be a Design to suppress the Papers, it will be seen by their laying on such a Rate, as will disable the Printing them.

Defoe prophesies that if the Tories do succeed in stopping the opposition press, such an event will have a result contrary to expectation:

... the stopping the Press will be the opening the Mouth, and the Diminution of Printing will be the Encrease of Writing, in which the Liberty is tenfold, because no Authors can be found out, or Punished if they are; and this made King *Ch[arles]* II. say, and he understood those Things very well, That the Licenser of the Press did more harm than good, and that if every one was left to Print what they would, there would be less Treason spread about, and fewer Pasquinades—And I take up[on] me to say, that let them stop the Press when they will—What is wanting in Pamphlet, will be made up in Lampoon.

In the first paper of Volume VII (March 28, 1710), Defoe

writes that he is very sorry to start a new volume by opening the highly controversial subject of Dr. Sacheverell.[338] But "there is no Help for it, we must either defend our Cause, or give our Cause up." He is "satisfied, the Cause of Liberty is the Cause of Truth; and it is from this Principle only" that he opposes "the High-Church Darling Dr. Sacheverell," and does it "in the Teeth of his Mob, when his Cause would be thought Rising, and when [he sees] Men that pretend to be for Revolution-Principles, cow'd and afraid." Defoe has nothing to say to the man Sacheverell himself: "it is the Temper of insulting the Laws, and preaching up Tyranny: 'tis this I oppose, and this I will oppose, if the Tyrant were an Emperor."

Having thus thrown down the gauntlet, Defoe carried on his warfare bitterly against Sacheverell and his Tory supporters, boldly denouncing individuals and not sparing the Lord Mayor or certain aldermen. In No. 5 (April 6, 1710, in the London issue) we find him incorrigibly continuing the little joke[339] that had once sent him to the pillory: "we Tories and High-Flyers," he writes, propose certain fundamental changes in the English government, of which one project is: "We will cause the Articles of the late Union, and the unhappy Settlement of the pretended Succession, which are so contrary to the true Doctrine of Non-Resistance and Passive-Obedience, to be laid before our most free Parliament, in order to be repeal'd in a legal Way."

In a series of some half-dozen numbers[340] he attacked the extreme Tories in one of those well-sustained allegories of which he was a master, and represented their army and his own drawn up in battle.

The Enemies Army have in their first Line the *High-Church* in the Center, a Party of select *Domino-Dominoques* on their Right, and the Mob on the Left. In their second Line *Non-jurors* in the Center, *Papists* on their Right, and the *Pretender* with his Mercenaries on their Left; and two Bodies of *Tackers* and *Bigotts* make the reserves. *The Army they fight against* . . . [has the Commons of Britain in the Center] the QUEEN and the Nobility on the Right Wing . . . and all fighting under the Command of that Old General CONSTITUTION.[341]

Such boldness could hardly go unnoticed or unpunished. That it was noticed appears clearly enough from the diary kept by that outspoken Tory and Oxford antiquary, Thomas Hearne, whose entry for March 6, 1710, not only shows the violent feeling against the Whigs at the time of Sacheverell's trial, but specifically mentions the *Review* as one of the principal offenders.[342]

To what extent Defoe's bold attack was unpunished we cannot be sure. Punishment by the national government would perhaps not be expected, for the Whigs were still in power. But censorship of the press had to be reckoned with, and there were also the City authorities to consider.[343]

We have Defoe's definite statement[344] that the Tories had tried every possible method of suppressing his paper and that they had urged both the government and the grand jury to take action. "Great Endeavours have been us'd to stifle and suppress this Paper; . . . sometimes they carry it to *this* Grand-Jury to get it presented, sometimes to *that*; sometimes the Government is sollicited to discourage and silence it."[345] We have also his word[346] that his enemies had seized the issue of April 25, 1710, and had so thoroughly intimidated his printer, Matthews, that Defoe changed to John Baker, whose imprint appears beginning with No. 13. Careful students[347] of Defoe's life and of the *Review* have not been able to discover that he was actually brought to trial or even summoned to appear for examination by the Common Council. But his sweeping statement that his enemies had tried every way to silence him may well mean that he had been so summoned. Furthermore, there is a curious detail in *Review*, VII, No. 14 (London issue), which must be dwelt on for a moment.

In the course of that paper (and therefore in *News from the Moon*) we learn that the poor tailor was seized and carried "into a great Assembly of that City," which assembly "is call'd in their Language the *Momonciculoc*: I will not pretend to Knowledge enough in the Lunar Language to translate—Some think, it may resemble a *Common Council*." Then, "of a sudden," various persons began to complain that "*the Coat is made for me*," until, "to be short with my Story, no less than 114 of them challeng'd the poor Man for bringing this Coat out to expose them in particular."

Why *one hundred and fourteen?* As has already been pointed out, Defoe had less to fear from the Government than from the authorities of London. In a case of this sort the City would naturally act through the Lord Mayor, the aldermen, and the common councilmen, who together constituted the Court of Common Council. If, therefore, this body numbered one hundred and fourteen men, we have a fact of considerable interest. Consulting the standard contemporary authority, John Chamberlayne's *Magnae Britanniae Notitia: or, the Present State of Great Britain* for the year 1710 (pp. 630–632), we find that this body did in that year number exactly 114 men.[348]

Taking all the evidence together, there is therefore a distinct possibility that Defoe may have come up before the City authorities and that the dialogue between the tailor and his questioners may to some degree represent Defoe's version of an actual hearing.[349] Even if this possibility be disregarded, we may fairly enough say that anyone in Boston in 1721 who knew Defoe's *Review* would more or less fully have realized that this periodical and its author represented Nonconformity, active resentment of intolerance, freedom of the press, and advanced ideas in general, to say nothing of such vigorous, informal, and prolific journalism as could hardly be found anywhere else in the world.[350]

However significant it may have proved to examine Defoe's possible reasons for printing *News from the Moon* just when he did, it is now time to ask just what a "character" is and whether some knowledge of the ways of certain English "character"-writers before 1721 may not help us to unravel Mr. Davis's "mystery." Some years ago in examining John Dunton's use of the "character"[351] I said that the "character" was "a well-recognized, prolific, popular, and influential form in English literature of the seventeenth century." More is known about the "character" now than was the case at that time (1912); but still the form may well be defined in the words of a schoolmaster named Ralph Johnson, who in 1665 published *The Scholars Guide from the Accidence to the University*.[352] Johnson there (p. 15) defines the "character" as "a witty and facetious description of the nature and qualities of some person, or sort of people." In his rules for making of "characters"[353] Johnson emphasizes the selection, as subjects, of those sorts of men whom one would naturally treat with a considerable degree of disapproval; the delineation of their reprehensible natures by a series of "tart nipping jerks about their vices or miscarriages"; and a constant effort toward "wit and pleasantness." In the remaining pages of this article, the word "character" will, unless otherwise indicated, always be used (without quotation marks) with the meaning Johnson here gives it.

The general impression left by Johnson's definition and rules could easily be confirmed, if space permitted, by other contemporary definitions and comments, as well as by many examples. One must not, however, suppose that characters are regularly adverse or that they are necessarily of persons: they may be, and often are, favorable; and they not infrequently take for their subject such impersonal topics as a coffee-house or a prison.

Before leaving our definition of the character let us try to clarify it still further by examining the boundaries between it and the portrait, often called a character, of some individual who is named and is openly characterized. Richard Flecknoe, in the preface to his *Heroick Portraits* (1660), thinks that "the *Portrait* has this advantage of the *Character*, that it gives the Bodies resemblance together with the disposition of the Minde." And Sir Charles Firth,[354] comparing the portraits by Clarendon with those of Burnet, regards the latter as stronger in observation, though weaker in insight. "Clarendon's description of the exterior of the personages he mentions is usually vague," Firth observes, whereas Burnet, "notices a number of minor particulars of every kind which Clarendon neglects or disdains." Firth goes even further: he accounts for this difference by observing that Clarendon, "instead of individualising his personages by noting the little peculiarities which differentiated them from other men, . . . seems to endeavour to generalise, and to reduce them all to certain universal types." Thus we may say that although portraits, as Flecknoe remarked, tend to differ from characters in being more concerned with externals, we must not forget that the extent of this difference varies greatly with the individual writer and that in the case of Clarendon's portraits this variation, in the direction of the method more typical of the impersonal character as defined by Ralph Johnson, is so great that Firth well observes that "in reading the *History of the Rebellion* one is continually reminded that the description of *imaginary*[355] types of character was a popular literary exercise in Clarendon's day." Moreover, we may well remember that portraits like Burnet's, as well as those like Clarendon's, were, in spite of Flecknoe's distinction in terminology, habitually called characters throughout the seventeenth and eighteenth centuries.

Between 1608, when Bishop Joseph Hall published his *Characters of Virtues and Vices*, and 1721, when *News from the Moon* appeared in Boston, there were literally thousands of characters, singly and in collections, published in England. To a certain extent one may arrange them in periods. Let us attempt to do so, always remembering that the pattern is not quite so regular as it appears in any brief summary.

From 1608 until about 1642, the essay-character flourished, after a fashion the norm of which is pretty well indicated by Ralph Johnson's definition. This is the period of Hall (1608), the Overbury group (1614), Earle (1628), and Fuller (1642), to mention only a few great names. Even in this period the character was made use of by dramatists, sermon-writers, and others, as well as by the large number of those who may fairly be called essayists. Sometimes they published essays and characters (as did Earle and Mynshul) in the same volume. Sometimes they illustrated to excess (as did Nicholas Breton) the idea of euphuistic style that was stressed in Ralph Johnson's definition.

In the period from 1660 to 1688, the pattern becomes even less distinct. There are survivals in plenty of the essay-character; there are numerous examples of the type of character or portrait represented by Clarendon; there are frequent instances where the character is used by dramatists and writers of various sorts of prose treatises; and there are examples—Dryden is a notable one—of poets who write, usually with a satirical intent, characterizations in verse of individuals or of imaginary types. But—numerically, at least—the most important form of character in this period is what may be called the pamphlet-character, like Halifax's Character of a Trimmer, though that is longer, better written, and more fair-minded than most examples of its class. The pamphlet-character tends to be a justification of belief, or, much oftener, an attack upon the beliefs of others, which for greater effectiveness borrows the name and some of the hall-marks of the essay-character.[356]

In the period which begins, roughly, in 1688, when La Bruyère's *Caractères* first appeared, and which runs along until, in the 1740's its path can hardly be followed further because of the rise of the novel of character, we have, as before, an abundance of survivals and, out-topping them in importance, if not in numbers, a new sort of character. Of the survivals we can pause only long enough to say that they represent every variety of the character that has previously been mentioned. But with a much more entertaining kind of character that is found for the first time in this period we must deal somewhat more particularly.

Broadly speaking, the character has up to this point been a sort of composite photograph of a number of people who, though spoken of as "he" or "she," are intended to represent what is true of all Puritans, pedants, or Whigs. The subject of the character has no individual name; he rarely speaks; he is a sort of mounted specimen, who is the subject of an analysis. But in the work of such writers as La Bruyère, Ned Ward, and Addison we are now to see something quite different. The nature of this difference can best be shown by examples.

In 1628, John Earle's *Microcosmographie* appeared, a collection of fifty-four characters, one of which was "An Antiquary." One of the sentences in this character runs thus: "He would give all the books in his study (which are rarities all), for one of the old Roman binding, or six lines of Tully in his own hand." The other thirteen sentences in the character are like this one: they all refer to the antiquary; they are all in the present tense; they all help to build up a somewhat artificially consistent picture of one whose "humor" is a love of old times and ancient objects. And the whole, despite its unity and its pleasant tone, has an air of unreality: we do not quite believe that the antiquary does these things, though we grant that if he were sufficiently alive to do anything, these are the things that he might be expected to do. Furthermore, the writer is as much outside of his subject as a historian or an essayist would be. So, though to read this character gives us a certain pleasure, it is not at all the kind of pleasure that we should take in a play by Ben Jonson or a novel by George Eliot that presented us with a pedant as one of its characters. And the pedant of Earle does not greatly tempt the reader to ask which of Earle's friends sat for the portrait.

In 1710, Joseph Addison, in the *Tatler*, No. 158, represented a pedant in quite a different fashion. A part of the difference lies in the fact that the paper is supposed to consist of the observations of one Isaac Bickerstaff, who, being a fictitious character, can walk right in among Addison's other characters and carry the essay well on toward a scene from a novel, whenever it suits his purpose.[357] Again, Addison's pedant has a name, "Tom Folio," which helps to enliven him. Furthermore, no inconsiderable part of the essay consists of a little scene, with conversation, between Isaac Bickerstaff and Tom Folio. "I had yesterday morning a visit from this learned ideot," Addison makes Mr. Bickerstaff say. In the course of the visit we have this very revealing dialogue, as narrated by Addison through Isaac Bickerstaff:

Knowing that Tom had not sense enough to give up an opinion which he had once received, that I might avoid wrangling, I told him, "that Virgil possibly had his oversights as well as another author." "Ah! Mr. Bickerstaff," says he, "you would have another opinion of him, if you would read him in Daniel Heinsius's edition. I have perused him myself several times in that edition," continued he; "and after the strictest and most malicious examination, could but find two faults in him; one of them is in the Aeneids, where there are two commas instead of a parenthesis; and another in the third Georgic, where you may find a semicolon turned upside down." "Perhaps," said I, "these were not Virgil's faults, but those of the transcriber." "I do not design it," says Tom, "as a reflection on Virgil; on the contrary, I know that all the manuscripts reclaim against such a punctuation. Oh! Mr. Bickerstaff," says he, "what would a man give to see one simile of Virgil writ in his own hand?" I asked him which was the simile he meant; but was answered, any simile in Virgil. He then told me . . . of many amendments which are made, and not yet published; and a thousand other particulars, which I would not have my memory burdened with for a Vatican.

At length, being fully persuaded that I thoroughly admired him, and looked upon him as a prodigy of learning, he took his leave.

This technique speaks for itself, and we see at once that the old formal character is now well on its way toward the novel of character.[358]

Before we attempt to indicate the relation of *News from the Moon* to the situation in Massachusetts in 1721, two other questions require attention. First, to what degree was the aim of the character-writer general and to what degree was it individual? And to what degree did the reading public seek "originals" for characters, whether such originals were or were not in the mind of the writer? Second, was the character something that Massachusetts people in 1721—Cotton Mather, for example—knew nothing about?

There is more than a little evidence that the character-writer sometimes drew the picture of an individual. Ralph Johnson, it will be remembered, defined the character as "a . . . description . . . of *some person*[359] or sort of people." "L. G.," who in 1661 published a volume of Essays and Characters, assures his readers that he does not reflect "upon any particular Person, save only in the Character of a Scandalous Minister, . . . whom I had some cause to know in the Country."[360] Richard Flecknoe's titles seem occasionally to indicate a personal application, as in "Of one that shall be namelesse," "Of a certain Nobleman," and "Of an other" (*i.e.*, another nobleman).[361] And there are fairly numerous additional examples of this sort, not to speak of such characters as those "Of a Protector," "A Duke of Bucks," or "A true Character of the illustrious James Duke of York," where portraiture of an individual is more than implied.

Usually, however, the evidence makes rather in the direction of a generic aim for the character-writer, or, at any rate, expresses his wish to be understood as speaking of a class, not of an individual. Of his *Seventy-Eight Characters* (1677) Flecknoe says that "the subject of them is taken from the observations of several *Natures*, *Humors*, and *Dispositions*; and whilst I name no body, let no body name themselves, if they be wise." And Sir Roger L'Estrange[362] writes that "a *Character* . . . Shoots *Hail-Shot*, and *Strikes* a great many *more* than ever the *Marks-man*, either *Aim'd* at, or *Dreamt* of." Addison (in the *Spectator*, No. 34) begs

every particular person, who does me the honour to be a reader of this paper, never to think himself, or any of his friends or enemies, aimed at in what is said: for I promise him, never to draw a faulty character which does not fit at least a thousand people; or to publish a single paper that is not written in the spirit of benevolence, and with a love to mankind.

And to the same purpose, in No. 262, Addison writes:

I believe my Reader would still think the better of me, if he knew the Pains I am at in qualifying what I write after such a manner, that nothing may be interpreted as aimed at private Persons. For this Reason when I draw any faulty Character, I consider all those Persons to whom the Malice of the World may possibly apply it, and take care to dash it with such particular Circumstances as may prevent all such ill-natured Applications. If I write any Thing on a black Man, I run over in my Mind all the eminent Persons in the Nation who are of that Complection: When I place an imaginary Name at the Head of a Character, I examine every Syllable and Letter of it, that it may not bear any Resemblance to one that is real. I know very well the Value which every Man sets upon his Reputation, and how painful it is to be exposed to the Mirth and Derision of the Publick, and should therefore scorn to divert my Reader at the Expence of any private Man.[363]

But in spite of such protestations, a certain proportion of mankind has persisted in believing that many characters and similar portrayals were in fact aimed at, or derived from, individuals. Eustace Budgell, a cousin of Addison, prefaced his translation of the characters of Theophrastus (1714) with the observation that "Theophrastus was the *Spectator* of the age he lived in. He drew the pictures of particular men." Dr. Johnson believed that the personages introduced in the *Tatler* and the *Spectator* "were not merely ideal; they were then known, and conspicuous in various stations."[364]

In view of all this conflicting evidence, the question can never be really settled whether such a writer as those whom we have been considering copies from individuals and then corrects his results by comparison with his more or less abstract idea of the class, or whether he conceives an abstract idea and then modifies it by comparison with individuals. Often, no doubt, separate features are taken from different individuals and assembled in a portrait which cannot, without a kind of surgery to which it ought never to be subjected, be got into either of the two groups of character-portraits, which, after all, do tend to run into each other. Let us therefore take leave of this part of our subject without putting too much trust in any single witness, but with a fair degree of confidence that Sir Roger L'Estrange was not far wrong when he said:

A *Character* . . . Shoots *Hail-Shot*, and *Strikes* a great many *more* than ever the *Marks-man*, either *Aim'd* at, or *Dreamt* of. There is a great deal of *Difference*, I know, betwixt the *Whipping* of the *Vice*, and of the *Man*; and betwixt the *Whipping* of the *Vice* for the *Man's* sake, and the *Whipping* of the *Man*, for the sake of the Vice. But be it as it will; 'tis *nonsense* to *Imagine*, that a man draws a Figure in the *Air*, and Means No body; or that he had not *some One Man* more in his Thought then *Another*, toward the *Instructing*, or the *Finishing* of the *Piece*.[365]

We may, without hesitation, answer in the negative the question whether a Boston printer was giving his Massachusetts readers of 1721 too hard a task when he expected them to know enough about the character to see the more technical side of the point in *News from the Moon*. Let us merely outline the case.

In the first place, we know that by 1721 both the *Tatler* and the *Spectator* had reached New England. Steele had personally sent "all the *Tatlers* and *Spectators* being eleven volumes" to Yale in 1714.[366] The *New England Courant* began to appear in August, 1721, less than five months after *News from the Moon* was advertised. In No. 48 of the *Courant* (July 21, 1722) the "office library" is advertised, containing both the *Spectator* and the *Guardian*. It is possible that these two periodicals were not imported until after *News from the Moon* appeared. But one doubts that: the *Spectator* is from the outset so clearly a model for the *Courant* that one feels reasonably sure that the books had been in Boston for some little time.

At all events, there was one man in Boston who, by August, 1713, had not only heard of the *Spectator* and the *Guardian*, but who at that time recorded in his diary the hope that "perhaps, by sending some agreeable Things, to the Author of, *The Spectator*, and, *The Guardian*, there may be brought forward some Services to the best Interests in the Nation." The writer of this entry was, as it happens, Cotton Mather.[367] It is possible that Cotton Mather knew, or knew of, Defoe's *Review*, for it is certain that by May, 1711,[368] he had had "some epistolar Conversation with Mr. *De Foe*," and had resolved "in . . . [his] Letters unto him, [to] excite him to apply himself unto the work of collecting and publishing an History of the Persecutions which the Dissenters have undergone from the Ch[urch] of E[ngland]." Certainly the *Review*, and the very part of it where the original version of what was later called *News from the Moon* had appeared, was a work from which Mather would instantly perceive what a champion the Dissenters had in Defoe.

Putting aside conjecture, however, let us note a few solid facts. Cotton Mather had before 1721 used the word "character" frequently; had imitated an English book containing characters; and had himself written more than one work containing characters. For the sake of brevity the evidence for the first statement is given in a footnote,[369] and only a few examples are mentioned to show that Cotton Mather had found the character a fit instrument for the Lord's business, as many an English clergyman had found it before him.

Cotton Mather's *Ornaments for the Daughters of Zion, Or the Character and Happiness of a Virtuous Woman* (1691)[370] is interesting for our purpose because here and there it literally follows an English book which contains characters[371] and because it contains a character by Cotton Mather. Mather's funeral sermon on the Reverend John Baily (*A Good Man Making a Good End*, 1698) has as the running title of its last thirty pages "The Character of a Christian." His *Desiderius* (1719) may fairly be called a character also, though it is the sub-title and the framework, rather than the details, that make it one. And in Mather's *Benedictus: Good Men Described, with some Character & History of Mr. Thomas Bridge* (1715) the character certainly plays a part: the word is used on the title-page; the purpose of the work is declared (p. 4) to be "to set a lively Pourtraiture of a GOOD MAN before you"; and the general run of the part from the fourth to the top of the nineteenth page is that of the character as applied to the funeral elegy of the time in both England and America.

If Cotton Mather's works do not more frequently contain outright characters of the more satirical and "literary" kind, it would therefore seem to be merely because he did not often employ the more secular forms of writing in which such portraiture would naturally appear.

When *News from the Moon* came out in March, 1721, the condition of affairs in Massachusetts was one of intensely opposed opinions, almost one of warfare, upon a number of questions.

Religious questions, as always in the early days of Massachusetts, were burning. Those who upheld the conservative side found that their ancient authority had somehow weakened. Of one among the radicals, John Wise,[372] Williston Walker writes that

he presented a new and forceful treatment of Congregationalism, ... basing its merits ... on the broad principles of democracy which were to be the mainspring of so much of American thought and action. In so doing he emphasized the democratic element in Congregationalism as no previous writer had done.[373]

Not unnaturally, therefore, Cotton Mather thought Wise "a furious Man," and his book, though "a foolish libel," most dangerous nevertheless, because "some of our People, who are not only tenacious of their Liberties, but also more suspicious than they have cause to be of a Design in their pastors to make abridgments of them; are too much led into Temptations, by such Invectives."[374]

The small-pox was raging, and the pros and cons of inoculation were debated with great acrimony. Here, as is well known, Cotton Mather was on the liberal side. The controversy was by no means limited to those who understood the technical aspect of the matter. How it embittered the thoughts of Cotton Mather his *Diary* testifies: the opposition to his counsels in this matter has, he writes, "been carried on, with senseless Ignorance and raging Wickedness."[375]

Governor Shute and his legislature were violently at loggerheads over the choice of a Speaker, the freedom of the press, and other issues. Shute presently went back to England and "arraigned the conduct of the Massachusetts assembly in a long memorial to the King," in the course of which he expressed the general belief that the people of Boston "were too much inclined to be levellers, and to give a mutinous and disorderly support to the house in its encroachments."[376]

The year 1721 also marked one of the crises in a long series of discussions about currency and banking. The merits of various banking projects were vigorously debated, so vigorously that the question of restraining the press became one of the chief issues of the moment.

As would naturally be expected, the number and importance of these questions greatly increased the amount of publication in Massachusetts and tended somewhat to change its tone. Before the year 1721 was over, the *New England Courant* had begun and the newer journalism had really come to Massachusetts. But some little time before that the change had already become perceptible. By March, 1721, it is fair to say that such men as in a few months were to start the *New England Courant*—in certain cases the very men who did start it[377]—were doing something more than merely arguing for their own views. They were attempting a more familiar style and a less formal presentation of their authorities and arguments. They were introducing various means to enliven New England pamphleteering—the imaginary dialogue, the imaginary letter, the character, and other devices of that sort.

Certain English writers, as we have seen, had for some years before 1721 been taking that line, with the result sometimes of winning a readier acceptance for their views, and sometimes with the result, no doubt, of drawing upon their heads a sharper counter-attack from their opponents or a sterner punishment from the government than would have followed had their opinions been less facetiously expressed. Swift's tone, nearly as much as his views, in *A Tale of a Tub* had injured his chances of advancement in the church. And Defoe had stood in the pillory partly because both friends and foes resented their slowness on the uptake when they had to make up their minds about his ironical *Shortest Way with the Dissenters*. So it may well be that some Massachusetts conservatives disapproved of the manner as well as the opinions of their opponents. In the case of Cotton Mather we have an explicit defense of his own "more Massy Way of Writing" as against the style of the coffee-house wits.[378]

Whatever its grounds, we know that resentment against the utterances of the liberals took the form not only of a host of pamphlets on the conservative side and bitter forebodings in Cotton Mather's diary, but of certain actual prosecutions. John Colman's *Distressed State of the Town of Boston* (April, 1720) caused his arrest and prosecution; and Benjamin Gray, a Boston bookseller, was prosecuted in 1721 for publishing *A Letter to an Eminent Clergyman in the Massachusetts Bay* (1720). The prosecution of Colman was dropped, but he was held under bonds until July, 1720. Gray, having declared that he meant no evil and having expressed regret, was discharged in May, 1721.[379] The cases, therefore, may be said to have gone against the conservatives. The House of Representatives, though it was willing enough to declare it "an unhappy Circumstance attending a well Regulated Government, when they have Seditious and Scandalous Papers printed and publicly Sold or Dispersed,"[380] was most unwilling to grant the governor the power of the press that he claimed as the king's representative. And Duniway, reviewing these two cases and the later case of James Franklin, writes that they mark the end "of an attempt to revive and enforce censorship in Massachusetts."[381]

Since some have regarded *News from the Moon* as a burlesque of one of these trials, it will be well to examine briefly the language of the charges against Colman and Gray. The former was charged with the authorship of a pamphlet containing passages "reflecting upon the Acts & Laws of the Province, & other proceedings of the Governm^t" and having "a Tendency to Disturb the Administration of the Government, as well as the Publick Peace."[382] Gray was charged with having published the pamphlet already mentioned, and with causing a certain advertisement to appear, the language of which showed contempt of the Council, whose vote of censure (declaring that the pamphlet contained "many vile, scandalous, and abusive expressions") had been printed in the newspapers.

The advertisement in question (which appeared in the *Boston Gazette* of March 13, 1721) reads as follows:

Just Published, The Mount Hope Packet. And News from the Moon, both to be Sold by Benjamin Gray *Bookseller, at his Shop opposite to the Brick Church, where all Gentlemen, Trades-men and others may be supply'd by Wholesail or Retail at reasonable rates, with all Letters, Postscripts, News, Dialogues, and other Pamphlets, which come out from Time to Time.*[383]

Now just what relation to all this has *News from the Moon?* That it is a "burlesque" of the proceedings against either Colman or Gray seems improbable. Why not take it for what it is—a perfectly clear, though perhaps disingenuous, attempt to controvert the belief that when a character-writer portrays a certain kind of person, he primarily or merely aims at an individual? If by the publication of *News from the Moon* the person responsible for it intended thus to lessen the objections to certain parts of recent publications, he was doing something worth while for his cause. And there are several passages in the then recent publications on the liberal side that may fairly be called characters and that probably caused personal application and resentment. The passage in *Reflections upon Reflections* (1720) about "one whose *Scribendi Cacoethes* has made him famous on both sides of the Atlantick"[384] is certainly a good case: it can fairly be called a character, and

[176]

it would almost certainly be thought to point toward Cotton Mather. Another case, in *New News from Robinson Cruso's Island* (1720), is the short remark, very brief but nevertheless a character as far as it goes, about "the great DON-DAGO, the *Primate-wou'd be* of our Island," who "like the famous Dr. S——l has long ago *burst his Orb, and become Eccentrick.*" [385] And the passage in this same pamphlet about covetousness, envy, pride, and hypocrisy [386] is also pertinent: it is not, as a whole, strictly a character, but it is at times very near it indeed, for example:

. . . *Religion* is made a *Stalking-Horse*, whereby *some Men* serve the most vile and unworthy Ends; cloaking their Designs of *Covetousness, Ambition,* or *Revenge,* with pretence of *Conscience* and *Zeal*; and under the specious Umbrage hereof, the most *execrable Villanies* have been acted.

It is not unreasonable to imagine that Cotton Mather regarded that as a character aimed at him.

But there is a much more striking case than any of these. John Colman's *Distressed State of the Town of Boston* was one of the pamphlets which caused legal proceedings, as we have seen, and which most enraged the conservatives. [387] In that pamphlet he boldly expressed dissatisfaction with many members of the House of Representatives and hoped

our good Friends in the Country will consider our miserable circumstances, & send such Men to Represent them next *May* as may be Spirited for our Relief, not Sheriffs and Lawyers, who are the only Men who are benefited by the straights of their Neighbours, else I fear Ruin and Destruction will come upon us. [388]

This charge, that many in the House were not men of public spirit, was taken up and flung back and forth. On April 18, 1720, the *Boston News-Letter* printed "The Country-Man's Answer, to a Letter Intitutled, *The Distressed State of the Town of Boston Considered.*" The writer, who is thought to have been the Reverend Edward Wigglesworth, took up Colman's challenge about the members of the House:

As to your Advice about the choice of our Representatives, which seems the main Spring and design of your Letter, we shall endeavour to choose Men of a Publick Spirit that understand and design the good of the Country in General, Men of good Substance and Interest in the Country.[389]

On the same conservative note, the writer of *A Letter from One in the Country to his Friend in Boston* (1720) has his fling at Colman's stinging words. He quotes Colman's sentence about "men Spirited for our Relief," and replies: "I hope also Men of a Publick Spirit, and heartily concerned for the Welfare of their Country will be sent." *The Letter from a Gentleman,* "Containing some Remarks upon the Several Answers" to Colman, bears the date 1720 on its title-page and the more specific date May 16, 1720, at the end of its text. It is supposed to have been written by Dr. Oliver Noyes.[390] He likewise joins in the hope "that the several Towns will chuse to Represent 'em in the General Court, Men of a Publick Spirit," and prays God "to direct the Governour and General Court in some proper Measures for our Relief."[391] Thus the phrase "Men of a Public Spirit" was made so familiar that each successive use of it in the controversy called up the preceding arguments, in which both sides had claimed the term for themselves and denied it to their opponents.

Then came *Some Proposals to Benefit the Province* (1720).[392] The copy at the American Antiquarian Society bears the initials "S. S." (Samuel Sewall) and, in Sewall's handwriting, a date which is, apparently, November 9, 1720. The pamphlet is signed "F. M." Its great importance for us consists in the fact that it has a "Postscript" consisting of a pair of contrasted characters. Here we are not required to guess whether the author is consciously using the character form: he actually

[178]

entitles one of them "A Character of a Publick Spirit," and the other, "A Character of a Private Spirit." The relation of those characters to the preceding controversy must have been perfectly clear. The character of a "Public Spirit" is the portrait of an ideal. The one of a "Private Spirit" is reprinted here:

A CHARACTER OF A PRIVATE SPIRIT

A Private Spirit is a selfish, narrow, contracted, little Spirit; it's the Devil form'd in us: *ye are of your father the Devil*; taking advantage from the Execution of the Divine Sanction, *viz.* (the loss of the Image of GOD) which Satan was the author of, and is; our setting up self to be equal with or above GOD, which is Idolatry; and self, both the Idol & Medium, by which we serve the Devil: we are by him hurried with all our powers to possess Idol-self, with the profits, pleasures, and honours of this Life, and therefore substitute Religion, Reason and Nature to effect it; for while we remain in our Apostacy, we can act from no other being, nor to any higher end than self, that is the spring, and all our actions center therein, how Religious soever we be: This Self Idolatry is the Ruining of all Societies, and all Men of what Rank or Degree soever, Sacred or Civil, either Wholly or in Part are the Subjects thereof; the effects, fruits and evidences of Self, are Tyranny, Oppression, Wrath, *&c.* with all Moral and Penal evils. And frequently Hypocritical Covetous Men, makes [*sic*] the greatest show of Religion. Our All-glorious Saviour was not Wise and Holy enough for such Men, but by them most vilely and falsely contradicted, accused, persecuted and executed for one of the greatest Sinners, even when the Gentile Judge Justified Him, and wrought by all Means (save force) for His deliverance.

In view of all that had gone before, this character could easily have been so received by members of the House of Representatives and their friends as to create exactly the kind of situation that would be most effectively met by reprinting the paper from Defoe's *Review*. That, I believe, or something very like it, is the genesis of *News from the Moon*. If so, the reprinting of Defoe's clever defense is certainly no "mystery," but a notably shrewd move—pertinent,[393] entertaining, and less easily punishable than almost any other kind of counter-stroke that one can imagine.

Did Joseph Addison Write
"The Play-House"?

ALTHOUGH more than two hundred years have passep
since Addison's death, the editing of his complete works
has progressed but little beyond the point where Tickell left
it when in 1721 he issued the four well-known quarto volumes which constitute the first collected edition. The latest
and on the whole the best of Addison's editors is Henry G.
Bohn, who in 1856 reprinted the material included in the
handsome edition of Bishop Hurd (1811) "with large additions, chiefly unpublished." Among these additions,[394] as
well as elsewhere,[395] there appears as probably written by
Addison a poem called "The Play-House." The reasons for
questioning Addison's authorship of this poem seem not to
have been carefully examined.

"The Play-House," written in one hundred and ten lines
of heroic couplets, is a fairly amusing and effective satire upon
the Covent-Garden Theatre, the stinginess of Christopher
Rich, its unpopular owner, the shabbiness of its stage setting
when seen at close quarters, the greasy realities of make-up
and costume, and the quite unroyal nature of those who play
the part of kings and queens. The prince is thus portrayed:

> The prince then enters on the stage in state;
> Behind, a guard of candle-snuffers wait;
> There, swoln with empire, terrible and fierce,
> He shakes the dome, and tears his lungs with verse;
> His subjects tremble; the submissive pit,
> Wrapt up in silence and attention sit;
> Till, freed at length, he lays aside the weight
> Of public business and affairs of state;

Forgets his pomp, dead to ambition's fires,
And to some peaceful brandy-shop retires;
Where, in full gills, his anctious thoughts he drowns,
And quaffs away the care that waits on crowns.

In like manner the stage soldiers, who

More than a thousand times have changed their side
And in a thousand fatal battles died,

are, along with the poor stage ghost and all the rest, allowed
their moment of glory

Till the kind bowl of poyson clears the stage,

and then the play is over, and "The Play-House" closed.

The tradition that this poem was written by Addison apparently goes back to the year 1707. The death of Sir Charles Sedley in 1701 had the usual effect of causing the publication of verses purporting to be by Sedley and his friends. Reckless as certain publishers then were in taking liberties with a man's verses while he was still alive, they felt even freer to do so after his death, and immediately thereafter was a favorite moment for unscrupulous publication. Among these "Sedley" collections there appeared in 1707 a volume entitled:

The | Poetical Works | Of the Honourable | Sir Charles Sedley Baronet, | And His | Speeches in Parliament, | With | Large Additions never before made Publick, | Published from the Original MS by Capt. Ayloffe, | a near Relation of the Authors. | With a New Miscellany of Poems by several of the most Eminent Hands. | And a Compleat Collection of all the Remarkable Speeches | in both Houses of Parliament: Discovering the Principles | of all Parties and Factions; the Conduct of our Chief Mi-| nisters, the Management of Publick Affairs, and the Maxims of the Government, from the year 1641, to the | Happy Union of Great Britain: By several Lords and | Commoners. | Viz.[396] | The Duke of Albemarle, Earl of Clarendon, Earl of Bristol, Lord Wharton, Earl of Pembrook, Lord Hollis, Lord Brook, Earl of Essex, Earl of Argile, Lord Melvil, Lord Haversham, Lord Belhaven, &c, Algernon Sidney Esq; Mr. Waller, Sir Francis Seymor, Mr. Pym, Richard Cromwell, Mr. Strode, Sir

William Perkins, Sir William Scroggs, Sir J— P—, And several other Lords and Commoners. | London, Printed for Sam. Briscoe, and Sold by B. Bragg, | at the Raven in Pater-noster-Row, 1707.

This volume contains (p. 202) our poem, headed "The Play-House. By J. Addison, Esq."[397] It is from this version that Park, Anderson, and Chalmers apparently derive: at least, their text approximates this "Sedley" volume and in each case they refer to it as their source.

But—although the fact has apparently escaped attention— "The Play-House" had thrice appeared before 1707, and in forms which make Addison's authorship of it difficult to accept.

In 1706 ("Sold by *B. Bragg*, at the *Raven* in *Pater-Noster-Row*") there had appeared our poem, the text printed in two columns on a single foolscap folio sheet, with the title *A Description of the Play-House in Dorset-Garden*, and with no indication whatever of authorship. This version, of which there is a copy in the Harvard College Library, will hereinafter be referred to as the broadside of 1706.

In 1705 there was published:

A New | Collection | Of | Poems | Relating to | State Affairs, | From | Oliver Cromwell | To this present Time: | By the Greatest | Wits of the Age: | Wherein, not only those that are Contain'd in | the Three Volumes already Published are | incerted, but also large Additions of Chiefest | Note, never before Published. | The whole from their respective Originals, | without Castration. | London, | Printed in the Year, MDCCV.

This volume contains (p. 486) "The Play-House: A Satyr. By Mr. A. D---n." Who Mr. A. D---n may be is a difficult question to answer; but the name[398] can hardly be meant for Addison: even in an ill-printed volume that would be an almost incredible typographical blunder if Addison were intending to appear as himself, and it would be an insufficient disguise if he were trying to conceal his authorship.

Still earlier, in 1702, the poem had appeared in a rare volume of miscellaneous pieces called:

A | Pacquet | From | Parnassus: | Or, A | Collection of Papers, | Viz. | ... | Vol. I, Numb. II. | London Printed by J. How, in the Ram-Head-Inn-Yard in Fanchurch-|Street; and Sold by most Booksellers, 1702.[399]

Here we find our poem as "The Play-House: A Satyr. By T. G. Gent."[400] Who was T. G. Gent?

In 1689 a poem called "The Play-House: A Satyr" had been published by Robert Gould.[401] Whether this earlier piece has any connection with our "Play-House" is doubtful. Gould's poem—as a whole an anti-vice tirade of a most ferocious and unpoetical sort, much longer than our poem, and closely corresponding to it at no particular point—does, however, go behind the scenes toward the end and does deal severely first with the actors and then with the actresses. In one or two details, even, the two poems are perhaps not too far apart to be looked at in connection with each other. Gould's reader is invited

> to go behind the Scenes,
> And take a turn among the *copper Kings and Queens.*
> Here 'tis our *Callow Lords* are fond of such,
> Which their own *Footmen* often scorn to touch,

all of which faintly resembles verses 28, 45, and 79 of the later poem. And it is a curious fact that our "Play-House," as reprinted in *Poems on Affairs of State* (ii. 374) in 1703, is immediately followed (p. 378) by "The Dream, to Sir Charles Duncomb, written by Mr. Gold." And "Mr. Gold" is no other than Robert Gould, author of the earlier "Play-House." In spite, however, of this evidence, it may well be doubted if the earlier poem served as more than a starting point for the later, if indeed it can be brought into the case at all.

Then there is a "T. G., Gent" who was author of a textbook entitled *Clavis Terentiana* and advertised in 1697.[402] But I can find no trace of this book in any English or American library, or any T. G. who seems a possible candidate for its authorship.

Still another T. G. Gent, who seems to be a ghost, brings into our story no less a person than Daniel Defoe. In 1702 there appeared a quarto entitled *Legion's New Paper: Being A Second Memorial To the Gentlemen of a Late House of Commons. &c. London, Printed; and Sold by the Booksellers of London and Westminster*. 1702. This is ascribed upon the highest authority to Defoe,[403] and as reprinted in the *Somers Tracts* of 1748 [404] it was furnished with a title-page on which are the words "by T. G. Gent." Was this pamphlet originally issued as "by T. G. Gent," and can the "T. G." of our "Play-House" possibly be Daniel Defoe?

Ten years ago, when I reported to Professor W. P. Trent that the Harvard copy of *Legion's New Paper*[405] did not have the T. G. legend anywhere about it, he replied: "I have the Huth and the Labouchère copies of the 20 pp. issue and one picked up by myself of the 18 pp. issue. 'T. G. Gent' figures in none of them, and I never saw a copy in which he did make his presence known." In view of this, one would greatly like to know if M. Paul Dottin has any better authority than the "Somers Tracts" of 1748 for his assertion (*Daniel Defoe et ses Romans* [Paris, 1924], p. 805) that *Legion's New Paper* is "signé T. G. Gent."

It is true, however, that in his *Review*, II, No. 26 (Thursday, May 3, 1705) Defoe discusses the significance of the fact that

We have lately Erected at the Cost and Charges of several Pious Charitably Disposed Christians, a Noble and Magnificent Fabrick, near the *Hay Market*, in the Liberties of *Westminster*.

The Name of this Thing (for by its Outside, it is not to be Distinguish'd from a *French* Church or a Hall, or a Meeting-House, or any such usual Publick Building) is a Theater, or in *English*, a Play-House.

From this beginning Defoe goes on to point out the contrast between the exterior of the theatre and the high purpose of its sponsors, on the one hand, and the vileness within the theatre, upon the other hand. "The Dimensions of this Noble Pile, its Beauty, its Stupendious Height, the Ornament and Magnificence of its Building, are Demonstrations of the Great Zeal of our Nobility and Gentry, to the Encouragement of Learning, and the Suppressing Vice and Immorality." But, thinks Defoe (who next drops into verse),

> Bless'd with Success, thus have their first Essays
> Reform'd their Buildings, not Reform'd their Plays.

The unreformed condition of the stage Defoe attributes to "the Taste of the Town": "But, Gentlemen and Ladies, if you would have a Reformation in the Play-house, you must Reform your Taste of Wit, and let the Poet see, you can Relish a Play, tho' there be neither Bawdy, nor Blasphemy in it."

And having expressed these and other excellently moral sentiments upon the question, Defoe reprints the "Prologue Spoken at the First Opening of the Queen's New Theatre in the Hay-Market,"[406] and following this prologue "a few hasty[407] Lines upon the same Subject, which are left to the Censure of the Readers."

Defoe thus appears as one who might have written satirically about "The Play-House" and as a writer to whom the pseudonym "T. G. Gent" has been attached. But so far as the present evidence is conclusive, it would seem to require agreement with the opinion expressed by Professor Trent, who in 1913 wrote:[408] "I see no reason to connect him [Defoe] with the publication [of "The Play-House"].

That the word "Gent" indicates the surname of the writer, and that G. is his middle initial seems to me extremely unlikely: middle names were very unusual in England in 1702, and I have found no trace of anyone named Gent who bore the initials T. G. and who was alive in or near that year.

At this point it is desirable to place the poem itself before the reader and to indicate all significant variants. The version of 1702, therefore, as the earliest and perhaps the rarest, is chosen for the text, and the readings of 1703, 1705, 1707, 1710, and 1716 are indicated in footnotes.[409]

(18)

The Play-House: A Satyr. By T. G. *Gent.*

Near to the *Rose* where Punks in numbers flock,
To pick up Cullies, to increase their Stock;
A Lofty Fabrick does the Sight Invade,
And stretches round the Place a pompous Shade;
Where sudden Shouts the Neighborhood surprise,   5
And Thund'ring Claps, and dreadful Hissings rise.

(19)

Here Thrifty *R*—— hires Monarchs by the Day,
And keeps his Mercenary Kings in Pay;
With deep-Mouth'd Actors fills the Vacant Scenes,
And draines the Town for Goddesses and Queens: 10
Here the Lewd Punk, with Crowns and Sceptres Grac'd,
Teaches her Eyes a more Majestick Cast;
And Hungry Monarchs with a numerous Train,
Of Suppliant Slaves, like *Sancho*, Starve and Reign.
But enter in, my Muse, the Stage survey,   15
And all its Pomp and Pageantry display;
Trap-Doors and Pit-falls, from th' unfaithful Ground,
And Magic Walls, encompass it around:

1-2 Near . . . the Stock: so (except as below) 1703, 1705, 1716; 1707, 1710 have Where gentle Thames through stately Channels Glides, / And Englands proud Metropolis divides.
2   their Stock: so 1702; the Stock, 1703, 1705, 1716.
4   round the Place: so 1703, 1705, 1716; o'er the waves, 1707, 1710.
5   Where: so 1703, 1705, 1716; Whence, 1707, 1710.
7   *R*——: so 1703, 1705, 1716; Rich, 1707, 1710.
7   Monarchs: so 1703, 1705, 1716; Heroes, 1707, 1710.
10 draines the Town: so 1703, 1705, 1716; rakes the Stews, 1707, 1710.
11 Punk: so 1703, 1707, 1710; Punks, 1705, 1716.

On either side maim'd Temples fill our Eyes,
And Intermixt with Brothell-Houses rise;   20
Disjointed Palaces in order stand,
And Groves Obedient to the movers Hand,
O'er shade the Stage, and flourish at Command.
A Stamp makes broken Towns and Trees entire:
So when *Amphion* struck the Vocal Lyre,   25
He saw the Spacious Circuit all around,
With crowding Woods, and Neigb'ring Cities Crown'd.

   But next the Tyring-Room survey and see,
False Titles, and promiscuous Quality,
Confusd'ly swarm from Heroes, and from Queens   30
To those that Swing in Clouds and fill Machines,
Their various Characters, they chose with Art,
The Frowning Bully fits the Tyrants part:
Swoln Cheeks, and Swaggering Belly makes a Host,
Pale meager Looks, and hollow Voice, a Ghost;   35
From careful Brows, and heavey down-cast Eyes,
Dull Cits, and thick-scull'd Aldermen arise:
The comick Tone, inspir'd by *F——r* draws
At every Word, loud Laugher and Applause:
The Mincing Dame continues as before,   40
Her Character's unchang'd, and Acts a Whore.

   Above the rest, the Prince with mighty stalks
Magnificent in Purple Buskins walks:
The Royal Robe his Haughty Shoulders grace,
Profuse of Spangles and of Copper-Lace: 45

27 So 1702; Neighb'ring, 1703, 1705, 1716; rising, 1707, 1710.
32 chose: so 1703, 1705, 1716; chuse, 1707, 1710.
34 Swaggering: so 1703, 1705, 1716; Swagging, 1707, 1710.
34 makes: so 1703, 1705, 1716; make, 1707, 1710.
35 Pale: so 1703, 1705, 1716; But, 1707, 1710.
38 *F——r*: so 1703, 1705, 1716; *Congreve*, 1707, 1710.
39 Laugher: *sic*; Laughter, in all other eds.
40 Mincing: so 1703, 1705, 1716; Whineing, 1707, 1710.
41 Character's: so 1703, 1705, 1716; Character, 1707, 1710.
44 Robe: so 1703, 1705, 1716; Robes, 1707, 1710.
44 Haughty: so 1703, 1705, 1716; Auful, 1707, 1710.

Officious Rascalls to his mighty Thigh,
Guiltless of Blood th' unpointed Weapon tye:
Then the Gay Glittering Diadem put on,
Pondrous with Brass, and Starr'd with Bristoll stone.
His Royal Consort next consults her Glass,   50
And out of twenty Boxes culls a Face;
The Whit'ning first her Ghastly Looks besmears,
All Pale and Wan th' unfinish'd Form appears;
'Till on her Cheeks the Blushing Purple Glows,
And a false Virgin Modesty bestows.   55
Her ruddy Lips the Deep Vermillion dyes;   ⎫
Length to her Brows the Pencils touch supplies,   ⎬
And with black bending Arches Shades our Eyes.   ⎭
Well pleas'd at length the Picture she beholds,
And Spots it o'er with Artificial Molds;   60
Her Countenance compleat, the Beaux she warms
With looks, not hers; and spight of Nature, Charms.
      Thus Artfully their Persons they disguise,
'Till the last flourish bids the Curtain rise.
The Prince then enters on the Stage in State;   65
Behind, a Guard of Candle-Snuffers wait:
There swoln with Empire Terrible and fierce,
He shakes the Dome, and tears his Lungs with Verse:
His Subjects Tremble, the Submissive Pit,
Wrapt up in Silence and Attention sit;   70
Till freed at length, he lays aside the weight,
of Publick Business, and Affairs of State:
Forgets his Pomp, Dead to Ambitious Fires,
And to some peaceful Brandy-Shop retires;

---

46   Rascal[l]s: so 1703, 1705, 1716; Vassals, 1707, 1710.
57   touch: so 1703, 1705, 1716; Art, 1707, 1710.
58   our: *sic*; her, in all other eds.
59   length: so 1703, 1705, 1716; last, 1707, 1710.
68   Dome: so 1703, 1707, 1710, 1716; Doom, 1705.

Where in full Gills his Anctious thoughts he drowns,   75
And quaffs away the care that waits on Crowns.
  The Princess next her pointed Charms displays,
Where every look the Pencils Art betrays
The Callow 'Squire at distance Feeds his Eyes,
And silently for Paint and Patches Dies: 80
But if the Youth behind the Scenes Retreat,⎫
He sees the blended Colours melt with heat,⎬
And all the trickling Beauty run in Sweat.⎭
The borrow'd Visage he admires no more,
And Nauseates every Charm he lov'd before: 85

(21)

So the same Spear, for double force Renown'd
Apply'd the Remedy that gave the Wound.
  In tedious Lists 'twere endless to Engage,
And draw at length the Rabble of the Stage,
Where one for twenty Years, has giv'n Allarms,   90
And call'd Contending Monarchs to their Arms;
Another fills a more Important Post,
And rises every other night a Ghost.
Thro the cleft Stage, his meager Face he rears
Then Stalks along, Groans thrice, and Disappears;   95
Others with Swords, and Shields, the Soldiers Pride,⎫
More than a thousand times have chang'd their Side,⎬
And in a thousand fatal Battles Dy'd.⎭
  Thus several Persons, several Parts perform;
Pale Lovers whine, and Blustring Heroes Storm.   100
The Stern exasperated Tyrants, rage,
Till the kind Bowl of Poyson clears the Stage.

75 Where: so 1703, 1705, 1716; There, 1707, 1710.
76 care that waits: so 1703, 1705, 1716; cares that wait, 1707, 1710.
77 pointed: so 1703, 1705, 1716; painted, 1707, 1710.
80 Paint and Patches: so 1703, 1705, 1716; Paints and Washes, 1707, 1710.
86 same: so 1703, 1705, 1716; fam'd, 1707, 1710.
94 meager: so 1703, 1705, 1716; Mealy, 1707, 1710.
96 Swords and Shields: so 1703, 1705, 1716; Shields and Swords, 1707, 1710.

Then Honours vanish, and Distinctions cease;
Then with Reluctance, haughty Queens undress.
Heroes no more their fading Lawrells boast,   105
And mighty Kings, in private Men are lost.
He, whom such Titles Swell'd, such Power made proud,
To whom whole Realms, and Vanquish'd Nations bow'd,
Throws off the Gaudy Plume, the purple Train,
And is in *Statu quo*, himself again.   110

110 And is in *Statu quo*, himself again: so 1703, 1705, 1716; And in his own Vile
   Tatters stinks again, 1707, 1710.

Let us now attempt a few generalizations upon the history
of the poem. The versions after 1702 fall, broadly speaking,
into two groups: first, those in the "State Poems" of 1703,
1705, and 1716; second, those in the broadside of 1706 and
the two "Sedley" collections of 1707 and 1710.

In the first group, very curiously, we have two appearances
of the poem (1703 and 1716) as by "T. G. Gent" and one
(1705) as by "Mr. A. D---n." Yet, excepting obvious misprints, all three are essentially the same. They retain the
coarse opening lines; they keep "*F—r*" and "*R—*" right
through, though Farquhar died in 1707 and Rich in 1714;
they keep the bad grammar in verses 34 and 44; and in some
twenty-four other little points they are identical, but different
from 1707 and 1710.

In the second group the opening lines are refined; "*R—*"
(v. 7) becomes "Rich"; Congreve (v. 38) takes Farquhar's
place; the bad grammar in verses 34 and 44 is corrected. But
in verses 10 and 110 the poem is made somewhat coarser
than it was in 1702.

The groups break up in v. 11, where all are coarse, but only
1705 and 1716 ungrammatical.

There are eight rhymes in "The Play-House" which seem
odd, not to say bad,[410] to a modern ear. But Addison's
rhymes are often such as can be explained only by some pro-

nunciation or poetic license quite different from our own.[411] On the whole, one feels that the rhymes in "The Play-House" are probably not incompatible with Addison's practice.

Thus we have to do with a poem for the authorship of which "T. G. Gent" and "Mr. A. D---n" seem just as eligible as "J. Addison." Furthermore, we have to do with a poem which certainly appeared as early as 1702. Therefore, if we accept Addison's authorship, we must be prepared to believe either (1) that he wrote the version of 1702, or (2) that someone else wrote the version of 1702 and that Addison very slightly altered the poem in 1705, or (3) that in 1707 he took a poem that had twice appeared as by others and put his name to a version of it that was in no important respect different from the earlier forms.

The first possibility is exceedingly difficult to accept. Addison's writings up to the year 1702 are, so far as we know, always acknowledged under his own name, carefully composed and printed, wholly free from indecency, academic in tone, and mainly concerned with classical subjects. Again, in 1702 Addison, so far as one can tell from his life and his acknowledged writings, knew nothing of London, the squabbles between the theatres, or the details of the Covent-Garden tiring-room:[412] he had been spending his time at Oxford and on the Continent.

That in 1705 he should have soiled his hands with such a poem as this one seems equally incredible: by 1705 Addison had made a secure place for himself by *The Campaign*; he was comfortably installed as Commissioner of Appeals and as Under-Secretary; and the last thing to be expected of a man so prudent and so auspiciously placed would be that he should imperil his reputation by taking a poem that was unworthy of him, making a few slight changes[413] but leaving nine-tenths of it exactly as it stood, and then publishing it as his own.

And at this point it should be noted that if those who

printed "The Play-House" in 1706, in 1705—and, to a somewhat less extent, those who printed it in 1702—had had the slightest reason to suppose that they could safely attribute the poem to Joseph Addison, they would in all probability have used his name instead of no name, "T. G. Gent," or "Mr. A. D---n."

The third possibility, that Addison in 1707 was willing to become the acknowledged father of the disreputable offspring of "T. G. Gent" and of "Mr. A. D---n," seems, if possible, even more difficult to accept, and for much the same reasons.

The validity of the foregoing argument seems hardly to be impaired at all by one concession that may fairly be made: some of the ideas in "The Play-House" are by no means unlike Addison's in *The Tatler* and *The Spectator*. We recall the amusing inventory of the stage properties at Covent Garden ("being the movables of Christopher Rich, Esquire") in *The Tatler*, No. 42 (July 16, 1709); the raillery on opera in *The Spectator*, No. 5 (March 6, 1711); and especially a passage in *The Spectator*, No. 42 (April 18, 1711):

Another Mechanical Method of making great Men, and adding Dignity to Kings and Queens, is to accompany them with Halberts and Battel-axes. Two or three Shifters of Scenes, with the two Candle-Snuffers, make up a compleat Body of Guards upon the English Stage; and by the Addition of a few Porters dressed in Red Coats, can represent above a dozen Legions.

But this is a later Addison, whose manner is wholly different from that of Robert Gould, Defoe, and T. G. Gent on the same subject.[414]

Finally, we know that the compilers and publishers of such miscellanies as those in which these three versions of "The Play-House" appeared were notoriously conscienceless.[415] We can readily believe that to charge the prudent and successful Mr. Joseph Addison[416] with the authorship of a poem like "The Play-House" would seem to them ethically permissible, commercially advantageous, and perhaps rather funny as well.

It therefore appears that in the absence of anything resembling proof of his authorship, "The Play-House" should be regarded as probably neither written nor revised by Joseph Addison.

New England Almanacs, 1766-1775, and the American Revolution[417]

FEW topics in modern history are more interesting than the American Revolution, especially if that revolution be defined in the words of John Adams as meaning not primarily the war, but that radical change, nearly complete before the war began, "in the principles, opinions, sentiments and affections of the people."[418] An unknown writer in the "Postscript" to the *Massachusetts Gazette and Boston Weekly News-Letter* for March 8, 1770, finds the beginning of this new attitude toward England almost immediately after the close of the Seven Years' War:

> In the year 1763, and before that unhappy period, so great was the veneration the Colonists had for the old countries, that it was by much, more easy to incense a Marylander against a Virginian, or any one Colonist against another, to such a degree, that they would decide their difference by fighting, than to stimulate any of them to fight with an Englishman; but the stamp-act, and subsequent revenue laws, have already raised a flame in the colonies, which will not now be speedily allayed.

To follow that change of feeling in the case of the leading men in the American colonies is sufficiently difficult, even though for most of them we have at least biographical outlines and a few letters, while in certain instances we are fortunately able to consult avowals of political theory, perhaps to know something about their reading at college, or possibly to have a partial catalogue of the books in their personal libraries.

But how shall we explain the well-drilled rank and file? We cannot assume a college education or much reading in books. Yet apparently they had pretty well formed their opinions and had somehow kept along not far behind their leaders through the period from 1766 to 1775. That they learned much from newspapers no one doubts. And that they learned much from the pulpit besides theology has been made clear.[419] But another possible source, the humble almanac, has hardly received sufficient consideration, though the extent and character of its circulation unquestionably lend great weight to whatever revolutionary propaganda it may contain. One cannot too strongly emphasize the point that throughout this paper material in almanacs is presented as important, even though it—or its equivalent—may have appeared elsewhere in more costly form, on account of the wide circulation of the almanac in homes where there was little or no other reading matter.

Daniel George, addressing the "Kind Reader" in his almanac for 1776, concludes thus:

I do not pretend to direct the Learned;—the rich and voluptuous may, perhaps, scorn my direction: But should this sheet enter the solitary dwellings of the poor and illiterate, where the studied ingenuity of the Learned Writer never comes, it will rejoice the heart of their most humble Servant, Daniel George.

And Joseph T. Buckingham (1779–1861), whose testimony is especially important on account of the meagreness of his facilities for reading, tells us what almanacs meant to him as a book-loving child.

But I had access, for amusement, (not on Sunday or Saturday night,) to another set of works, such as I have never seen since, and to which I was indebted for much useful instruction. We had on our book-shelf a regular file of *Almanacks*, for near or quite fifty years. Some of them were dated as far back as 1720, and some were made by "Nathaniel Ames, *Philomath*." These periodicals I read often, and with never-relaxing interest. They contained many fragments of history, scraps of poetry, anecdotes, epigrams, &c. One of them had a long poetical account of Braddock's Defeat. Others contained accounts of events which led to the Revolutionary War. One in particular made a deep impression on my mind. The title page had on it a large picture of a female, representing America, in a recumbent position, held down by men representing members of the British ministry, while Lord North was pouring Tea down her throat from an immense teapot. From his pocket was represented as falling out a roll of parchment, labeled "Boston Port Bill." The articles of Confederation between the colonies, Petitions to the King, the Declaration of Independence, and many other papers connected with the history and politics of the country, were preserved in these useful annuals, and afforded me ample food for study. But what excited my especial wonder was the calculations of the eclipses, and prognostications concerning the weather. To me these old periodicals were sources of delight and instruction.[420]

In the seventeenth century the almanac-maker seems to have been regarded—by the wits, at any rate—as a pretender to knowledge which he did not possess.

In 1614 one of the Overbury group of "character"-writers —possibly Sir Thomas Overbury himself—portrayed "An Almanac-Maker" as "the worst part of an astronomer," whose verses "have a worse face than ever had Rochester hackney" and whose prose is "dappled with ink-horn terms." As "for his judging at the uncertainty of weather, any old shepherd shall make a dunce of him." "To be brief, he falls three degrees short of his promises, yet is he the key to unlock terms and law days, a dumb mercury to point out highways, and a bailiff of all marts and fairs in England."[421]

From much the same point of view Richard Brathwait, in his *Whimzies* of 1631, creates "An Almanack-maker"[422] whose "usual dialect" includes "Horizons, Hemisphaeres, Horoscopes, . . . Astrolabes, Cycles, Epicycles, . . . ; yet I am perswaded they may bee something to eate, for ought he know . . . Hee would make you beleeve hee had a smacke of poetry, by the verses which hee fixeth above every moneth: but doe not credit him, hee is guiltlesse of that art: onely some stolen shreads he hath raked out from the kennell of other authors." Perhaps more can hardly be expected, for Brathwait is writing of one whose "yeerely pension upon every impression" is only forty shillings.

Readers of Swift will recall his devastating skit upon John Partridge, the almanac-maker, in "Predictions for the Year 1708," an attack no doubt made with added zest on account of Partridge's political leanings, which were the opposite of Swift's own. And there were many similar attacks, on the whole, no doubt deserved.

But by the middle of the eighteenth century, at least in New England, almanacs seem to have become much more respectable. The Ameses, father and son, were Harvard graduates; and in general the almanac of their day seems to represent honest calculation and writing of average journalistic quality, with perhaps some allowance here and there for bits of doggerel and humorous precepts about thrift that long remained traditional among almanac-makers.

The New England almanac of the 1760's and 1770's invariably had for each month a page of information about sunrise and sunset, tides, sessions of courts, weather predictions, and the like. At the top of the page there would be a few lines of verse, and sprinkled in the empty spaces short bits of verse or prose. Such was the body of the almanac.

More than equalling these twelve pages in bulk would usually be the varying contents of the front matter and end matter, which almost always included an address to the reader from the publisher, relating to the general state of public affairs; special articles; lists of important events, with dates; recipes; lists of public officials; tables of distances; and not infrequently poems and stories running to a considerable length. "Continued next year" occurs more than once, and seems to indicate that almanacs were usually not thrown away, but preserved as in the home of the youthful Buckingham, whose recollections have already been cited.

Thus the almanac fulfilled some of the purposes now served by the calendar, register or gazetteer, and magazine. That it was often used as a diary is clear from the annotations in many surviving copies. We shall probably not misconceive the past if we regard the almanac as read from cover to cover by many thousands of people whose other reading was very slight indeed.[423]

Just before our period the Seven Years' War had found New England rejoicing in the successes of British arms:

> AMHERST *with Glory triumphs o'er his Foes,*
> *And rests for want of Countries to oppose.*
> CANADA *conquer'd! Can the News be true!*
> *Inspir'd by Heav'n what cannot* Britons *do.*
> *The News with Haste to listning Nations tell,*
> *How* Canada, *like ancient* Carthage, *fell.*[424]

And in his issue for 1762, Ames addresses the ladies with a light article in praise of tea-drinking. "There may," he admits, "be some considerable political Objections against the Utility of so great a Consumption of a foreign Commodity; *but as I meddle not with Politicks, so I shall not pretend to answer this Objection."*[425] The whole passage—unfortunately too long to quote—is extraordinarily at variance with the attitude so soon to be taken on the subject of politics in general and tea in particular.

Let us now run through typical New England almanacs from 1766 to 1775 to see what they say about public affairs.

1766

With the Stamp Act, the protests against it made at the New York meeting of delegates from nine colonies, and the Virginia Resolves freshly in mind, and with the writings of

Otis and Patrick Henry only a little less so, an almanac-maker preparing his copy for the year 1766 could hardly keep silent on public affairs.

Nathaniel Ames's address to the "Generous Reader" for this year is highly interesting:

... Here I should conclude, did I not share in the general distress of my countrymen, and think it out of character, not to condole with them in their present distressed circumstances, who not only groan, but almost sink beneath a load of debt; our merchants continually breaking; no money to be had, even for the most valuable articles; and all threatened with ruin, without the lenity and assistance of our superiors; yet so far from this, that we are shocked with a new demand, which, it is thought by many, all the current specie among us is not able to satisfy; and after that is gone, then go houses and lands, then liberties! and all the land that we can then get will be only in vassalage to some hungry Lord, which Heaven avert! But this is only a conjecture of what might be, should we prove very tame and easy at putting on the yoke ... But, above all things, let us rely on the goodness of that Power ... who ... , as long as we do our duty, will continue to defend us from foreign and domestic enemies, and *stamp* with eternal infamy and disgrace, those who would oppress or tyrannize over us.

For January, 1766, Ames has these verses:

Columbian Genius hear our pray'r:
O! let us all with lustre rise
Beneath thy tutelary care;
Retain our dear bought liberties;
Let not the voice of native freedom sound
Alone in realms which Albion's shores surround.

For April, 1766, he gives us the familiar political maxim: "The sole end of government is the happiness of the people." And for November, 1766, this jingle:

If each blade, would mind his trade,
Each lass and lad in home-spun clad,
Then we might cramp the growth of stamp.

[200]

West's almanac (Providence, Rhode Island) publishes "A Short View of the present State of the American Colonies, from Canada to the utmost Verge of His Majesty's Dominions. July . . . 1765," containing:

(1) Evidence that "the whole of English America" is "in the Depths of Despair upon the Loss of Privileges, the most dear and invaluable."

(2) The conclusion that "such being the deplorable Situation of this Country, once renown'd for Freedom, it is hoped a Review thereof will excite such a universal Spirit of Patriotism in every Inhabitant, that our Liberty and Property may be yet rescued from the Jaws of Destruction."

(3) These final thoughts: "I can now only add the following political Sentences, which I hope will be duly considered, viz.

1. Power, like Water, is ever working its own Way; and, wherever it can find or make an Opening, is altogether as prone to overflow whatever is subject to it.

2. Though Matter of Right overlooked, may be re-claimed and reassumed at any Time, it cannot be too soon re-claimed and re-assumed.

3. And if the Representative Part of Government is not tenacious almost to a Fault, of the Rights and Claims of a People, they will, in a Course of Time, lose their very Pretensions to them."

1767

The greatest recent public event was of course the repeal of the Stamp Act, in March, 1766, though the jubilation thereat was no doubt a little clouded by the Declaratory Act whereby Parliament still asserted its right to tax the colonies. The name of William Pitt naturally stood out as the colonists thought of the victory for their cause.

West's *New-England Almanack* in the dedication "To my Countrymen": first thanks his patrons for buying the almanac, and then acknowledges this higher obligation to them:

It is to you, my countrymen, I am in a great measure, indebted for my freedom; it was you, that so nobly exerted yourselves to bring about a repeal of the Stamp-Act, that so lately hung over our heads like a heavy cloud; an Act, in its nature detestable; plotted and contrived by a set of wicked designing men; and had it taken place among us, would have enslaved millions of loyal subjects, and subverted the whole constitution of *English America*. It is generally believed those wicked fowlers had something of a worse nature in view; but thanks be to GOD! the snare is broken,[426] and we are escaped; and we may well say, the Lord hath done great things for us; whereof we are glad.

Ames's general address to the Reader for 1767 is especially important. In part it runs thus:

Reader,

I most heartily congratulate thee on the happy prospect of the publick affairs of this Country, so different from what it was last Fall, as nearly to exceed the most sanguine expectation; and which, however unwilling some few may be to own it, was produced by the exertion of that noble spirit of *Freedom*, which every thinking honest Man that has never been galled with the *chain* of *slavery* is possessed of—a spirit which GOD grant no tyrant may ever be able to extinguish amongst us: to the first exciters of which we are so superlatively indebted on so many accounts, as would far exceed the limits of my page to express. I only hope that you will always show your sense of the obligation by rewarding them and their posterity, so long as they shall hold their integrity, with all the most important posts of honour and profit that you are capable of bestowing; and that whenever a *Virginian* shall visit this part of the *Land of Freedom*, you will be no niggard of *Hospitality*. Having these matters so far settled according to our wishes, let us turn our thoughts on the arts of peace.—Oh! ye husbandmen, too happy would ye be, did ye know your own advantages; did ye turn your minds to the cultivation of ingenious arts, that soften the manners and prevent our being brutish; did ye neglect the vain amusements and idle tattle of the town and rather strive to know the life and manners of young prince *Heraclius* of *Georgia*, than whether neighbour *Such-a-one* married a month too late to be honest. What fine opportunities have ye to improve yourselves by study above tradesmen and mechanicks, whilst your fruits and herbage are growing? At the intervals of cultivating your fields, ye might be enriching your minds with useful knowledge— by perusing the *Roman* history, ye might learn how gradually a rough and ignorant people, by cultivating the study and practice of useful arts and manufactures, did emerge from obscurity to a state of grandeur and affluence inconceivable; so great that their relicks are at this day the wonder of the world—how at last, they became indolent and luxurious, and therefore vitious and ignorant, which made them a prey to tyranny; and tyranny always ends in the extinction of a nation, as is evident to those that take notice of what passes in the great world, that is, read history. Ignorance among the common people is the very basis and foundation of tyranny and oppression. With what absolute and despotick sway did that grand tyrant and impostor the Pope of *Rome* rule the consciences and purses of mighty sovereigns and most of the people of *Europe*, *Britons* among the rest, so long as he kept them in ignorance, making them pray in *Latin* like a parcel of parrots, nor suffering the common people to keep Bibles in a language they understood.—But happy for the world he is dwindling away, many nations have thrown off his saddle, and are not quite so much priest-ridden. Let us then, my countrymen, study not only religion but politicks and the nature of civil government; become politicians every one of us; take upon us to examine every thing, and think for ourselves; striving to prevent the execution of that detestable maxim of *European* policy among us, *viz*. That the common people, who are three quarters of the world, must be kept in ignorance, that they may be slaves to the other quarter who live in magnificence: and for this end I should recommend to you, first, the study of Geography, that is, the situation, extent, government, commodities, &c. of all countries upon earth. *Salmon's* [427] or *Gordon's* Geographies are as good as any that are published; and in *Salmon's* Gazeteer you have in few words an history of any country in alphabetical order, that you may turn to it in a moment. An *English* dictionary will be a vast help to you. The Knowledge of geography will fit you for reading history: it is proper to begin with the history of your own nation; *Rapin's*, *Echard's*, or *Hume's* histories of *England* are most approved of.—Yet let not these amusements intrude upon the more important occupations of life: our bodies must be fed and clothed. But that is not all; we must do more; we must raise something to sell for exportation, if we would increase in wealth. We are not tenants but *lords* of the soil, and may live as genteel tho' not in such splendour, as lords, by increasing trade and commerce, which are as necessary to a state as wings to a bird; encouraging all kinds of tradesmen and artificers among us, diligence and industry in every one, keeping all sorts of lawful business constantly going on, every wheel in the grand system continually moving; despising foreign luxury and effeminacy, banishing from among us immorality and idleness. He that will not work, neither shall he eat.

The remainder of the address (a full page) is of the greatest interest to the student of economic history: it is a plea for the home manufacture of potash and for the planting of mulberry trees, the culture of silk worms, and the manufacture of silk.

Ames's almanac for March, 1767, calls attention to the anniversary (March 18) of the repeal of the Stamp Act, and in the following doggerel proposes Pitt's health:

> *Let's drink to* PITT
> *The English pearl;*
> *May he shine yet*
> *Tho' made an earl.*[428]

1768

For the year 1768, just after the Townshend duties, Ames is again an important witness as he eloquently sets forth the grievances of the colonists and bids them be frugal and stout-hearted:

Friends and Country-Men! Our Fathers came into this Wilderness, encouraged by the word of a King, that they shou'd enjoy their Civil & Religious Liberties! They lived upon Boil'd Corn and Clams, and laboured hard to clear and cultivate the Country they purchased of the Natives, and defended the same at the Expence of their own Blood and

Treasure: We have often aided the Crown with Men and Money; and by the Conquest of Cape-Briton, gave Peace to Europe: Our Taxes, till very lately, have been granted by our own Representatives for the Support of Government; and we have given Old England Millions of Money in the way of Trade: Our Growing Extravagancies have run us amazingly into Debt; and the Moneys that should go in Payment, are now to be taken from us, *without our Consent*, to support, independent of the People, and in greater Affluence, the Officers of the Crown; as also to maintain & keep up a large body of Regular Troops in America. Duties, unknown to our Fathers to be paid here upon Sugar, Molasses, Wine, Rum, Tea, Coffee, Cocoa, Paper of all kind, Painters Colours, Window and other Glass, &c. will carry off all our Silver and Gold, without other Taxes, which are talk'd of upon Salt & Land, to the Ruin of Trade, and in the end of the whole Province, unless prevented by the Virtue of the People. Boston has set a noble Example for the Encouragement of Frugality and our own Manufactures, by the Agreement *unanimously* come into; and may it be followed by all the other Towns: Nay, let them go further by agreeing not to sip that *poisonous Herb*, called Bohea Tea as also not to purchase any sort of Woolen Goods made abroad, for 12 or 18 Months to come, but to wear their old patch'd Cloaths, till our own Manufacture can be bought, as many in New-York, Connecticut and Philadelphia are now doing.—If this Saving is not made, Interest must rise, Mortgages cannot be cleared, Lands will fall, or be possess'd by *Foreigners:* Families impoverish'd and our Goals filled with unhappy Objects.—If these wise Measures should be come into, a whole Province will be saved from Slavery, and this dreadful Ruin, and we shall become a Free, Rich, and Happy People!—That the Things which belong to our political Peace, may not be hid from the Eyes of Americans, as it seems to be from the Eyes of Britons, is the hearty wish of—A NEW ENGLAND MAN.

On the leaf facing December in this same issue, Ames reprints the vote of the Town of Boston, October 28, 1767, on "Measures to encourage the Produce and Manufactures of the Province, and to lessen the Use of Superfluities."

1769

The New England almanacs of 1769 naturally made use of such momentous events of the preceding twelve months as the non-importation agreements in response to the Townshend Acts, the Circular Letter of the Massachusetts House of Representatives and the order to rescind it, the arrival of military forces, the case of John Wilkes, and the publication of Dickinson's "Letters of an American Farmer."

"Abraham Weatherwise," in the final paragraph of his address to the "Courteous Reader of 1769," observes that his "Almanack[429] being printed on Paper manufactured in this Colony . . . , those who may be kindly pleased to promote and encourage its Sale, in Preference to *others*, published out of the Government, and done on Paper of the Manufacture of Europe, will do a singular Service to their Country, by keeping among us, in these Times of Distress, large Sums of Money, which will otherwise be sent abroad for this Article."

The front cover of this "Weatherwise" almanac for 1769 is adorned by a crude portrait of John Wilkes, with verses underneath as follows:

Hail Wilkes, immortal in the List of Fame,
Thy hateful Foes shall hide their Heads in Shame,
When you the Sweets of Liberty *restore*
To Britain's *Isle, and who can wish for more?*

This is followed by two pages and a half of matter on Wilkes, entitled "Anecdotes of Mr. Wilkes." The ending is: ". . . it will never, can never be denied, that his steady opposition to illegal general warrants, has been, and ever will be, of lasting benefit to the subjects of Great Britain; that, if he is not virtuous, he is a lover of virtue; and a friend to the civil and religious liberties of mankind; which we have no doubt of his displaying upon all future occasions, if he should sit in the House of Commons." Considering the rather un-promising nature of the material, from the moral point of view, and the fact that Wilkes' seat was still in question, the New England writer has done about all that he could.

Edes and Gill's almanac for 1769 gives us an extended piece of political allegory, inspired by the extreme unpopularity of the Governor, "An Extract from the History of Publius Clodius Britano Americanus" which begins thus:

> Publius Clodius Britano Americanus was born in one of the European Islands, his Parents were probably obscure Persons, as upon the most careful Enquiry I can find no one able to give an Account of them; but the great Bustle which our Hero has occasioned in the World, renders it not improper to transmit him down as a Warning to Posterity.[430]

In the end-matter of this same issue we have "The Charter of the Province of the Massachusetts-Bay" (18½ pages), followed by "The Explanatory Charter granted by His Majesty King George" (2½ pages). This is a good example of one very important feature of the New England almanacs of the period: they put before a very large body of readers the actual text of certain important public documents.

Low's (Boston) almanac for 1769 gives its readers this bit of political theory in a quotation from *Cato's Letters*:[431]

> . . . unlimited Power is so wild and monstrous a Thing, that however natural it be to desire it, it is as natural to oppose it; nor ought it to be trusted with any mortal Man be his Intentions ever so just: For besides that he will never care to part with it, he will rarely dare.— A FREE PEOPLE will be shewing that they are so, by their FREEDOM OF SPEECH.

Among the contents of Ames's almanac for 1769 are: A general article "On the Manufacture of Silk" (2 pages).

For February, eight lines of verse, beginning:

> *What! Shall a Tyrant trample on the Laws.*

For March, these outspoken verses:

> *Lives there a Wretch whose base degenerate Soul,*
> *Can crouch beneath a Tyrant's stern Controul?*
> *Cringe to his Nod, ignobly Kiss the Hand,*
> *In galling Chains that binds his native Land!*
> *Purchas'd by Gold or aw'd by slavish Fear,*
> *Abandon all his Ancestors held dear!*

These verses for April are equally significant:

> *Tamely, behold that Fruit of glorious Toil,*
> *The People's Charter made the Ruffian's Spoil?*
> *In Luxury's Lap, lie screen'd from Cares and Pains,*
> *And only toil to forge the Subjects Chains?*
> *Hear, unconcern'd, his injur'd Country's groan,*
> *Nor stretch an Arm to hurl them from the Town.*[432]

The page for April also contains this rhetorical question: "Who would sell his Birth Right for a Mess of Soup, or risque his Constitution for a Sip of Tea?"

Not least interesting in Ames's almanac for 1769 are the crude lines which follow: they show that desire to discover Americans equal to the great British names in literature that is so evident in the poetry and journalism of the early national period of our literature.

> *Some future Locke with Reason's keenest Ray,*
> *Pierce the rich Font of intellectu'l Day.*
> *The subtil Ties of Complex Thought unbind,*
> *And fix each Movement of the varying Mind.*
> *Some second Newton trace Creation's Laws,*
> *Through each Dependance to the Sov'reign Cause.*
> *Some Milton plan his bold impassion'd Theme,*
> *Stretch'd in the Banks of Oxellana's Stream.*
> *Another Shakespear shall Ohio claim,*
> *And boast its Floods allied to Avon's Fame.*
> *There too shall Sculpture warm the featur'd Stone,*
> *And Canvas glow with Beauties not its own.*

1770

A New England almanac for 1770 would naturally be to some degree a reflection of such events as the Virginia "Resolves" and the departure of the unpopular Governor Bernard. Edes and Gill's (Boston) almanac has been selected as a good representative of that year: its ample contents are especially significant in relation to the economic grievances of New England.

The imprint of this almanac is significant: "Boston: Printed [upon Paper Manufactured in this Country] and Sold by Edes & Gill."

Of similar import is a list of eleven merchants "who AUDACIOUSLY continue to counteract the UNITED SENTIMENTS of the BODY of Merchants thro'-out NORTH-AMERICA; by importing British Goods contrary to the Agreement" and the text of the votes passed "At a Meeting of the Merchants & Traders at *Faneuil* Hall, on the 23d January 1770," whereby certain merchants are designated as "obstinate and inveterate Enemies to their Country, and Subverters of the Rights and Liberties of this Continent." It is proposed "that all who with us are exerting themselves to maintain and secure the invaluable Rights of our Country, may refuse to sell to, buy of, or have any intercourse with the said [persons, whose names are given, being four merchants of Boston[433]] not only during the present Struggle for Liberty, but *for ever* hereafter."

The proceedings of this meeting next recite that

Whereas John Bernard, James & Patrick McMasters and Company, Anne & Elizabeth Cummings, and John Mein, most of whom being Strangers in this Country, have set themselves in open Defiance to the Body of Merchants and others throughout this Continent, by importing British Goods contrary to the known Sentiments of the Merchants, Freeholders, and Inhabitants in every Colony:

Therefore *Voted*, That they have in the most insolent Manner *too long* affronted this People, and endeavored to undermine the Liberties of this Country, to which they owe their *little* Importance, and that they deserve to be driven to that Obscurity, from which they originated, and to *the Hole of the Pit from whence they were digged.*

The proceedings of this meeting also include a record of the following vote concerning the use of tea:

Whereas the greatest Part of the Revenue arising by Virtue of the late Acts of Parliament, is produced from the Duty paid upon TEA, and it appearing to be the Determination of the Ministry to continue the said Duty:

Voted, That we will each of us strictly and religiously enjoin it upon our respective Families, totally to abstain from the Use of Tea upon *any Pretence whatever;* and each of us will also recommend to his Country Customers and Friends not to buy, sell, or use it, until the said Duty shall be taken off.

The annual editorial address, usually the most important single feature in the almanacs of this period, runs in part as follows:

We congratulate you that the most infamous G. B. [presumably Governor Bernard] has now come to the End of his Tether; and may all such Governors and Enemies of our natural and Charter Rights and Privileges meet with no better a Fate. The Time to elect Town Officers and Representatives approaches: If you regard the Well-being of your Posterity, do not promote such Men as have kept *a base Neutrality* in these Times of *Danger*, any more than you would those who have *appeared openly against your Rights* and on the Side of *Power*, and who for Pensions, Commissions and other Bribes, would have sold us all long ago; but on the contrary, advance *those* to Places of *Honor* and *Trust* who have nobly given up their Ease, their Time, and personal Advantage to preserve America from Slavery and Ruin. By proper Votes and Resolves, strengthen the Hands of the Merchants, who are worthy of double Honor, for shewing themselves so wise and virtuous as to call upon you not to purchase any Goods, that may be imported contrary to an Agreement they have come into, as the most *easy and sure Method* to get clear of the *present imposed Duties*, and to prevent *future ones* being laid upon us to pay American standing Armies, and to support Commissioners and a swarm of dirty Placemen and Pensioners, who we have already experienced to be Disturbers of the Peace, and the proper Caterpillars of the State. Encourage Religion and Virtue, Frugality and Industry in your several Towns: Follow the Example of those Ladies of Boston, Charlestown, Leicester, and other Places, who knowing that the Duties laid on Foreign Teas, is the chief Support of the Commissioners, &c. and that the Use of it is the Cause of all our nervous Disorders, will not now taste it at Home or Abroad, any more than they would Ratsbane: Purchase no *Foreign* Nicknacks and Fopperies and as little as possible of any *outlandish* Wares; for remember, that saving your Money is saving your Country.—Go on as you have wisely begun, to increase your Flocks of Sheep, and the Growth of Flax; and let Ministers and People still go Hand in Hand in encouraging every kind of Home-made Goods; and when you see a Rag on the Floor or in the Street let it remind you that two new Paper Mills have lately been erected. And remember it to be a certain Truth, that with the Blessing of God, manufacturing will soon make you a rich and *independent* People. To be sure instruct your Representatives to continue steady in the *good Cause* now we are coming to *the Pinch . . . the Game*, as it should be remembered for our Warning that many a free People have been *coaxed* to give away or sell those *invaluable* Rights, which their Enemies had in vain attempted to deprive them of by *Force*.—If these few short and broken Hints are regarded as they ought to be, we may then hope that the late Revenue Acts will be repealed, and the Soldiers and Commissioners, &c. removed, when all will be well.

Even the verses at the top of the twelve pages, one for each month, which constitute the workaday part of the almanac, are evidence of its preoccupation with public affairs.

> *'Tis gone, the memorable Year is past,*
> *And honest Execrations seal'd its last;*
> *Plagues, Taxes, lawless Rage and ranc'rous Foes*
> *Distract our Cities, and forbid Repose;*
> *Tho' Heav'n's rich Bounties load the generous Land,*
> *They snatch the Harvest from the Labourer's Hand.* (JANUARY)

E'en yet one Hour of Freedom, one blest Hour,
May sure be rescu'd from the Gripe of Power;
Let us improve the poor, the scanty Space,
The mock Reprieve, the Penury of Grace;
Assert your Rights and brave the menac'd Rod,
Wouldst thou be free and happy, hope in God.   (FEBRUARY)

What shall we think, can People give away
Both for themselves and Sons, their native Sway;
Then they are left, defenceless, to the Sword
Of each unbounded, arbitrary Lord;
And Laws are vain by which we Right enjoy,
If Kings unquestion'd can those Laws destroy.—Dryden.
(SEPTEMBER)

The end-matter begins with lists of officers of the government of Massachusetts Bay; Members of the House of Representatives; Officers of the Courts; Justices of the Peace; Harvard College; Ministers; Military Officers; the Ancient and Honourable Artillery Company;[434] Officers of the Town of Boston, etc., etc.

Finally comes "A List of Commissioners and other Officers of the Revenue, with their respective Salaries." The list begins with the five commissioners whose salaries at £5000 each amount to £25,000 (Old Tenor). Messrs. Green and Russell are listed as Printers and Messrs. Mein and Fleming as Stationers to the Revenue Office. Their salaries come to £10,900. To that the addition for "blanks," incidental charges, and secret services is estimated at £25,320, making £76,220. Then come Admiralty, Judges, etc., after all which we are told:

We cannot say that these are all upon the American Pension List; as a Veil of Darkness is carefully thrown over it, to prevent if possible the Public Odium, and to answer other Purposes of Ministry.

A Number of new Revenue and Custom-House Officers thro' the Colonies, which cannot be distinctly enumerated;—Add to these a

Swarm of petty Officers, Spies and Informers, whose Pay and Rewards cannot yet be ascertained.

Behold Americans part of a List of Officers and Placemen unknown to the Colonies before the late Revenue Acts, all supported by Taxes drawn from you, without your Consent.—A small Specimen of what you are to expect, if these Acts should be continued.

1771

To represent the New England almanacs for 1771, a significant article from Ames on non-importation will serve. Under the title "A Discourse on what is not done, and on what may be done, from a late eminent writer," it begins thus: " 'Let the world go as it will, do your Duty indifferently and always speak well of the Prior,' is an ancient maxim among the Monks; but it is capable of leaving the Convent in mediocrity, negligence and contempt." It ends:

What fruit is the good seed sown likely to produce in the minds of our great, who can supinely behold the Philadelphians not only outstrip us in the liberal arts but also in the mechanic Arts, who instead of importing immense quantities of British manufactures, have their ships enter their ports laden with cash and manufactures from England. Golden Fruits of the Non-importation Agreement!

1772

Among the claims of the New England almanac upon the student of history is the fact that it so frequently enlarged the reader's knowledge by telling him who the eminent writers on Liberty were, both in the American colonies and in England. Ames's almanac for 1772 does that in two important cases.[435]

The first is John Dickinson of Pennsylvania, "The Patriotic American Farmer . . . Who with Attic Eloquence, and Roman Spirit, hath asserted the Liberties of the British Colonies in America." Below an atrocious engraving of Dickinson, who stands with his elbow resting on "Magna

Charta" and with a scroll inscribed "Farmer's Letters" in his hand, are these lines of bad but historically interesting verse:

> *'Tis nobly done to Stem Taxation's Rage,*
> *And raise the Thoughts of a degenerate Age,*
> *For Happiness and joy, from Freedom spring;*
> *But Life in Bondage is a worthless Thing.*

These lines, curiously enough, are a reminder that Addison's *Cato*, at least as a political document, had a certain vitality in the Massachusetts of 1772. For they are obviously adapted from Eusden's verses to Addison on his *Cato*:

> *'Tis nobly done thus to enrich the stage,*
> *And raise the thoughts of a degenerate age;*
> *To show how endless joys from freedom spring,*
> *How life in bondage is a worthless thing.*

When Nathaniel Ames made these lines partly his own and decorated his almanac with them, he perhaps remembered that performance of *Cato*, and the rehearsals for it, which he certainly witnessed and perhaps took part in, as a Harvard undergraduate in 1758.[436]

The other friend of Liberty to whom Ames's almanac pays the tribute of a very badly executed engraving is Catharine Macaulay Graham (1731–1791), whose violently republican *History of England* (1763–1771), handsomely printed and bound in the style of his "republican classics," was presented to the library of Harvard College by Thomas Hollis, who wrote in the first volume: " 'Liberty the Nurse of all great Wits,' as see beautifully illustrated, o Youth, ingenuous, of Harvard College, in the *Areopagitica* of the MATCHLESS John Milton.—T.H."

In recommending Mrs. Macaulay to his readers, Nathaniel Ames was endorsing one of the very outspoken liberals of the time. For in the introduction (p. xi) of her first volume Mrs. Macaulay had written: "Whoever attempts to remove the limitations necessary to render monarchy consistent with

Liberty, are rebels in the worst sense; rebels to the laws of their country, the law of nature, the law of reason, and the law of God." And on the execution of Charles I she had gone so far as to declare (IV. 433 [437]) that "to attempt the defence of that eminent act of justice, the King's death, on the narrow bottom of constitutional forms, is to betray the cause of Liberty, and confound both truth and reason.[438]

1773

We shall again let the New England almanacs of a year be represented by Ames, whose issue for 1773 has a certain grave force, especially to be seen in his general article of a page and a half on "How a Nation may be ruin'd and reform'd." Two topics are discussed: "There are two pernicious things in the government of a nation which are scarce ever reme-died. The first is an *unjust* and too *violent authority* in Kings: the other is *luxury*, which viciates the morals of the people."

The first topic is thus treated:

When Kings acknowledge no law but their own will, and give a loose to their most exorbitant passions, they may do any thing; but by this very power they usurp of doing any thing, they sap the foundation of their regal power; they go by no certain rules, and govern by no fixed maxims; all try who shall flatter them most: they loose their people and have nothing left them but slaves, whose number diminishes every day. Who shall tell them the truth? Who shall set bounds to this torrent? Every thing falls before it: the wisest fly away, hide themselves and groan in secret; nothing, but a sudden violent revolution, can bring back this exorbitant power into its natural channel; nay some times the very means made use of to reduce it, irrecoverably destroy it. Nothing threatens so fatal a fall as an authority that is strain'd too high: it is like a bow that is bent, which at last breaks on a sudden if the string be not slacken'd. But who is he that will dare to slacken it? A King thus cor-rupted can scarce expect to be reformed without a kind of miracle.

The tone is quiet enough, but the writer is not afraid to mention the possibility of "a sudden violent revolution."

Outspoken also were the following verses which appeared on the front cover of the almanac, and which, we happen to know,[439] were written by Ames himself:

Our great Forefathers, fir'd with virtuous Rage,
Did all the Perils of the Deep engage,
To fly those Realms where proud tyrannic Sway,
And horrid Persecution scout for Prey;
Their native Soil and youthful Scenes they fled,
Where bounteous Nature all her Blessings shed,
And sister Art had ransack'd foreign Shores,
Made every Dainty croud their British Stores,
Had rais'd the ample Dome and lofty Spire,
And spacious Theatre, w[h]ere Crouds admire
The mighty Feats perform'd in ancient Days,
That spring to Life, reviv'd in English Plays.
These Pleasures all, our Fathers left behind,
But bro't the Seeds of Science in their Mind,
Here planted first fair Freedom *with* Applause,
Which gives the Relish to all other Joys:
Guard then the Plant,—this savage Land adorn,
This Work they left their Children then unborn.

1775

Though the almanacs of 1774 are by no means uninteresting,[440] those of 1775 demand so full an account that we shall turn to them without delay.

West's *New-England Almanack* (Providence, Rhode Island) bears on its front cover twelve lines of verse, of which the last six are:

Americans! for Freedom firmly join,
Unite your Councils, and your Force combine,
Disarm Oppression—prune Ambition's Wings,
And stifle Tories, e'er they dart their Stings:
And then your plunder'd Rights shall be restor'd,
And Tyrants tremble when you grasp the Sword.

Later in the same number (November) are these lines:

THE GENIUS OF AMERICA TO HER SONS

Are Americans born to bear
The galling weight of Slav'ry's chain?
A patriot's noble ardor share,
And freedom's sacred cause maintain.
Arise, my sons, shew your unconquer'd might,
A freeman best defends a freeman's right.
Look back on every deathless deed
For which your sires recorded stand;
To battle let your heroes lead
The sons of toil, a hardy band;
The sword on each rough peasant's thigh be worn,
And war's green wreaths the shepherd's front adorn.

But much the most important feature of West's Rhode Island almanac for 1775 is a three-page general article entitled "A Brief View of the present Controversy between Great-Britain and America." It will be noted that "America" —not "the American colonies"—is here spoken of as if it were already a separate country. The complete text of this article follows:

In our last year's Almanack was inserted "a brief historical account of the rise and settlement of Rhode-Island government:" We then proposed to enlarge and continue that account in our present Almanack; but in the course of the preceding year some very surprizing and important events have taken place, which perhaps will render some observations upon another subject more useful and agreeable to our readers in general.

Never perhaps was there a period more important to America than the present. Great-Britain is now carrying into execution a claim, assumed but a little while since, and which, if acceded to, will involve us in the most abject slavery. The year 1774 [441] will hereafter be reckoned as a great æra in the history of America. The blocking up the port of Boston, the metropolis of a powerful government, will, in all probability, bring on a decision of the grand dispute now subsisting between Great-Britain and America. Britain claims the right of taxing America, whensoever, wheresoever and how much soever she pleases, without our consent, and of making *laws binding upon us in all cases whatsoever.* We think that we ought to have a voice in the disposal of *our own property.* The dispute is not whether the tea destroyed at Boston shall be paid for, or whether it shall cost us three-pence more in the pound; but, whether Great-Britain shall *tax America at all?* "If they have a right to levy a tax of *one penny* upon us" (says the illustrious Farmer) "they have a right to levy a *million*; for where does their right stop? At any given number of pence, shillings or pounds?—To attempt to limit their right, after granting it to exist at all, is as contrary to reason, as granting it to exist at all is contrary to justice. If they have any right to tax us, then whether *our own* money shall continue in our pockets or not, depends no longer *on us,* but on *them.*"

"Taxation and representation" (says the great Earl of Chatham) "are inseparably united: God hath joined them: No British Parliament can separate them; to endeavour to do it, is to stab our vitals. This position is founded on the laws of nature; it is more, it is itself an eternal law of nature:—For whatever is a man's own, is absolutely his own, and no man hath a right to take it from him without his consent, either expressed by himself or his representative; whoever attempts it, attempts an injury;—whoever does it, commits a robbery;—he throws down the distinction between liberty and slavery." These are the sentiments of the greatest men in the English nation, and of every man of sense and virtue in all North-America, except a few *narrow-soul'd* selfish tools, who would be glad "to owe their greatness to their country's ruin." The letters which some have written to people of influence in England, recommending the abolition of our charters—*"an abridgment of English liberties"*—and the introduction of an arbitrary power, sufficiently shew us who are our greatest enemies. Nothing can more deserve the just indignation and resentment of an abused people, than those infamous wretches, whose names will be execrated by all posterity, the *mandamus Counsellors* of a neighbouring government, who stubbornly continue to do their utmost to enslave their country. A few persons, with a view of aggrandizing themselves, and growing eminent by the misfortunes of others, have set on foot the destructive measures now pursued by the British Parliament; measures which, if persisted in, are big with the fate of Europe and America, and ruinous to both. The wisest men in Britain strongly recommend to us to oppose them by *every means*. We must oppose, or we must be slaves. It is possible that another revolution may soon take place—that Britain (as the patriotic and benevolent Bishop of St. Asaph [442] supposes) is blindly rushing on to her own destruction.

When a man, only because he has more strength and greater bones and sinews than his neighbour, undertakes to deprive him of his life, liberty or property, resistance is justifiable: So when a nation, only because they have more strength and power, attempt to invade the liberty, or unjustly to take the property of a weaker state, opposition with the sword for their defence, even unto blood, would be justified, nay even is commanded, by the laws of God and nature. Such is the importance and situation of North-America, that very probably war may be brought into our territories, even in our days. France and Spain remember their losses, and perhaps, did they deem themselves able, would be glad to add this whole continent to their dominions. Great-Britain, lead by mistaken principles, seems fond of exercising a despotic rule over this continent; she has established the Roman Catholic religion in Canada— in a country of greater extent, and capable of supporting more inhabitants than Great-Britain itself. All her dispositions towards America, lately, have seemed inimical. We know not what may be attempted; fire and sword may be unexpectedly sent into our country. If the Ministry succeed in their designs, the French and Indians of Canada will be at their disposal, to pour in upon our back settlements.

We ought therefore to prepare for our defence, and accustom ourselves to arms and discipline. These colonies, like the little kingdoms of ancient Greece, are growing into empire; they have spread and are spreading every day through many latitudes, over a vast extent of territory, of whose width as yet no bounds have been discovered, wherein are supposed to be five millions of inhabitants. The Americans are descended from brave ancestors; they inherit their spirit; they, in general, love their liberty; they want not courage: It is discipline alone in which they are exceeded by the bravest troops that ever trod the earth. From the martial spirit which seems lately to have diffused itself over the country, we may hope that our militia will soon be on a footing equal with any troops in the world. History shews us what a militia, fighting in their own country, even in a bad cause, and much more so in a good one, are capable of doing.—In the late rebellion in Scotland, the King's troops, though considerably superior in numbers, were beaten and put to flight in their pitched battles. The rebels were however finally conquered in the field, though they *now* seem to have the ascendency in the *cabinet.* The Rhode-Island *militia*, in the last war, were honourably distinguished by their bravery and courage. The taking the important fortress of Louisburgh, at Cape-Breton, which gave peace to Europe, in the year 1745—the defeat of the French army, commanded by Baron Dieskau, and taking their General by Sir William Johnson, in the year 1756—the defeat which Sir William Johnson with only 600 men, gave to the French army, consisting of 1700, commanded by M. D'Aubry—and the taking Niagara, on the twenty-fourth day of July, 1759—all which achievements were performed by the forces of the colonies, are sufficient proofs of the military courage of English Americans. Art and discipline are very necessary and important in war. —The histories of all countries shew us, that a few regular well-disciplined troops have worsted armies, not so well disciplined, very far superior in number to themselves.—It is not so much the multitude of numbers, and undisciplined courage, as art and regularity which carry the victory. It is therefore incumbent upon us all to study the art of war, that we may be ready, if necessitated to have recourse to arms. But at the same time it is a duty highly incumbent upon us to promote concord and unanimity—"as much as in us lieth, if possible, to live peaceably with all men," and never to apply to the *ratio ultima*, as long as it can possibly be avoided, and our liberty secured.—May the Parliament of Great-Britain see the *injustice* and *impolicy of taxing America*, before civil distraction, the result of imperiousness and oppression, shall enervate the English empire dividing against itself.—May they be induced to repeal all the acts which have caused such universal uneasiness throughout America.—May our land yet be a land of peace; a land of liberty—the seat of virtue—the asylum of the oppressed.—May there yet be a constitutional and perpetual union and harmony between Great-

Britain and America, and may they both for ever hereafter, in *one* great empire, be free, flourishing and happy.

Ames for 1775 is, as usual, important. Let three items suffice.

The first is the brief but suggestive observation opposite the day (January 30) which was the anniversary of the execution of Charles I: "K. Cha. I *established a Memento for Tyrants.*"

The second is the series of continuous verses at the top of the twelve pages (January to December) which constitute the body of the almanac. Not for their poetic quality are these lines especially important, or because no earlier almanac had contained such exhortations as

> *Stand forth the champions of your country's cause,*
> *Nor fear the traitors aided by their laws.*

What one does find important in these verses is, first, a certain practical realism and confidence about the manner and outcome of the actual fighting,—should fighting come. And this in spite of periphrases and an inept touch generally. For example:

> *Our practis'd huntsmen, sure of flying game,*
> *Ne'er fight in phalanx when they've surer aim.*
> *No dazzling arms our steady marksmen hold,*
> *No heavy panoply, or casque of gold.*
> *But sure as death, the trusty piece he bears,*
> *And fears no wild, or powder'd son of Mars.*

And, secondly, one commends the shrewdness of the author—poet though he may not be—for reminding his readers that not by mere physical bravery and good marksmanship could they gain their cause. He bids them also consider

> *How one grand centre must the whole survey,*
> *By posts and couriers it's resolves convey.*
> *How civil wisdom must the arms controul,*
> *To act in concert, like one mighty soul!*

The third item in Ames's almanac for 1775 is perhaps the most interesting of all. It is found on the page opposite that for the month of December and is entitled "The Method of Making Gun-Powder. By following which Directions every Person may easily supply himself with a sufficiency of that Commodity."[443]

To sum up: the New Englander who had saved his almanacs since 1766, possessed in 1775, even if he had nothing else to read, the means of becoming well prepared to take an intelligent part in the great events that lay just ahead.

1. He had a fairly adequate record of the recent great public events.

2. He had the text of various charters and other important public documents.

3. He had some hundreds of lines of the better English poets, especially of what they had written in praise of Liberty, and a lot of native verse, mostly on that theme.

4. He had been urged to become more politically minded, had been given a considerable amount of political doctrine about his rights and liberties, and had been told where he could find more.

5. He had been introduced to the idea of economic resistance and had been shown several practical methods of decreasing his economic dependence upon the Mother Country.

6. He had been told who his best friends were in England,—Chatham, Bishop Shipley, Wilkes, and Mrs. Macaulay. He knew about John Dickinson. He knew something about the Virginia statesmen and had been urged to greet a Virginian as his brother.

7. He had even been introduced to the idea of armed resistance and told how he could make his own little store of gunpowder.

All this, barring occasional quips and doggerel verse, had been presented to him with a fairly creditable dignity and restraint, tending to arouse a patriotism not incompatible with a love of God and of peace.

Therefore, it is submitted, the New England almanacs from 1766 to 1775 establish a presumption that the body of almanacs of which they form a part deserve more attention than they have apparently received from those who would understand the growth, among the rank and file, of American thought just before the Revolution.

Characters of Nations

I

THAT the articles of food upon our breakfast tables often originate in exceedingly remote places and undergo striking changes of form before they reach us has been made a sufficiently familiar idea. It is less generally realized, perhaps, that the pages of a great modern writer, like Macaulay or Parkman, who belongs both to history and to literature, sometimes contain kinds of material the origins and early traditions of which are by no means historical. When, for instance, Parkman in the first chapter of his *Conspiracy of Pontiac* sketches the typical Indian, or Macaulay in his famous third chapter turns out those brilliant composite photographs of the English family chaplain or the country squire of 1685, there recurs—far from its original setting—that ancient and historically most interesting kind of discourse that used to be called a "character." Upon that essentially "literary" type a few observations are here offered, with special regard to one sub-species of it which may be termed "characters of nations."

The essays, plays, poems, pamphlets, travels, and other miscellaneous writings of the seventeenth and eighteenth centuries, especially those of a satirical and facetious sort, contain many such generalizations.

In 1615, for instance, an almost unknown writer named I. Cocke, in the sixth edition of that famous collection of characters that passed for Overbury's, wrote thus of one national type:

A Braggadocio Welshman

Is the oyster that the pearl is in, for a man may be picked out of him.

[224]

He hath the abilities of the mind in *potentia*, and *actu* nothing but boldness. His clothes are in fashion before his body, and he accounts boldness the chiefest virtue. Above all men he loves an herald, and speaks pedigrees naturally. He accounts none well descended that call him not cousin, and prefers Owen Glendower before any of the Nine Worthies. The first note of his familiarity is the confession of his valour, and so he prevents quarrels. He voucheth Welsh a pure and unconquered language, and courts ladies with the story of their chronicle. To conclude, he is precious in his own conceit, and upon St. David's Day without comparison.

Some eighty-five years later Edward Ward in his *London Spy* (1698–1700) sets forth "The Character of an Irishman" in these words:

He is commonly a huge Fellow, with a little Soul; as strong as a *Horse*, and as silly as an *Ass*; very poor, and yet proud; lusty, and yet lazy; foolish, but yet knavish; impudent, but yet cowardly; superstitiously devout, yet infamously wicked; very obstinate in his Faith, but very loose in his Morals; a loyal Subject to his Prince, and an humble Servant to his Master; for he thinks 'tis his Duty to make a Rogue of himself at any time to serve the one, and a Fool of himself at any time to serve the other; that is, to back a *Plot*, or make a *Bull*, he's the fittest *Calf* in *Christendom*.[444]

Slightly different is the point of view of one J. Gaillard, Gentleman, "Who hath been Tutor Abroad to several of the Nobility and Gentry": he published, in 1678, *The Compleat Gentleman: or Directions for the Education of Youth*, which contains "a character of some Nations, out of which a Traveller may receive some Lights and Directions how to behave himself when he comes amongst them" (pp. 178 ff.). The author cautions his readers that, "As there is no Rule without exception, so in every Country some are of a temper different from what is here represented" (p. 183). In general, however, Gaillard instructs his complete gentleman to regard the French, Spanish, Italians, and Germans as differing thus:

In Learning

The French knows a little of every thing,
Spanish hath a deep learning,
Italian like a Doctor,
German like a Pedant.

In Religion

French zealous.
Spanish superstitious.
Italian ceremonious.
German indifferent.

In Promises

French light.
Spaniard deceitful.
Italian advantageous.
German true and faithful.

Josiah Dare, in his *Counsellor Manners his Last Legacy to his Son* (1673), is equally willing to trust everything to a single adjective: he advises his son, if he travel, to "*note* the *Virtues* of the *people* and *imitate* them; their *Vices* and *Vanities* likewise, but to *avoid* and *abhor* them. There are many *young Sparks* that travel abroad, who leave the *English Gentleman* they *carried out* with them, and bring home again nothing, unless it be a *formal Spaniard*, a *drunken Dutchman*, or an *airy Frenchman*" (p. 149).

In Cornelius Arnold's *Commerce. A Poem* (1751) we have another instance of nations pigeon-holed by a single adjective. The poet, after dwelling upon the glories of the Royal Exchange

> *Where various nations of the peopl'd earth*
> Transact *the* Business *of the* bustling *Globe,*

brings thither

> . . . *the furr'd* Russian, *and the turban'd* Turk,
> *The trowser'd* Dutchman, *and the* buskin'd Swede,

The plain, rough German, the Italian soft,
The slow, grave Spaniard, and the Frenchman gay.

This summary classification is here, be it noted, the expression of one who, though no poet—as "the peopl'd earth" amply shows—is no satirist either, but one who "can smile on all benevolently good."

Occasionally, though not often, such generalizations are used in actual praise. Bishop Sprat, early in his *History of the Royal Society*[445] (1667), thus sketches his "idea of a perfect philosopher":

He should not be all of our *Clime*, but have the different Excellencies of several Countries. First, he should have the *Industry*, *Activity*, and *inquisitive Humor* of the *Dutch*, *French*, *Scotch*, and *English*, in laying the ground Work, the Heap of Experiments: And then he should have added the cold, the *circumspect*, and *wary* Disposition of the *Italians* and *Spaniards*, in meditating upon them, before he fully brings them into Speculation.

Many other examples might have been selected; but these are fairly representative. They hardly tend to present the "character" as a medium well adapted to give anything like a complete, objective, fair-minded view of their subject. Rather, they leave us, do they not, with some such feeling as this: granted, we say, that some of these pieces are not intended to be taken very seriously, and granted also that still greater unfairness is to be seen in those generalizations about nations that took the form of satirical prints and drawings, do not most of these writings show an obvious hostility? And is not the writer usually speaking with a witty exaggeration which tends to take certain definite forms or patterns? Is not the convention of the single epithet in Arnold's verses, for example, and the conscious balance in Ward's portrait of the Irishman much too strongly in evidence—at least, too strongly if their purpose be to tell what an historian would call the truth?

To such a judgment upon the "character" a person like Edward Ward might well reply that only one wholly ignorant of the origins and conventions of the "character" would expect it to be dignified, complete, objective, or fair-minded. Therefore let us briefly consider those origins and conventions.

II

Students of the history of criticism know how the tradition of a "rule" of three "dramatic unities"—of time, place, and action—was gradually built up until before the end of the sixteenth century Aristotle's precept of unity of action, together with his simple statement about the usual length of the dramatic time involved in a Greek tragedy, had, in spite of his complete silence in respect to any unity of place, become expanded to the "Rule of the Three Unities." Not unlike that was the development of a theory of characterization.

The chief steps were somewhat as follows. Aristotle, in the *Poetics*, intending to legislate mainly for tragedy and epic—and definitely excluding history—had merely required that characterization should be good, true to life, consistent with itself (or at least consistently inconsistent), and true to type. There is, he said, for example, a type of womanly gentleness, and it must be observed. This is central in Aristotle's theory as the representation of the universal.

In his *Rhetoric* Aristotle also has something to say about character. Here he is not discussing poetry, but oratory. The orator, he says (ii. xii), must, to make a successful appeal to his audience, know the distinctive character of youth, middle age, old age, and so forth. To this end Aristotle gives "characters" of these three types and of certain others. Later in the *Rhetoric* (iii. viii) he makes the point that style must have the virtue of being "ethical," that is, of representing facts by the proper characteristic sign as regards age, sex, or country. Here, clearly enough, Aristotle recognizes the existence of national characteristics: "the difference between Laconian and Thessalian" are his words in the Jebb-Sandys translation. Aristotle is here merely pointing out that the successful orator will in general take account of existing characteristics in his audiences and subjects. He is not suggesting that a good speech should have "characters" in it. Still less is he intending to stereotype the lines of such "characters."

But with Horace this rhetorical advice comes over into Poetic, and *decorum* becomes a principle which should govern the writing of tragedy, necessitating fidelity to the manners (*mores*) characteristic of childhood, youth, manhood, or old age. These four "ages of man" are briefly and well summarized. The whole passage runs to about twenty lines. By 1684, John Oldham freely imitated this part of Horace in these lines:[446]

> *Observe what Characters your persons fit,*
> *Whether the Master speak, or* Todelet:
> *Whether a man, that's elderly in growth,*
> *Or a brisk Hotspur in his boiling youth:*
> *A roaring Bully, or a shirking Cheat,*
> *A Court-bred Lady, or a tawdry Cit:*
> *A prating Gossip, or a jilting Whore,*
> *A travell'd Merchant, or an home-spun Boor:*
> Spaniard, *or* French, Italian, Dutch, *or* Dane;
> *Native of* Turky, India, *or* Japan.

The last two lines show how important a phase of the idea the "character of a nation" had become.

To indicate fully the many pseudo-classic variations that were played on this Horatian theme would open a very large subject, involving all the countries that felt the Renaissance influence. Limiting ourselves to England, we note merely two early examples.

The first is George Whetstone, who, writing in 1578, urges that comedy keep to its Unity of Time, and that it also submit to *Decorum*, not allow fools to give grave counsel, and not forget that "old men should instruct, young men should show the imperfections of youth, boys should be unhappy, and Clownes should speak disorderlye."

The second is William Webbe, whose *Discourse of English Poetrie* (1586) follows the Horatian precepts that the speech of each character must be suitable to "the dignity, age, sex, fortune, condition, place, *Country, etc.*"[447] Also, that it is necessary that the nature of each character shall observe fitness: thus, "it is meete and agreeable everywhere a man to be stoute [*i.e.*, bold], a woman fearefull, a servant crafty, a young man gentle."

III

All this was by way of general *poetical* precept while as yet there were, we may say, hardly any formal, intentional "characters" in England. But soon after 1600 there began to be many "characters" published, singly and in collections —their production accelerated and modelled to some degree, no doubt, by these critical doctrines that we have been considering. Here and there among this "character" literature one finds indicated the point of view of the writer, and sometimes an actual definition—a "character of a character," one may say. Let us assemble some of this material topically.

As regards length, there is ample testimony that the character should be exceedingly brief and pithy. "Here a man writes a great deal in a little room," says one author.[448]

In actual practice, if not by definition, the character strongly tended to be either wholly favorable or wholly unfavorable. In perhaps four cases out of five it was wholly unfavorable.

Obviously this brevity and the avoidance of mingled praise and blame create a serious danger of unfairness. In the vast majority of cases it is perfectly clear that fairness was not intended. The character, says Richard Flecknoe in 1665, either "extols to *Heaven*, or depresses into *Hell*; having no mid-place for *Purgatory* left." And Edward Ward wrote of one of his books of characters (1709): "'Tis true, the Picture is but half drawn, and only the unagreeable Side is exposed to our Reflexions."

But the character also exaggerates, intentionally, by its very form. At the end of the preface to his *Collection of the Choicest Epigrams and Characters* (1673), Flecknoe expresses his opinion that epigrams and characters may be aptly coupled, "since these are only Epigrams in Prose, as the others are onely Characters in Verse." Character-writers differ in their style, of course, as do writers in general. But in a large number, if not in the majority of cases, the character manifested so curious a fondness for alliteration, balance, conundrums, puns, paradoxes, and ideas arranged in sets of three or four that it early developed stylistic conventions tending toward other ends than telling what an historian would call the truth.

To make matters worse, the rhetoricians had got hold of the character and made it one of the forms regularly practised in schools. That was true even in Roman times, continued through the middle ages, and ran right on almost up to our own time.[449] By way of indicating the degree to which rhetoricians had formalized the "character," three cases—all English—may serve.

The first is that of Thomas Wilson, the popularity of whose *Arte of Rhetorique*, first published in 1553, may be judged by the fact that it reached at least a fourth edition by 1585. He regarded the "character," which he called "description," as a valuable ornament to discourse, especially if the style were artfully considered: "It much avayleth to use this figure in divers matters," wrote Wilson,[450] "the which whosoever can doe, with any excellent gift, undoubtedly he shal much delite the hearers." But Wilson bids the young writer note that "similitudes, examples, comparisons, from one thing to another, apt translations, and heaping up of

Allegories, and all such figures as serve for amplifying, doe much commend the lively setting forth." He specifically indicates that this figure of the "description," or "character," is suitable not only for representing conditions, such as "the pleasure of Plowmen, and the care that a King hath," but by it "men are painted out in their colours, yea, . . . Kingdomes, and Realmes are portured, places and times are described. The Englishman for feeding and chaunging for apparell. The Dutchman for drinking. The Frenchman for pride & inconstance. The Spanyard for nimblenes of body, and much disdaine: the Italian for great wit and policie: the Scot for boldnesse, and the Boeme for stubbornesse."

It is reasonably safe to imagine the pupils of Thomas Wilson sedulously aping in their themes the master's suggestion that all Italians are as notable for wit and policy as Dutchmen are for drinking.

The second case is that of Joshua Poole, M.A., of Clare Hall, Cambridge, who, in 1657, in his preface to *The English Parnassus*[451] says of that whole group of literary types in which he includes the "character" that it is all

a facetious kind of writing, full of spirit, humour, and fancy. . . . It is full of mirth and salt, *sententious*, *directive* as to *Morality*, *proverbiall*, *Mythologicall*, *Enigmaticall*, in a word hath all humane actions and accidents to work upon, closing up all with a certain smartnesse of *conceit*. The numerous brood of it, are, *ingenious fallacies* in, and *extra dictionem*, *Encomiasticks*, *Vituperatories*, *Scoffs*, *Sarcasms*, *Jeers*, *Jests*, *Quibbles*, *Clinches*, *Quippes*, *Bulls*, *Anagrams*, *Chronograms*, *Acrosticks*, *Criticismes*, in a word whatever is of Succinct and concise Poetry, on what subject soever, handsomely couched, and worded.

This passage perhaps raises more questions than it answers. But at least it puts the "character" with the more conceitful literary forms. And Poole was in his own day important enough[452] to make his attitude toward the "character" significant.

Our third rhetorician, who was also a schoolmaster, is Ralph Johnson, whose *Scholars Guide* (1665) aims "in a low and familiar language, such as a Child doth readilyest apprehend" to supply "Short, Plain, and Easie Rules for performing all manner of Exercises in the Grammar School," including the writing of "characters" (p. 15). Johnson's definition of a "character" emphasizes the "witty and facetious" element in it; his suggestions of possible subjects strongly imply adverse characterization, as does his final rule—that the "character" should conclude by leaving the persons characterized "to the effect of their follies or studies." And Johnson's directions for making the body of the character,[453] especially if they are considered in the light of his earlier rules (pp. 8–11) for "amplification," "allusion," "imitation," and "observation," strongly enforce the impression, already given by Wilson and Poole, that the "character" was presented to schoolboys as a form of prose or verse to be practised with studious regard to certain effects, among which are to be found neither fairness in considering substance nor plainness in considering style.[454]

One must not suppose that only the learned writers in the seventeenth and eighteenth centuries would have known the earlier authors well enough to make ready use of their diction. As a matter of fact, there were, in addition to dictionaries, a number of well-known books which codified the usage of earlier writers, especially that of the poets, with regard to synonyms, epithets, and periphrases. The influence of such books upon the style of both prose and verse has hardly received sufficient attention. It will be well, therefore, to consider the nature of that influence upon "characters of nations."

Such phrase-books were especially used to suggest the proper epithet. Dr. Johnson, in his famous *Dictionary* (1755), defines an epithet as "an adjective denoting quality good or

bad: as the *verdant* grove, the *craggy* mountain's *lofty* head."
A collection of epithets, therefore, to go with such a word as
"Italian," "Spaniard," or "Englishman" may be regarded as a
very useful—perhaps dangerously useful—source of information for a schoolboy who has been told to write a character.

An especially well-known book of this sort was the *Epi-
thetarum Thesaurus* of Johannes Ravisius Textor (who died
in 1524). In the edition of 1595 Textor catalogues various
nations as follows:

Angli: Brutiades, angligenae, brutigenae, armipotentes.
Belgae: Armiferi, audaces, pugnaces, crudi.
Galli: Feroces, truces, bellicosi, Romanis infesti, armorum avidi,[455]
rebelles, acres, stolidi, fortes,[455] timidi,[455] leves, alacris, saevi, atroces,
efferi, ardentes.
Germani: Invicti, atroces, potentes, feroces, bellaces, truces, caerulei.
Helvetii: Feri, armipotentes, saevi, truces.
Hispani: Venales, feroces.
Itali: Superbi, praefulgidi.
Scoti: Truces.
Turcae: Infidi, immanes, improbi, atroces, immites, feroces, fortes,
potentes, armipotentes, pharetrati, minaces, audaces, horribiles, truci,
mahometigenae, orthomanigenae.

Generally speaking, these epithets seem to have been carried over from a much earlier period, to consider primarily
the warriors of the various nations, and not to embody the
observations of recent visitors.

Rather different are the epithets in Joshua Poole's *English
Parnassus*, the introduction to which has already been considered. Poole wrote in English. He regarded the English
themselves as "stout, courageous, valiant, true-hearted,
hardy, bold, audacious, adventurous, warlike, apish, imitat-
ing." For the French he suggests "warlike, courtly, generous,
ingenious, deviseful, active, industrious, lascivious, wanton,
stately, courteous, cavalering, courageous, complementive."

Germans should be called "fierce, warlike, audacious, daring, adventurous, valiant, ingenious, industrious, rebellious, thirsty, drunken." The Italian he finds "spruce, neat, amorous, proud, courtly, complimental, ceremonious, jealous, suspicious, proud, insolent."

Compared with earlier phrase-books, Poole's *English Parnassus* seems based, as we know that it was based, on a rather large and varied body of English literature. In Poole's list of authors read,[456] three earlier books of "characters" appear —Earle's (called Blount's), the Overbury collection, and Fuller's *Holy and Profane State*.

The "character" of a "braggadocio Welshman" in the Overbury collection, it will be remembered, emphasized the Welshman's boldness and his love of pedigree. Therefore it is interesting to note that Poole's "Welshman" is "valiant, furious, genealogicall." There could hardly be a better example of the stereotyping influence of these phrase-books in fixing supposed national traits. And two of the epithets in Arnold's *Commerce* (1751)—the "furr'd Russian" and the "turban'd Turk"—are to be found in Poole.

Even more widely used was the *Gradus ad Parnassum*, which first appeared about 1687,[457] ran through a very large number of editions, and, judging by the names and dates in many extant copies, was relied on as an aid in hammering out Latin verses until well on in the last century. The "*Gradus* epithet" has become a byword among hostile critics of eighteenth-century verse. The *Gradus* epithets for the principal nations of the world are but little changed from those of Johannes Ravisius Textor of nearly two centuries before, though they are considerably more numerous: the Scots are still "truces," the Germans are "invicti," the Italians are "superbi," the Swiss have fourteen epithets, of which the first four are exactly those in the earlier book and are printed in the same order.

It would be a serious error to suppose that those who thus recommended the pigeon-holing of nations by means of a few approved traits were at variance with the great body of critical tradition in their time. What we have found true of the "character" was generally true throughout the pseudo-classic period.

The English were less consistently pseudo-classical than the French, and John Dryden was less consistently pseudo-classical than some other English critics. It is, therefore, a very important fact that in his preface to *Troilus and Cressida* (1679) Dryden not only recognizes such differences in type as we have been considering, but argues for their fundamental importance in all poetry, shows that his ideal poet would gather his knowledge of these type-characteristics from reading far outside the boundaries of literature, and emphatically remarks that no one who ignores this phase of his equipment deserves to be called a poet. So important a passage deserves to be quoted here:

The manners, in a poem, are understood to be those inclinations, whether natural or acquired, which move and carry us to actions, good, bad, or indifferent, in a play; or which incline the persons to such or such actions. . . . To produce a villain, without other reason than a natural inclination to villainy, is, in poetry, to produce an effect without a cause; and to make him more a villain than he has just reason to be, is to make an effect which is stronger than the cause:

The manners arise from many causes; and are either distinguished by complexion, as choleric and phlegmatic, or by the differences of age or sex, of climates, or quality of the persons, or their present condition. They are likewise to be gathered from the several virtues, vices, or passions, and many other commonplaces, which a poet must be supposed to have learned from natural philosophy, ethics, and history; of all which, whosoever is ignorant, does not deserve the name of poet.[458]

If space permitted, one could easily produce other passages from English critics whose emphasis upon *decorum* naturally led them to stress its importance in characterization. From Jeremy Collier's *Short View* (1698) one could, for example, cite that amusingly emphatic paragraph[459] about "propriety of *Manners*" in which the dramatist is bidden "to hold his *Persons* tight to their *Calling* and pretentions." Or one might in Thomas Rymer's two well-known critical treatises[460] discover an abundance of instances to show that Rymer habitually takes *decorum* to include the representation of that which may be supposed poetically probable in the case of a fictitious person of a given rank, profession, or nation, without regard to the occasional exceptions presented by history.

But even without this additional support, Dryden's great prestige makes his testimony suffice, perhaps, to show that we are considering a theory that was not far from the very foundation of seventeenth-century literary thought.

One does not venture to be sure exactly what Dryden intended by his vague wave of the hand toward a whole library of books in the fields of "natural philosophy, ethics, and history" which every real poet ought to read. He may have meant to include—at all events they are too important to omit—some of the authors who, from Greek times down through Montesquieu and later, wrote upon the deeply interesting question of the influence of geographical location and climate upon national character.

There was Pierre Charron (1541–1603),[461] for instance, whose *De la Sagesse* (1601) was widely influential[462] and was twice translated into English.[463] At the beginning of his forty-second chapter in the first book (1653 ed.), Charron sets forth his belief that "as fruits and beasts are divers, according to the divers countries wherein they are; so men are born more and less warlike, just, temperate, docible, religious, chaste, ingenious, good, obedient, beautifull, sound, strong" (pp. 153 ff.).

"Following this foundation," says Charron, "we may in

grosse, divide the world into three parts, and all men into three kinds of nature." His three divisions of the world—northern, middle, and southern—have, in his opinion, the result that

the natures of men, are . . . different in every thing, body, soul, religion, manners, as we may see in this Table: for the

	Northern People are	*Middle are*	*Southern are*
1. *In their bodies*	High and great, phlegmaticke, sanguine, white, and yeallow, sociable, and voice strong, the skin soft and hairy, great eaters and drinkers, puissant	Indifferent and temperate in all those things, as neuters or partakers a little of those two extremities, and participating most of that region to which they are nearest neighbours	Little, melancholick, cold, and drie, blacke, Solitarie, the voice shrill, the skin hard, with little hair, and curled, abstinent, feeble
2. *Spirit*	Heavy, obtuse, stupid, sottish, facile, light, inconstant		Ingenious, wise, subtile, opinative
3. *Religion*	Little religious and devout		Superstitious, contemplative
4. *Manners*	Warriers valliant, painfull, chaste, free from jealousie, cruell and inhumane		No warriours, idle, unchaste, jealous, cruell and inhumane

After much interesting comment on various examples of these differences, Charron thus concludes (p. 158):

By all this discourse we may say see [*sic*] that generally those of the North do excel in body, have strength for their part; and they of the South in spirit, and have for their part subtiltie; they of the middle Regions partake of both, and are temperate in all. So likewise we may see that their manners, to say the truth, are neither vices nor virtues, but works of Nature, which to amend or renounce altogether is more then difficult; but to sweeten, temper, and reduce the extremitie, to a mediocritie, it is a work of virtue.

Charron was translated into English in 1707 by George

Stanhope, D.D., "Dean of Canterbury, and Chaplain in Ordinary to Her Majesty," a fact which seems to show that by that time he was not considered especially dangerous. It is important to notice, however, that Charron not only furnished epithets for characterizing various nations, but expressed views which tend to transfer the discussion of national traits from the moral to the natural realm.

Montesquieu and other exponents of this theory who followed Charron might be discussed if space permitted. That such theories amused some people, the opening lines of Richard Tickell's *Project* (1778) may perhaps be admitted to prove:

> *Since sage philosophers aver,*
> *That* climate *forms the* character;
> *And prove each nation, tame, or bold,*
> *Just as its air is hot or cold;*
> *What schemes might crafty statesmen lay,*
> *If such a system they'd obey?*

> *Suppose the Turks, who now agree*
> *It would* fatigue *them to be free,*
> *Should build an ice-house, to debate*
> *More* cooly *on affairs of state,*
> *Might not some Mussulmen be brought,*
> *To brace their minds, nor shrink at thought?*
> *How, as their blood began to cool,*
> *Would nature scorn despotic rule?*
> *The silken sons of slavish ease,*
> *Would glow for freedom, while they* freeze;
> *And in proportion to the coldness,*
> *Discover latent fire and boldness.*

IV

Only a few have been selected from the many known cases in which writers on poetics, rhetoricians, and makers of phrase-books have fostered the tradition of characterization with strict fidelity to type and of emphasizing fixed national traits as one phase of that tradition. But perhaps enough has been said to show how well supported by precept were the great army of practitioners who in widely scattered regions contributed to that enormous mass of observations about human beings, real and fictitious, for which the seventeenth and eighteenth centuries are so notable.

The authors of the travel books and the courtesy books, though as a rule more urbane than the average, are likely to show their confidence in the superiority of their own country-men and the adequacy of a stock epithet or two by way of labelling outsiders. Thus John Macky thought in 1714 that the English were "free from the Vanity and Insincerity of the French, the Haughtiness of the Spaniard, or the Moroseness of the Dutch."[464] And the reader of James Howell's *Instructions for Forraigne Travell* (1642) learns that the wise travel-ler will "from the *Italian* . . . borrow his *reservednesse*, not his *jealousie* and *humor* of *revenge*; . . . from the *Spaniard* his *Sobriety*, not his *lust*: from the *German* (cleane contrary) his *Continency*, not his *Excesse*, the other way."

The comedies, periodical essays, and novels were, of course, crowded with fictitious persons, sometimes based on real ones, whose natures were more aggressively unified than present taste commends. Only after a very thorough study of them could one confidently generalize on the non-English characters. But one's impression is that long after the Eng-lish characters had been liberated from their comparatively rigid conformity to type, the foreigners continued to person-ify the characteristics of their nation as handed down in a convention that had little relation to actual life. They tended, on the whole, to supply elements of evil in the tragic or melo-dramatic novel, for example, and of comic in the lighter sorts of stories. Italians and Spaniards, generally speaking, served the former purpose, and Irish and French served the latter, though of course there are alternatives and exceptions.

One might expect that the eighteenth-century professional man would view his fellow-professionals, even when they were not British, with comparative freedom from this tendency to apply national epithets indiscriminately. Probably he did so in many cases; but not always. David Fordyce (1711–1751), for instance, was an eminent professor of moral philosophy at Aberdeen, whose *Dialogues concerning Education* (1745–1748) and *Theodorus: a Dialogue concerning the Art of Preaching* (1752) received a good deal of attention in the American colonies as well as at home. In the second of these works Fordyce generalizes as follows on the sermons of French, Italian, and Spanish preachers. In them he finds much to praise, but even more to remind him of the national characteristics of their authors:

The *French* are a lively, loquacious, and witty People: Accordingly, we find their Preachers wonderfully warm, diffuse, full of Action in the Pulpit, as in Conversation; fanciful and picturesque in their Descriptions, and rather elegant and wordy, than deeply strong in their Conversations. The *Italians*, who are of a more severe, cautious, and reserved Cast in their Temper and Conversation, shew a proportionable Difference in their Manner of Speaking and Preaching. Their Preachers are subtil, acute, and refined, of a less vivacious, yet more commanding Action than the *French*: Full of Spirit and Passion, yet more smooth and artful in managing them. Though this may be generally true of the common Rule, yet both Nations have given us good Models of strong Reasoning and masterly Eloquence, equally accommodated to please the most refined Taste, and to affect the most Vulgar. The *Spanish* Manner, like that of the Nation, is more solemn, stately, and full of Figures formed for Ostentation, and proudly swelling with all the Pomp of Rhetoric. Their Genius is piercing, and sublime; and though, perhaps, as full of Fire as any of their Neighbours, yet more chastened by the Stiffness and Haughtiness of their Manners.

Political events in the eighteenth century were, as every-

one knows, often treated allegorically, and the result sometimes had a very strong effect in perpetuating national traits
and nicknames. Of such works Arbuthnot's *John Bull* is de-
servedly best known, and has several "American descendants."[465] The very numerous satirical prints and drawings
have a similar relation to our subject.

Meanwhile it must not be supposed that writers in other
countries failed to make their contribution. The "perfidious-
ness" of the English was a convention which received the imprint of Scaliger's authority[466] in the mid-sixteenth century.
In 1571, De la Porte's *Les Epithètes* set down the English as
"ennemis des françois, . . . superbes, rouges, furieus, hardis,
audacieus."[467] And in 1640 Jules de la Mesnardière's *La
Poétique* (pp. 122–123) finds the English "infidelles, cruels,
ennemis des etrangers."

It is rather a pleasure to find Dr. Johnson commending
Shakespeare's characters because they are represented as human beings rather than as inhabitants of particular countries.
In spite of Dennis and Rymer, who "think his Romans not
sufficiently Roman," Shakespeare seems to Johnson to "make
nature predominate over accident."

His story requires Romans or Kings, but he thinks only on men.
He knew that Rome, like every other city, had men of all dispositions;
and wanting a buffoon, he went into the senate-house for that which
the senate-house would certainly have afforded him. . . . a poet over-
looks the casual distinctions of country and condition, as a painter, satisfied with the figure, neglects the drapery.

But in spite of this resonant good sense, and in spite of
all that novelists like Miss Edgeworth and Scott must have
done some fifty years later to humanize English notions of
Irishmen and of Scots, we must not suppose the old-fashioned
set "character" to have disappeared with the rise of romanticism. Keats—perhaps not altogether seriously—writes in one
of his letters that "a Scotchman will go wisely about to de-

ceive you, an Irishman cunningly." And he shrewdly adds:
"It seems to me they are both sensible of the Character they
hold in England and act accordingly."

So it goes, right down into our own lifetimes. As recently
as 1892 the distinguished French critic, Ferdinand Brune-
tière, though he quite frankly admitted the difficulties in so
doing, ventured to summarize in a single word the character of French literature, which he found *sociable*, as well as
that of the Italian (*artiste*), Spanish (*chevaleresque*), German
(*philosophique*), and English (*individualiste*).[468] Nearer still
are the very interesting but questionable generalizations of
Salvador de Madariaga, whose *Englishmen, Frenchmen, Spaniards: an Essay in Comparative Psychology* (1928) is founded
upon the belief that "in international psychology, by far the
most important factor is national character." Those who delight in sharply contrasted generalizations about national
characteristics will here find them in abundance: "while
English thought is concrete and vague, French thought is
abstract and precise" (p. 67); or, "the Englishman goes to
action, the Frenchman to thought, the Spaniard to passion,
spontaneously" (p. 112).

V

To affirm that most of the foregoing generalizations about
nations are ill founded might very well be merely to add another dangerous generalization upon an exceedingly difficult
subject. Yet surely we have, while tracing in brief outline
certain formative influences that went into the making of
these "characters of nations," observed forces at work that
seem ill calculated to promote the discovery of any serious
truth. More than once, indeed, we have overheard the schoolmaster instructing his pupils or the writer declaring the purpose of his book in words which seemed explicitly to disclaim
even the intention to be what the historian would call truth-

ful. Certainly a tradition so deeply affected by rhetorical considerations would seem to tend toward increasing the difficulties presented by love of country, hatred of other peoples' religion, trade rivalry, and many other powerful human forces which stand in the way of the dispassionate portrayal of foreigners.

Yet portrayal of foreigners will doubtless go on indefinitely: for no amount of good advice can ever make painful the contemplation of our own excellences or the perception of what looks like a mote in our brother's eye.

How, then, should one face this not entirely trivial matter? Sir Leslie Stephen once said that "the conventional picture made by one nation of another is a mere random putting together of hasty guesses and rash assumptions."[469] Hume, in his essay "Of National Characters," took a somewhat more moderate position: "The Vulgar," he wrote,

are apt to carry all *national characters* to extremes; and having once established it as a principle, that any people are knavish, or cowardly, or ignorant, they will admit of no exception, but comprehend every individual under the same censure. Men of sense condemn these undistinguishing judgments: Though at the same time, they allow, that each nation has a peculiar set of manners, and that some particular qualities are more frequently to be met with among one people than among their neighbours.

More bluntly, an anonymous writer of a letter to the editor of the *London Chronicle* (September 16–18, 1760) declared: "Ever since I have had an opportunity of examining mankind a little with my own eyes, I have found myself very liable to a good deal of scepticism, as to the general Character I find given of any people antient or modern, from whatever pen it has flowed."

One may, then, be assured of respectable company if one decides to be systematically sceptical on this whole subject. Or one may decide to regard all such generalizations as merely amusing when one finds them in funny papers, and harmlessly wrong when one finds them elsewhere. It will not do, however, to believe seriously that, although conventional generalizations about other countries are true and important, the stage American in a foreign play is a monstrous exaggeration about which something ought to be done at once.

John Galsworthy
1867-1933

JOHN GALSWORTHY, who was elected a Foreign Honorary Member of the Academy on May 13, 1931, died January 31, 1933.

He was born in 1867, of an old Devonshire family, went from Harrow to Oxford, studied law and travelled. But chiefly he wrote, from 1897, when his first work appeared, under a pseudonym, until *Over the River* closed the great Forsyte series in 1933. The resulting body of novels, plays, short stories, sketches, poems, and letters will not soon cease to inspire all good workmen, whatever may be their special calling. For all that he did and was Galsworthy deserved and received many honors, though he was not able to accept all the distinctions that were offered. Honorary degrees came to him from St. Andrews, Manchester, Dublin, Sheffield, Oxford, and Princeton; the O.M. was awarded him in 1929 "for services to literature and the drama." The Nobel Prize was also awarded him, but ill health prevented his going to Stockholm to receive it. He declined knighthood in 1918.

Galsworthy's aim—characteristically put by him in the third person—was simple, exacting, and appropriate: he wished "to present truth as he sees it, and gripping with it his readers or his audience, to produce in them a sort of mental and moral ferment, whereby vision may be enlarged, imagination livened, and understanding promoted." This aim Galsworthy was able to realize because in him great artistic gifts were joined with a remarkable endowment and balance of human qualities.

The justice which presides over his work has more than a

little that is Greek about it: "all are bound to their own natures, and what a man has most desired shall in the end enslave him." Thus his plots seem to unroll without the author's manipulation, always in the direction of a "doom" which is strangely inevitable on account of the skill with which it is made to seem the negative of the virtues punctiliously granted to each class. The art is quite marvellous with which, as from a chorus, public opinion is made to surround the central action: "Society stands to the modern individual as the gods and other elemental forces stood to the individual Greek."

But in Galsworthy justice is constantly balanced by sympathy. His hatred of cruelty is intense: "of all attributes of the human creature," he says, "cruelty is to me the most abhorrent." At the end of *Swan Song* he can think of nothing more poignant to compare Fleur with, after her father's death and her terrible remorse, than a bird that "had been shot with both barrels, and still lived; no one with any sporting instinct could have hurt it further. Nothing for it," thinks the wronged but deeply chivalrous Michael, "but to pick her up and mend the wings as best he could." A subtler form of pity, shading off into a luminous irony, runs through his depiction of such people as the Forsytes, the Carádocs, and the Pendyces. This kind of pity is so far above mere partisanship that it can embrace two opposed characters or social systems at once. It makes the feeling of the others toward De Levis in *Loyalties* seem snobbish yet difficult wholly to avoid. It nicely qualifies its approval of Courtier (in *The Patrician*) and its distaste for the rigidity of Miltoun. "Human nature has room for both and a good deal besides."

Galsworthy was intensely English: witness among a thousand passages, the feeling for one's own part of the land in "Devon for Me!" and in the final pages of *Over the River*. Therefore he was, usually, very reserved: witness his statement that he habitually creates "characters who have feelings that they cannot express." Yet the line in "Donkeys" where God's creation of these patient beasts is described as "One of the best of His numerous chores" is not, merely because its humor happens to be of the sort that we sometimes call American, any the less perfect as an expression, on one of its sides, of his extraordinarily well rounded nature.

The authenticity and significance of Galsworthy's people can perhaps be traced, in part, to the fact that they do not always seem wholly individual. In many of his sketches, especially, we meet them as type-studies, not yet ready to take a living part in novel or play. That some of Galsworthy's people seem not to have got quite far enough from this original state is perhaps their "doom." Yet he would probably reply—and perhaps rightly—that our significance, if we have any, arises to some extent from the fact that we are all less individual than we imagine ourselves to be. For he wrote of one of his characters: "When he met himself about the town (which hourly happened) he had no knowledge that it was himself; on the contrary he looked on himself as specially designed, finding most other people 'rather funny.'" In the great gallery of his portraits, therefore, these studies of types and classes, though sometimes weighed down by their responsibility of representing so many besides themselves, do tend to document Galsworthy's best work, even if they are not quite a part of it. They show us how he labored to bring his best characters into a life the completeness of which requires some thought of their representative value as well as of their individuality.

It has often been pointed out that John Galsworthy, like his father before him, was himself a bit of a Forsyte. Obviously, or he could not so remarkably have done the Forsytes both from the outside and from within. But so are we all, all Forsytes, in our several ways. "As surely as a dog will bark at a brass band, so will the essential Soames in human nature ever rise up uneasily against the dissolution which hovers round the folds of ownership." By this fact of their universality, together with the equally certain fact that they are solidly planted, with their houses and their dogs and their flowers, as well as their prisons and their slums, in an England which a great writer loved yet wished to better, these books, at this short distance from them, seem extraordinarily well fitted to endure.

Notes

Notes

1. By Martha Pike Conant, Ph.D. Columbia University Studies in Comparative Literature. New York: The Columbia University Press, 1908.

2. For example, the chapter closes thus: "There only remains to inform our *Readers*, That 'tis not onely *Books*, but *Maps*, *Monuments*, *Bas-Reliefs*, *Medals*, and all Antient Descriptions, that mightily strengthen and confirm History."

3. *The Post-Boy Robb'd of his Mail*, second edition, 1706, p. 229.

4. Opposite the title-page of the first edition of Swift's *Tale of a Tub* (1704), among several other "Treatises writ by the same author . . . ; which will be speedily published," is "A Voyage into England, by a Person of Quality in Terra Australia incognita, translated from the Original." This probably explains Swift's well-known comment on *Spectator*, No. 50, in his letter to Stella of April 28, 1710. Another South Sea Islander is the supposed author of No. 15.

5. Cf. *Spectator*, No. 50, and Nos. 8 and 13.

6. John Nichols, *Literary Anecdotes of the Eighteenth Century*, IV. 39 ff.

7. Nathan Drake, *Essays . . . illustrative of the Rambler, Adventurer, and Idler*, etc., London, 1810, especially Parts IV and V.

8. *Catalogue of a Collection of Early Newspapers and Essayists, . . . presented to the Bodleian Library by the late Rev. Frederick William Hope, M.A., D.C.L.*, Oxford: Clarendon Press, 1865.

9. A similarly unguarded statement is (p. 173) that in the *Connoisseur*, No. 21 "is the only example of deliberate parody in all the eighteenth-century periodicals." It is of no great moment to point out the entirely deliberate parody of "L'Allegro" in *Looker-On*, No. 53; it is of importance, however, that a general warning should be issued against reckless generalizations concerning such a vast and—to American scholars—such an inaccessible body of material.

10. Among others, Palfrey, *History of New England*, III. 60 note, 69 note, 487 note; Sibley, *Harvard Graduates*, II. 17, 130, 240, 266, 280, 304; Winsor, *Memorial History of Boston*, II. 199, 413 note, 433, 495, 500, IV. 531; G. E. Littlefield, *Early Boston Booksellers*, pp. 139–143; S. G. Drake, *History and Antiquities of Boston*, 1856, pp. 459–467, 472 note, 595 and note.

11. "In the description of the Boston old maid—which must be

taken entire if we would comprehend its truthfulness and its characteristic revelation of the time—the gay traveller [Dunton] records what
he saw" (W. B. Weeden, *Economic and Social History of New England*,
I. 299–300). This particular portrait, of which we shall say more later,
may be found in the *Letters from New England*, pp. 98–102, or in the
Life and Errors, I. 102–103.

Whitmore (Introduction to the *Letters*, p. xxiv, Boston, Prince Society, 1867) regards these letters "as unique sketches of New-England
life, honestly drawn, and defective rather than erroneous." Whitmore
also (p. xviii) thinks that "the portraits of Mrs. Breck, Mrs. Green, and
Comfort Wilkins, are descriptions of such Puritans as we may be proud
to claim for Massachusetts."

Throughout this article references to Dunton's *Letters from New
England* are to Whitmore's edition made for the Prince Society, and—
unless the contrary is stated—references to Dunton's *Life and Errors*
are to J. B. Nichols's edition, in two volumes, London, 1818.

12. The sketches of his life in the *Dictionary of National Biography*,
in John Nichols's *Literary Anecdotes of the Eighteenth Century*, v.
59–83, in John Bowyer Nichols's introduction to the 1818 edition of
the *Life and Errors*, in Whitmore's introduction to the *Letters from
New England*, and elsewhere, all rest upon Dunton's own account in
the *Life and Errors*, first published in 1705.

13. Arber, *Term Catalogues*, I. 458.

14. *Life and Errors*, I. 79.

15. In the *Life and Errors* (I. 87) Dunton gives the date November 2; in the *Letters from New England* (p. 16) he has it November 20.
But Sewall (*Diary* for January 28, 1686) records that "Jenner came
from Ile Wight the 13, of November" (5 *Massachusetts Historical Collections*, v. 119). Dunton says (*Letters*, p. 22), "It was on Friday, the
29th October, we began to sail from the Isle of Wight." It happens
that in 1685 the 29th of October fell on Thursday.

16. "Being laid down upon the Bed one Day to repose my self,
Palmer [Dunton's apprentice and servant] comes down to me, and tells
me, I had lost the sight of a very great and strange Creature, which our
Captain call'd an Alligator; this Creature is of a vast length and breadth,
(some say many yards in length:) in colour he is of a dark brown, which
makes him the more imperceptable when he lies as a Trapan in the
Waters. He is of so vast a strength that no Creature is able to make his
Escape from him, if he gets but his Chaps fastened in them; for he has
three Tere of Teeth in his Chaps and so firmly sealed and armed with

Coat of Male, that you may as well shoot at a Rock, or strike against Bars of Iron, as offer to wound him" (*Letters*, p. 35).

17. Introduction to *Letters*, pp. xi, xxii.

18. *History of New England*, III. 487 note 2.

19. *Literary Anecdotes of the Eighteenth Century*, v. 63.

20. *Life and Errors*, I. xi.

21. *Id.*, p. 89. In the *Letters* (p. 49) he says "almost four months." Compare note 23, below. This is disproved by the fact (see p. 22 and note 29, below) that on February 16, 1686, Dunton was given the freedom of Boston and signed his name to the record.

22. *Letters*, p. 69.

23. "I came from Boston on the Fifth of July and was in London on the fifth of August; which was three months shorter than my passage thither" (*Letters*, p. 302).

24. *Letters*, p. 26; *Life and Errors*, I. 86, 88.

25. *Letters*, pp. 53–54; *Life and Errors*, I. 89–90.

26. Captain Roger Clap, Governor of the Castle.

27. On account of the critical state of affairs in England and their bearing on the matter of the charter, the arrival of a ship was just then an event of even more consequence than usual. It is not unlikely that Captain Jenner was particularly expected, for we know that just one year before, on January 28, 1685, "at the opening of this Court the Gouerno^r declard it, y^t on the certeine or generall rumo^{r}s in Mr Jenner, lately arrived, y^t o^r charter was condemned, & judgment entred vp, &c, they lookt at it as an incumbent duty to acquaint the Court wth it, & leaue the consideration of what was or might be necessary to them, &c" (*Massachusetts Colony Records*, v. 465).

Our associate Mr. Henry H. Edes has kindly called my attention to the fact that there is much information about the Jenners in Wyman's *Genealogies and Estates of Charlestown*, I. 551–553.

28. 5 *Massachusetts Historical Collections*, v. 119.

29. *Letters*, p. 65 note. The record, which is herewith reproduced, is as follows:

Witnesse these presents that I ffrancis Burrowes of Bostone Merchant doe binde my selfe, my Execut^{rs} and Administrat^{rs} to Edward Willis Treasurer of the Towne of Bostone in the sume of ffortie pounds in mony that John Dunton booke seller nor any of his ffamilie—shall not be chargable to this towne duringe his or any there abode therein. Witnesse my hand the 16th of ffebruary 1685.

That is sd Burrowes bindes him selfe as aboue to sd Willis & his success[rs] in the Office of a Treasurer, omited in ye due place aboue

Fran: Burroughs

John Dunton

The date in this entry is, of course, 1685–6. The entry is found in a small quarto book in the office of the City Clerk of Boston, who has kindly allowed it to be examined and photographed. The book is that described on p. 12 of City Document No. 171 (1899) as containing Bonds for Security against Strangers, 1679–1700.

30. *Letters*, p. 301; *Life and Errors*, I. 137.

31. *Life and Errors*, I. 138.

32. *Id.*, p. 139.

33. *Id.*, p. 151.

34. "I am informed, that worthy citizen and bookseller, Mr. John Dunton, has made a faithful and painstaking collection [of speeches], which he shortly designs to publish in twelve volumes in folio, illustrated with copper plates. A work highly useful and curious, and altogether worthy of such a hand" (Swift's *Works*, ed. Nichols, London, 1803, III. 65).

35. VI. 182.

36. *Life and Errors*, II. 760 note.

37. John Nichols (*Literary Anecdotes of the Eighteenth Century*, V. 78 note) has "auction bookseller," which J. B. Nichols (*Life and Errors*, I. vi) repeats. But the reading in the annotated *Dunciad* (second edition) of 1729 (p. 107 note) is "broken bookseller." So it is in Elwin and Courthope's edition (IV. 140 note).

38. Pope's *Works*, ed. Elwin and Courthope, IV. 140 note.

39. *Life and Errors*, II. 465.

40. *Id.*, chap. XII, *passim*.

41. *Id.*, II. 759. The two letters from Key which Nichols reprints (*Life and Errors*, II. 758–759) are distinctly those of a boon companion, not of a malicious critic.

42. The fourth "Project" in the second part of *Athenianism* (1710), for example.

43. Nichols, *Literary Anecdotes of the Eighteenth Century*, IV. 88 note.

44. *Remarks and Collections of Thomas Hearne*, ed. C. E. Doble, Oxford (Oxford Historical Society), 1886, II. 26.

45. "Philaret (or Lover of Vertue) was the Name that Cloris gave me in all the Letters she sent to me during the Time of our Correspondence" (Dunton's *Athenianism*, 1710, p. 5 note). Cloris was Elizabeth Singer, afterwards Mrs. Rowe, "die göttliche Rowe," with whom Dunton enjoyed a Platonic correspondence, if the evidence of his "Character of Madam Singer" (the first of the "Projects" in his *Athenianism*) can be relied upon.

46. *Letters*, pp. 56–57.

47. His own word.

48. Now Chelsea.

49. Now Weymouth.

50. *Letters*, p. 221.

51. Pp. 129, 130.

52. *Letters*, p. 249.

53. In it, however, Dunton writes, "In a few weeks I hope to take my Leave of this New World" (*Letters*, p. 298).

54. The | *Life and Errors* | Of | *John Dunton* | *Late Citizen of London;* | *Written by Himself in Solitude.* | *With an Idea of a New Life;* | *Wherein is Shewn* | *How he'd Think, Speak, and Act, might he* | *Live over his Days again:* | *Intermix'd with the* | *New Discoveries* | *The Author has made* | *In his Travels Abroad,* | *And in his* | *Private Conversation at Home.* | *Together with the Lives and Characters of a Thou-|sand Persons now Living in London, &c.* | *Digested into Seven Stages, with their Respective Ideas.* | *He that has all his own Mistakes confest,* | *Stands next to him that never has transgrest,* | *And will be censur'd for a Fool by none,* | *But they who see no Errors of their own.* | *Foe's Satyr upon himself, P. 6.* | London: Printed for S. Malthus, 1705.

The copy formerly owned by Charles Eliot Norton is now in the Harvard College Library.

On the verso of p. 251 is advertised—

Preparing for the PRESS,

A Ramble through Six Kingdoms,

BY

JOHN DUNTON

LATE

Citizen of LONDON

Wherein he relates, 1. His *Juvenile* Travels. 2. The History of his *Sea Voyages*. 3. His *Conversation* in Foreign Parts.

With *Characters of Men and Women*, and almost ev'ry thing he Saw or Convers'd with.

The like Discoveries (in such a Method) never made by any Traveller before.

Illustrated with *Fourty Cuts*, representing the most pleasant Passages in the whole Adventure.

With *Recommendatory Poems*, written by the chief Wits in both Universities.

This Work will be finish'd by next *Michaelmas* and will be 2s. 6d. bound.

55. Second Series, II. 97–124. About one-third of the account is omitted without notice, the text is "improved" somewhat in the manner of Sparks, and the paragraphing is greatly changed.

56. Even the edition of 1818, however, has omissions, generally not indicated: p. 98, character of Mr. C. (cf. ed. 1705, p. 131); p. 114, a paragraph omitted (cf. ed. 1705, pp. 156–157, and *Letters*, pp. 141–142); p. 122, one clause omitted (cf. ed. 1705, pp. 168–169); p. 133, a dialogue of about two and one-half pages on Platonic love omitted (cf. ed. 1705, pp. 125–128). These omitted passages, if restored, would make the book coarser and more discursive; in other words, more like the Chester MS. of the Letters.

57. MS. Rawl., Miscel. 71 and 72. See *Life and Errors*, II. 753–760. These manuscripts contain Dunton's version of the Letters from New England, and more than eighty other pieces, most of which seem to be either actual letters to or from Dunton, or parts of fictitious correspondence. Often they are love letters, with answers in shorthand. There would seem to be material here for a more thorough study of Dunton's life and works than has yet been made.

58. This transcript, which I shall refer to as the Chester MS., is now in the possession of the New England Historic Genealogical Society, the Librarian of which has kindly allowed me to consult it. The different letters are paged separately; in referring to the MS., accordingly, the letter as well as the page is specified.

59. *Letters*, pp. 24 ff.

60. There is no description of Medford in the *Letters*: perhaps because Josselyn has none. Whitmore noted (pp. 66–69) that Dunton's description of Boston is borrowed from Josselyn.

61. The question where Josselyn got his descriptions of these towns

is interesting. Some of them (Boston, Charlestown, New-Town, Lynn, Dorchester, Roxbury, Wenham, and Ipswich) he could have got, either wholly or in part, from Johnson's *Wonder-Working Providence* (1654); in all of them except the description of Wenham he may have borrowed from Wood's *New Englands Prospect* (1634). But of the three books (Wood, Johnson, and Josselyn) we know that Dunton must have used Josselyn. For convenience a list of these descriptions of towns is added, with page references to Wood (as edited by Charles Deane in 1865 for the Prince Society), Johnson (ed. J. F. Jameson, New York, 1910) and Josselyn (Veazie's edition):

Boston	Wood	41–42	Johnson	70–71	Josselyn	124–125
Charlestown	"	43	"	68–69	"	126
New-Town	"	43	"	90	"	127
Winnisimet	"	44	"	—	"	128
Lynn	"	45	"	73	"	128
Nantascot	"	3	"	—	"	122–123
Wissaguset	"	40	"	—	"	123
Braintree	"	40	"	—	"	123
Dorchester	"	41	"	69–70	"	123–124
Roxbury	"	41	"	71–72	"	124
Wenham	"	—	"	226	"	129–130
Ipswich or Agawam	"	48–49	"	96	"	129

It is curious that Josselyn follows Wood's order very closely in describing these towns, and that Dunton follows Josselyn's order with equal closeness.

62. So in Whitmore.

63. Genuineness *as letters*, I mean. The identity of the author is not being called in question.

64. P. iv.

65. Pp. 305–306.

66. P. 259.

67. *Letters*, p. 65.

68. Everett Kimball, *The Public Life of Joseph Dudley* (Harvard Historical Studies), New York, 1911, pp. 24–25.

69. *Letters*, p. 137.

70. Sewall's *Diary* for May 14, 1686 (1. 137–139). What Randolph brought was the exemplification of the judgment against the charter and the commission for the new government. Sewall (*Diary* for May 17, 1686) describes the meeting at which Dudley showed these papers

and announced to the General Court that he "could treat them no longer as Governour and Company."

71. *Letters*, pp. 194 ff.

72. Sibley, No. 32. Cotton Mather's *Life of John Eliot* was first published at Boston in 1691. In the same year Dunton brought out a second edition in London. According to advertisements in the *Athenian Mercury* this second edition seems to have appeared on or about August 3, 1691 (*Athenian Mercury*, III, Nos. 2 and 3). There was a third edition (London: John Dunton) in 1694, and the work was also reprinted in the *Magnalia*. Which of these Dunton used I do not know.

73. "Having taken my leave of Mr. Cotton and Nathaniel Mather (whose Life I afterwards Printed) and after that, of their Reverend Father, I return'd home hugely pleas'd with my first Visit" (p. 75).

74. Sibley, No. 7. This work, "Printed by J. Astwood for J. Dunton, 1689," was entered in Trinity Term, 1689 (Arber, *Term Catalogues*, II. 268). Nathaniel Mather died October 17, 1688.

75. *Magnalia*, ed. 1702, bk. iii. pp. 194–195.

76. *Letters*, p. 75.

77. *Diary* for August 20, 1697 (7 *Massachusetts Historical Collections*, VII. 227). It seems almost impossible that "a Church-History of New England" can refer to any of Cotton Mather's works except the *Magnalia*, which is regularly referred to by that title in the *Diary* and which is outlined under that title ("A Schæme of his Church-History of New England") in Cotton Mather's *Johannes in Eremo*, 1695 (Sibley, No. 52).

78. *Letters*, p. 112.

79. P. 112. In the first edition of the *Life and Errors* (p. 147) "Sir Daniel" and "More Reformation" are printed in capitals; in the Chester MS. (Letter iii, pp. 52–53), they are not.

80. Arber, *Term Catalogues*, III. 371. The Harvard College Library has a copy which, though quite clearly of the first edition, has the date trimmed off. Note that the motto on the title-page of the *Life and Errors* is from Defoe's *More Reformation*, which is there referred to by its sub-title (see p. 257 note 54, above).

81. Possibly an exception should be made to this generalization. In his account (p. 194) of John Eliot, Dunton, who is following Cotton Mather's account very closely, writes: "And this Wife of his Youth [Eliot's] became also the Staff of his Age, and left him not *until about half a year ago.*" The italics are mine. Cotton Mather had written

(*Life of Eliot*, London [John Dunton], 1694, p. 7; *Magnalia*, ed. 1702, bk. iii. p. 173), "she left him not until about three or four Years before his own Departure unto those Heavenly Regions where they now together see light." This is very puzzling. John Eliot's wife died March 22, 1687 (Savage, *Genealogical Dictionary*, II. 110). "About half a year" after that takes us to September, 1687, as the approximate date when that particular sentence was written. But Dunton is quoting an account which, presumably, was not accessible to him before 1691. Why, when he was changing Mather's words, he did not put the date back so that it would agree with the supposed date of his letter, is very hard to see.

82. "And thus, Reader, I have given you the humours of a far different sort of Ladies from the former" (p. 116). So on pp. 102 and 105. The word "Reader" is used in the corresponding passages (pp. 103, 106, 108) of the *Life and Errors*. I conjecture that Dunton neglected to remove the word when he elaborated these passages from the *Life and Errors*.

83. The point is made clearer by an examination of the Chester MS. The parts which Whitmore omits are, in almost every case, destructive of the idea that Dunton's chapters are actual letters.

84. Chester MS., Letter i, p. 12. The poem, if inserted in the *Letters*, would be on p. 13, after the sentence which now concludes the paragraph.

85. This was Alexander Radcliffe's *Bacchanalia Cœlestia: a Poem, in Praise of Punch, compos'd by the Gods and Goddesses*, 1680. It was reprinted in *The Ramble: an anti-heroick Poem. Together with some Terrestrial Hymns and Carnal Ejaculations*, 1682. There is a short sketch of Alexander Radcliffe in the *Dictionary of National Biography*. It is to be noted that the sub-title of Radcliffe's poem explains the sentence referred to in the previous note.

86. Including one as important as Randolph, whom Dunton calls Randal (*Life and Errors*, ed. 1705, p. 152). He also has Higgins for Higginson and Geery for Gerrish (*Letters*, pp. 254–255, 272), although he says that he was entertained by both. Yet of course the spelling of proper names in the seventeenth century, even by their owners, was vagarious.

87. Sewall's *Diary* for March 17, 1686 (I. 128).

88. *Letters*, pp. 118 ff. James Morgan, for the crime of murder, was executed on March 11, 1686.

89. "But before I leave off this subject, I must bring Morgan to his

Execution, whither I rid with Mr. Cotton Mather, after the Sermon was ended. Some thousands of the People following to see the Execution. As I rid along I had several glimpses of poor Morgan, as he went" (*Letters*, p. 135).

90. "Mr. Cotton Mather accompanied James Morgan to the place of Execution and prayed with him there" (Sewall's *Diary*, March 11, 1686, 1. 126).

"There has been since, a second Edition of the Book [the sermons on Morgan's crime and punishment preached by Increase Mather, Joshua Moody, and Cotton Mather. First edition, Boston, 1686; second edition, Boston, 1687], with a Copy of my Discourse with the poor Malefactor walking to his Execution added at the End" (Cotton Mather's *Diary* for February 12, 1686, 7 *Massachusetts Historical Collections*, VII. 123). Mather's note is written in the margin. For an account of this book see Sibley, No. 5, and also p. 268 note 138, below.

91. "But from the House of Mourning, I rambled to the House of Feasting; for Mr. York, Mr. King, with Madam Brick, Mrs. Green, Mrs. Toy, the Damsell [Comfort Wilkins] and my self, took a Ramble to a place call'd Governour's Island, about a mile from Boston, to see a whole Hog roasted, as did several other Bostonians. We went all in a Boat; and having treated the Fair Sex, returned in the Evening" (*Letters*, p. 137).

92. Sewall's *Diary*, February 1, 3, 7, 12, 13; March 12 (1. 120, 121, 126–127).

93. Sewall's *Diary*, March 11, 1686 (1. 126).

94. *Letters*, p. 105. On his title-page (p. [5]), Dunton announces "Particular Characters of Men and Women"; in outlining his third letter he proposes to write "The Character of my Boston Landlord, his Wife and Daughter" and to "conclude with the character of Madam Brick as the Flower of Boston, and some other Ladyes" (p. 57). And cf. pp. 61, 63, 88, 93, 98, 102, 110, 112, 281.

95. The character becomes more intelligible as a manifestation of its time if we recall the fact that the influence of classicism was favorable to characterization by rather strict adherence to type. From Aristotle onward, in fact, there is a series of explicit instructions and criticisms on this point. The following passage, from Jeremy Collier's *Short View of the Immorality and Profaneness of the English Stage* (1698), is a good seventeenth-century example:

The propriety of *Manners* consists in a Conformity of Practise and Principle; of Nature, and Behaviour. For the purpose: An old Man must not appear with the Profuseness and Levity of Youth; A Gentleman must not talk like a Clown, nor a Country Girl like a Town Jilt. And when the *Characters* are feign'd 'tis *Horace's* Rule to keep them Uniform, and consistent, and agreeable to their first setting out. The *Poet* must be careful to hold his *Persons* tight to their *Calling* and pretentions. He must not shift, and shuffle their Understandings; Let them skip from Wits to Blockheads, nor from Courtiers to Pedants. On the other hand. If their business is playing the Fool, keep them strictly to their Duty, and never indulge them in fine Sentences. To manage otherwise, is to disert *Nature*, and makes the *Play* appear monstrous, and Chimerical. So that instead of an *Image of Life*, 'tis rather an Image of Impossibility (third edition, 1698, pp. 218–219).

96. P. 15.

97. *Sir Thomas Overbury | His | Wife. | With | Addition Of | many new Elegies upon his | untimely and much lamented death. | As Also | New Newes, and diuers more Characters, | (neuer before annexed) written by him-|selfe and other learned Gentlemen. | The ninth impression augmented. | London, | Printed by Edward Griffin for Laurence L'isle, and | are to be sold at his shop at the Tigers head in | Pauls Churchyard, 1616* (British Museum, 12331. aa. 46).

98. *Overbury's Miscellaneous Works*, ed. E. F. Rimbault (Library of Old Authors), London, 1856, pp. 168–169.

99. Overbury himself has a character of a prison; Earle (1628) has characters of a tavern, a bowling-alley, Paul's Walk, and a prison; and of the thirty-six characters in Donald Lupton's *London and the Country Carbonadoed, and Quartred into Seuerall Characters* (1632) only nine are of people. The last book, however, is exceptional in this respect.

100. There are definitions of the character in S. Person's *An Anatomicall Lecture of Man . . . in Essays and Characters*, 1664; Richard Flecknoe's *Fifty-five Enigmatical Characters*, 1665; *Seventy-eight Characters of so many Vertuous and Vitious Persons*, 1677; Sir Roger L'Estrange's "A Brief History of the Times . . . in a Preface to the Third Volume of Observators," 1687.

101. "Every line is a sentence, & every two a period . . . ; tis all *matter*, and to the *matter*, and has nothing of superfluity, nothing of circumlocution" (Flecknoe).

"Here a man writes a great deal in a little room" (Person).

102. That the character strives for wit has already appeared from the definitions of Overbury and Johnson.

103. "It not only delights but teaches and moves withall, and is a *Sermon* as well as Picture to every one" (Flecknoe).

104. "It is the Counterpane of Natures Book, and also of each Individuum" (Person).

"The subject of them is taken from the observations of several *Natures*, *Humors*, and *Dispositions*; and whilst I name no body, let no body name themselves if they be wise" (*Seventy-eight Characters*).

"A Character . . . Shoots *Hail-Shot*, and *Strikes* a great many *more* than ever the *Marks-man*, either *Aim'd* at, or *Dreamt* of" (L'Estrange).

This last phase of the matter is excellently put in the dialogue about the "Character-Coat" in Defoe's *Review* (vol. VII, No. 15) reprinted in Mr. Andrew McFarland Davis's "A Bibliographical Puzzle" (*Publications of the Colonial Society of Massachusetts*, XIII. 9–10).

105. "It extols to *Heaven*, or depresses into *Hell*; having no mid'-place for *Purgatory* left" (Flecknoe).

106. To bring to a close this explanation of the character there is reprinted below John Earle's portrait of "A Modest Man," which appeared in 1628 in the *Microcosmography*:

A MODEST MAN

Is a far finer man than he knows of; one that shewes better to all men then himselfe, and so much the better to al men, as lesse to himselfe: for no quality sets a man off like this, and commends him more against his will: And he can put up any injury sooner then this, (as he cals it) your Irony. You shall heare him confute his commenders, and giving reasons how much they are mistaken, and is angry almost, if they do not beleeve him. Nothing threatens him so much as great expectation, which he thinks more prejudiciall then your under-opinion, because it is easier to make that false then this true. He is one that sneaks from a good action, as one that had pilfered, and dare not justifie it, and is more blushingly deprehended in this, then others in sin. That counts al publike declarings of himselfe but so many penances before the people, and the more you applaud him, the more you abash him, and he recovers not his face a moneth after. One that is easie to like anything of another man's, and thinkes all hee knowes not of him better then that he knowes. He excuses that to you, which another would impute, and if you pardon him, is satisfied. One that stands in no opinion because it is his owne, but suspects it rather, because it is his owne, and is confuted, and thankes you. Hee sees nothing more willingly then his errors; and it is his error sometimes to be too soone perswaded. He is content to be Auditor, where hee only can speake, and content to goe away, and thinke himselfe instructed. No man is so weake that he is ashamed to learne of, and is lesse ashamed to confesse it: and he findes many times even in the dust, what others overlooke and lose. Every man's presence is a kinde of bridle to him, to stop the roving of his tongue and passions: and even impudent men looke for this reverence from him, and distaste that in him, which they suffer in themselves, as one in whom vice is ill-favoured, and shewes more scurvily then another. And hee is coward to nothing more then an ill tongue, and whosoever dare lye on him hath power over him, and if you take him by his looke, he is guilty. The maine ambition of his life is not to be discredited: and for other things, his desires are more limited then his fortunes, which he thinkes preferment though never so meane, and that he is to doe something to deserve this. Hee is too tender to venter on great places, and would not hurt a dignity to helpe himselfe. If he doe, it was the violence of his friends constrained him, and how hardly soever hee obtaine it, he was harder perswaded to seeke it.

107. E. C. Baldwin's bibliography of character-books (*Publications of the Modern Language Association of America*, New Series, XII. No. 1, pp. 104–114), though the largest in print, could be supplemented by hundreds of other titles. The collections and notes of Philip Bliss, appended to his edition (London, 1811) of Earle's *Microcosmography*, are very useful. Some of the best characters are collected in Henry Morley's *Character Writings of the Seventeenth Century* (Morley's Universal Library, London, 1891).

108. *Letters*, pp. 88–89.

109. I have used Pickering's edition, London, 1840. The character there occupies pages 88–91.

110. Lib. 13 de Trinitat. c. 3. The footnote is Fuller's.

111. Of the Class of 1669. Sibley (*Harvard Graduates*, II. 266) cites Dunton's character of Epes.

112. I. 128. Cf. note 140 on p. 268, below.

113. The last sentence is from "A Contemplative Man"; the rest is from "A Downright Scholar" (*Microcosmography*, ed. 1811, pp. 61–63, 93).

114. *Letters*, pp. 11–12, 120–121, 169–170. The sources are indicated in the table (pp. 49–54).

115. Whitmore has "Beds." Here, and several times elsewhere, Dunton is so faithful to the original that one can safely emend Whitmore's text.

116. The three others are Mrs. Ab——l; Doll S——der; and Mrs. ——, who in the *Life and Errors* (I. 110–111) is called Mrs. H. For their sources, see the table, pp. 49–54.

117. *Letters*, p. 106 note.

118. The First Church of Boston. Whitmore might have added that Dunton's Madam Brick had been a widow two years (*Letters*, p. 110). Whether this is true of Mrs. Robert Breck I do not know.

Joanna Mason, the daughter of Arthur and Joanna (Parker) Mason, was born March 26, 1664 (*Boston Record Commissioners' Reports*, IX. 92). The date of her marriage to Robert Breck seems not to be known. Of her two children, the elder, Joanna, was born June 12, 1681 (IX. 154), and the younger, Robert, on April 30, 1683 (IX. 159). The Widow Brick married Michael Perry on July 12, 1694 (IX. 218).

119. The first edition appears to have been printed at Oxford in 1673. The British Museum has a copy of the second edition (Oxford, 1673) and of the third edition (Oxford, 1675). The Harvard College Library has a copy of the fifth edition (Oxford, 1677) as well as a folio volume, very well printed "at the Theater in Oxford" in 1684, containing *The Ladies Calling* as the first piece in *The Second Part Of The Works Of the Learned and Pious Author Of The Whole Duty of Man*.

On the much disputed authorship of *The Whole Duty of Man*, see the Introduction to Pickering's edition of it (1842); Hearne's *Remarks and Collections*, ed. C. E. Doble, Oxford Historical Society, I. 17, 19, 282, 324; II. 299; IV. 420; C. E. Doble in the *Academy* (1882), II. 348, 364, 382; and the articles in the *Dictionary of National Biography* on Richard Allestree, Richard Sterne, and John Fell. Mr. Doble thinks that *The Whole Duty of Man* was written by Sterne and revised by Fell.

120. It will be observed that Dunton uses, in addition to *The Ladies Calling*, two short passages from Thomas Fuller's character of "The Good Widow" in *The Holy and the Profane State* (1642).

121. Fuller, "The Good Widow" (*Holy and Profane State*, ed. 1840, p. 19).

122. *Id.*

123. So Whitmore, and so Chester MS., Letter iii, p. 48. One would expect "she," as in *The Ladies Calling*.

124. Whitmore notes: "Here the manuscript is imperfect."

125. But to be found on p. 8 of Chester MS., Letter i.

126. This character originally appeared in the sixth edition (1615) of the Overbury collection, and is regularly spoken of, in a loose way, as Overbury's. But in the second edition (1615) of John Stephens's *New Essayes and Characters*, a person who signs himself I. Cocke claims as his own three of the Overbury characters, of which one is the

Almanac-maker. There is a copy of Stephens's book in the Harvard College Library.

127. Omitted by Whitmore. Chester MS., Letter i, pp. 23–24.

128. John Josselyn, *An Account of Two Voyages to New England, Made during the years 1638, 1663*, Boston, William Veazie, 1865.

129. *Letter | From | New-England | Concerning their Customs, Manners, | And | Religion. | . . . . | London. | Printed for Randolph Taylor near Stationers Hall, 1682.* Reprinted in facsimile by the Club for Colonial Reprints of Providence, Rhode Island, Providence, 1905. Edited by George Parker Winship.

130. Dunton copies Josselyn's statements of the punishments; *i.e.,* p. 72, first paragraph as far as the colon; all of the second paragraph; the first sentence in the third; as far as the semicolon in the fourth; all of the last; the first sentence in the first paragraph on p. 73; the first sentence in the second paragraph on p. 73.

131. Omitted by Whitmore. Chester MS., Letter iii, pp. 28–29.

132. *A | Collection | Of the choicest | Epigrams | And | Characters | of | Richard Flecknoe. | Being rather a New Work, | then a New Impression | of the Old. | Printed for the Author 1673,* p. 34. There is a copy in the Harvard College Library.

133. In the *Life and Errors* (pp. 110–111) she is called Mrs. H——.

134. Bodleian Library. Wood 868. (5.)

135. Whitmore divides the third letter into two parts.

136. These borrowings are, of course, acknowledged by Dunton.

137. *A Sermon | Occasioned by the Execution of | a man found Guilty of | Murder | Preached at Boston in N. E. March 11th 168⅚ | Together with the Confession, Last Expressions, | & solemn Warning of that Murderer to all per-|sons; especially to Young men, to beware of those | Sins which brought him to his miserable End. | By Increase Mather, Teacher of | Church of Christ. | The Second Edition. | [texts: Deut. xix. 20, 21; Prov. xxviii. 17] | Boston, Printed by R. P. Sold by J. Brunning | Bookseller, at his Shop at the Corner of the | Prison-Lane next the Exchange. Anno 1687.*

This seems to serve as the general title for the volume; at least, the copy in the Harvard College Library, which is paged continuously, has no other title at the beginning. Increase Mather's sermon occupies pp. 1–36. Then comes "The | Call of the Gospel | Applyed | Unto All men in general, and | Unto a Condemned Malefactor in particular. | In a Sermon, Preached on the 7th | Day of March. 1686. | At the Request, and in the Hearing of a man under | a just Sentence of Death for the

horrid Sin of / Murder. / By Cotton Mather. / Pastor to a Church at
Boston in N. E. / The Second Edition. / [text] / [motto] / Printed at
Boston, by Richard Pierce. 1687." Cotton Mather's sermon occupies
pp. 37–82, and is followed by "An / Exhortation / To A Condemned /
Malefactor / Delivered March the 7th 1686. / By Joshua Moody,
Preacher of / the Gospel at Boston in New-England. / [texts] / Printed
at Boston, by R. P. Anno 1687." Moody's sermon occupies pp. 83–113.
Then follows (p. 114) an address from "The Printer to the Reader,"
which is signed "R. P." Then comes (pp. 115–124) "The Discourse
of the Minister with / James Morgan on the Way to his Execution."

138. *A Key into the Language of America: Or, An help to the Language of the Natives in that part of America, called New-England. Together, with briefe Observations of the Customes, Manners and Worships,
etc. of the aforesaid Natives, . . . By Roger Williams . . . London, . . .
1643.* (Reprinted by the Narragansett Club, Fifth Series, Volume 1.
Providence, 1866). My references, like Whitmore's, are to the numbering of the volume, which contains other tracts besides the *Key*.

139. Through the kindness of Professor W. W. Lawrence of Columbia University, Mr. Will T. Hale transcribed for me from the copy
of the original edition in the New York Public Library the portions of
Eliot's book here used by Dunton. The text of Eliot is copied almost
verbatim.
On the date of the original, Sabin (No. 22148) remarks: "The date
of 1665 which has been assigned to it, is doubtless incorrect, as on page
25 following Eliot speaks of John Speen and Anthony as living in 1670,
whose 'Dying Speeches' are given in the tract named."

140. From his account in the Letters of the visit to Salem, Dunton
omits a character of Mr. Daniel Epes (*Life and Errors*, p. 128), which
is taken from Earle's "A Down-right Scholar" (*Microcosmography*,
1811, pp. 61–64). Whitmore (p. 256 note) notices the omission, quotes
the character of Mr. Epes and the two following paragraphs from the
Life and Errors, and observes that they "doubtless should be in the
text" of the Letters at this point. But he strangely fails to remember
that the third of these paragraphs, very slightly modified to make it fit
Boston instead of Salem, *had* been incorporated in the Letters and is to
be found on pp. 62–63 of his own edition.

141. By Whitmore, in his Introduction, p. xxiii.

142. Whether Dunton did this out of self-esteem and the desire to
steal a reputation, or with the wish to soften formal exposition into
something more entertaining, does not for the moment concern us.
Probably his motives were mixed.

143. "A King turn'd Thresher. By Mr. Dunton" (*Athenianism*, pp. 213–215; *Maggots*, pp. 94–96); "A Covetous old Fellow having taken Occasion to hang himself a little; another comes in, in the Nick, and cuts him down; but instead of thanking him for his Life, he accuses him for spoiling the Rope.—By Mr. Dunton" (*Athenianism*, p. 215; *Maggots*, pp. 68–70); "On the Bear-fac'd Lady. By Mr. Dunton" (*Athenianism*, pp. 218–220; *Maggots*, pp. 29–31); "The Innocent Fraud: Or, the Lyar in Mode and Figure. By Mr. Dunton" (*Athenianism*, pp. 221–222; *Maggots*, pp. 62–63).

144. *Maggots: | Or, | Poems | On | Several | Subjects, | Never before Handled. | By a Schollar. | London, | Printed for John Dunton, at the Sign | of the Black Raven, at the Corner of Princes | Street, near the Royal Exchange. 1685.*

There is a copy in the Harvard College Library.

145. *Life and Errors*, I. 187.

146. Among the earlier characters drawn on are Earle's "Grave Divine," which furnishes parts of the sketches of Mr. Spademan (pp. 140–141), Mr. Lobb (p. 175), Mr. Trail (p. 176); Earle's "Modest Man," which becomes Mr. Cleave (p. 228) and also furnishes a part of Mr. Samuel Hool (p. 255); and Earle's "Staid Man," parts of which go to make up Mr. Grantham (p. 246), Mr. Darby (p. 247), and Mr. Littlebury (p. 256). Bishop Hall's characters are also used: his "Humble Man" for parts of Mr. Merreal (p. 254) and Mr. Sheafe (p. 254), and his "Truly-Noble" man in Mr. Proctor (pp. 255–256) and in parts of Mr. Merreal (p. 254), Mr. Sheafe (p. 254), and Mr. Samuel Hool (p. 255). S. Malthus (p. 459), who published Dunton's *Life and Errors*, could hardly have been pleased to find on reading it that she was thought to combine the faults of Earle's "Detractor" and his "She Precise Hyprocrite."

147. See E. C. Baldwin, *Character Books of the Seventeenth Century in Relation to the Development of the Novel*, Western Reserve Bulletin, October, 1900; H. S. Canby, *The Short Story in English*, New York, 1909, especially Chapters viii and ix; F. W. Chandler, *The Literature of Roguery*, Boston and New York, 1907, especially Chapter vii; Martha Pike Conant, *The Oriental Tale in England in the Eighteenth Century*, New York, 1908, especially Chapter iv; W. L. Cross, *The Development of the English Novel*, New York, 1899; Rudolf Furst, *Die Vorläufer der Modernen Novelle im achtzehnten Jahrhundert*, Halle, 1897; Charlotte Morgan, *The Rise of the Novel of Manners*, New York, 1911 (good bibliography); Sir Walter Raleigh, *The English Novel*, New York, 1904.

148. *Overbury's Miscellaneous Works*, ed. E. F. Rimbault, London, 1856, pp. 168–169.

149. Geffray Mynshul, *Essayes and Characters of a Prison and Prisoners*, Edinburgh, 1821, pp. 14–17.

150. In *The Scholars Guide from the Accidence to the University*, p. 15.

151. Original editions of Breton's works are extremely rare. Most of them are reprinted in A. B. Grosart's *Works in Verse and Prose of Nicholas Breton*, 2 vols., Edinburgh, privately printed, 1879 ("Chertsey Worthies' Library"). My references are to this edition.

152. Grosart, II. *q*, 4.

153. *The Scholars Guide*, p. 17.

154. Of these Love only is consistently neuter: Peace and Honor are several times made feminine.

155. Like the final one in the extract on p. 64.

156. Grosart, II. *q*, 9.

157. *Id.*, *r*, 5.

158. It is proper to note, however, that Breton wrote some characters which are free from quadrumania. This is the case in *A Discourse of a Scholler and a Souldier*, 1599, and in *Fantasticks*, 1626. The latter work, by the way, throws some very interesting light on Jacobean daily life, especially on the question of the time at which various things were done. For example, at five o'clock in the morning "the Schollers are up and going to schoole" (Grosart, II. *t*, 13).

159. Grosart, II. *u*, 16.

160. *Id.*, *f*. A work called *The Figure of Foure*, licensed in 1597 (Arber's *Transcript*, III. 96), is presumed to be by Breton. No earlier edition than 1631–1636 is known, however, and of that only the second part (1636). That contains an address "To the Reader" which is signed N. B.

161. Perhaps quadrumania has seized me, but I cannot forbear suggesting that here Breton may have intentionally varied the familiar "century" by adding another four.

162. Grosart, II. *f*, 5.

163. *Id.*, *f*, 8.

164. The Council consisted of twenty-eight members, as follows: "for the Territory called the Territory of the Massachusetts Bay," James Bowdoin, Benjamin Greenleaf, John Hancock, Joseph Gerrish, Jedediah Foster, Michael Farley, Joseph Palmer, Jabez Fisher, James

Pitts, Caleb Cushing, John Winthrop, John Adams, James Prescott, Thomas Cushing, Benjamin Lincoln, John Whitcomb, Samuel Adams, Eldad Taylor; for the territory formerly called New Plymouth, William Seaver, Walter Spooner, James Otis, Robert Treat Paine; for the territory formerly called the Province of Maine, Benjamin Chadbourne, Enoch Freeman, Charles Chauncy; for the territory lying between the River Sagadahock and Nova-Scotia, Dr. John Taylor; at large, Moses Gill, Dr. Samuel Holten. (*A Journal of the Honorable House of Representatives*, etc., Watertown, 1775, p. 6.)

165. The original records (Massachusetts Archives, Vol. vi, f. 460, and cxxxvii, ff. 14–15) are in the office of the Secretary of the Commonwealth at the State House. The printed record, *A Journal of the Honorable House of Representatives*, Watertown, 1775, is in the Harvard College Library and the library of the Massachusetts Historical Society.

166. On the later changes in the seal (whereby the motto is not affected), see W. H. Whitmore in Commonwealth of Massachusetts, House Document No. 345 (1885); E. H. Garrett, "The Coat of Arms and Great Seal of Massachusetts" in the *New England Magazine* for 1901, xxiii. 623 ff. Mr. Garrett's article has to do wholly with the Indian and with the arm and sword in the crest. This arm, by the way, takes on additional significance when one remembers the first four words of the motto in their relation to the word *Ense*.

167. See C. E. Merriam, *A History of American Political Theories*, New York, 1906, especially Chapter ii; H. F. Russell Smith, *Harrington and his Oceana, A Study of a Seventeenth Century Utopia and its Influence in America*, Cambridge [England], 1914, especially Chapter viii.

168. *Works*, iv. 15.

169. The best short account of Sidney's life is that by Professor C. H. Firth in the *Dictionary of National Biography*. A fuller biography is A. C. Ewald's *Life and Times of the Hon. Algernon Sydney*, 2 vols., London, 1873.

170. Blencowe, *Sydney Papers*, p. 237.

171. On the phrase "in albo," see *Oxford Dictionary, s.v.* Album, 2.

172. Blencowe, *Sydney Papers*, pp. 209–211. Almost exactly the same version of the affair is given in an "extract from a manuscript of Lord Leicester in the possession of Mr. Lambard": "Saturday, 28 July, I returned his visit [Mr. Pedicombe's visit is meant], and falling into discourse about my said son, and of our King's displeasure to him, he sayed, that according to the usages of Germany and Denmark, the uni-

versity of Copenhagen had brought to my son a new Album, which is a book, wherein the university desired him to write some word or motto, and to sign his name in that booke, and that my said son had written in Albo, these words,

'*Manus haec inimica tyrannis,*'

and set his name to it, which, says Mr. Pedicombe, being written in the Album of the said university, must needs be knowne to many, and may doe your son somme hurt, because he hath declared himself to be a defender of the Commonwealth" (Blencowe, *Sydney Papers*, p. 210).

173. *Id.*, 216.

174. For a short general account (with a bibliography) of English political theory in the late seventeenth century, see A. L. Smith, in the *Cambridge Modern History*, vi. chap. 23. W. A. Dunning, *A History of Political Theories from Luther to Montesquieu*, New York, 1905, is clear and convenient, but often—as in his treatment of Sidney—slight. G. P. Gooch's *Political Thought in England from Bacon to Halifax*, London, 1914, is an excellent little book. Among the more thorough treatments of the subject two complementary volumes in the Cambridge [England] Historical Essays are pre-eminent: G. P. Gooch, *The History of English Democratic Ideas in the Seventeenth Century*, Cambridge, 1898 (see, especially, chap. x); and J. N. Figgis, *The Theory of the Divine Right of Kings*, Cambridge, 1896.

175. For a good account of Filmer, see Figgis, *Divine Right of Kings*, pp. 146 ff.

176. As Ewald does at considerable length in his final chapter. The page numbers in the following summary refer to the edition of 1704.

177. Chapter ii, Section 18, p. 125.

178. Chapter iii, Section 33, p. 369.

179. Chapter i, Section 19, p. 50.

180. *Id.*, Section 3, p. 61.

181. *Id.*, Section 2, p. 4.

182. Chapter iii, Section 11, p. 273.

183. *Id.*, Section 36, p. 376.

184. *Id.*, Section 25, p. 333.

185. *Id.*, Section 36, p. 379.

186. On Thomas Hollis of Lincoln's Inn the principal authorities are the Hollis Papers (especially Hollis's correspondence with Mayhew), in the possession of the Massachusetts Historical Society; Archdeacon

COLLECTED STUDIES

Blackburne's *Memoir of Thomas Hollis*, 2 vols., London, 1780; Josiah Quincy, *History of Harvard University*, II. 144–147; Edwin Cannan, in the *Dictionary of National Biography*.

187. "The library contained about five thousand volumes, all of which were consumed, except a few books in the hands of the members of the House; and two donations, one made by our late honorable Lieutenant-Governor Dummer, to the value of 50*l* sterling; the other of fifty-six volumes, by the present worthy Thomas Hollis, Esq., F. R. S., of London, to whom we have been annually obliged for valuable additions to our late Library; which donations, being but lately received, had not the proper boxes prepared for them; and so escaped the general ruin" (*Massachusetts Gazette*, February 2, 1764, quoted by Josiah Quincy, *History of Harvard University*, II. 482).

188. In regard to the bindings of his books Hollis wrote to President Holyoke, June 24, 1765: "The bindings of books are little regarded by me for my own proper library; but by long experience I have found it necessary to attend to them for other libraries; having thereby drawn notice, with preservation, on many excellent books, or curious, which, it is probable, would else have passed unheeded and neglected" (Blackburne's *Hollis*, II. 603).

On January 7, 1767, Andrew Eliot wrote to Hollis: "As a friend to Harvard College, I sincerely thank you for your liberality to that society. The books you have sent are vastly curious and valuable, and the bindings elegant. I hope their external appearance will invite our young gentlemen to peruse them, which I am persuaded was your principal design in sending them" (4 *Massachusetts Historical Collections*, IV. 402).

189. A plan of Harvard Hall showing these alcoves, drawn to scale, is in *Publications of the Colonial Society of Massachusetts*, XIV. 16.

190. Blackburne, *Hollis*, II. 603.

191. Printed in the *Boston Gazette*, April 7, 1766. See *Publications of the Colonial Society of Massachusetts*, XI. 59.

192. Addressed to Thomas Hollis, as a footnote to the poem indicates.

193. "The books he sent were often political, and of a republican stamp. And it remains for the perspicacity of our historians to ascertain what influence his benefactions and correspondence had in kindling that spirit which emancipated these States from the shackles of colonial subserviency, by forming 'high-minded men,' who, under Providence, achieved our independence.

"Doubtless at the favored Seminary her sons drank deeply of the writings of MILTON, HARRINGTON, SYDNEY, LUDLOW, MARVELL, and LOCKE. These were there, by Mr. Hollis's exertions, political text-books. And the eminent men of that day were—

> " 'By antient learning to the enlightened love
> Of antient freedom warmed.' "

William Jenks, *Eulogy on Bowdoin*, Boston, 1812, p. 21.

194. On May 21, 1760, Mayhew writes of certain books just received from Hollis that "they have afforded both me & my friends a great deal of pleasure" (*Hollis Papers*, p. 5).

195. *An | Account | Of | Denmark, | As it was in the Year 1692. | By the Right Honourable | Robert Lord Viscount Molesworth. | [motto] | The Sixth Edition. | Glasgow: | Printed by R. Urie, MDCCLII.* Boston Public Library, Adams, 223. 22.

196. *Franco-gallia: Or, An Account of the Ancient Free State of France, and Most other Parts of Europe, before the Loss of their Liberties. Written originally in Latin by the Famous Civilian Francis Hottoman, In the Year 1574. And Translated into English by the Author of the Account of Denmark.* London: 1721. The Harvard copy, presented by Thomas Hollis in 1764, has on the fly-leaf an inscription by Hollis which virtually constitutes a cross-reference to Molesworth: "The Translator's preface to the Franco-gallia, and the preface to the Acc. of Denmark are two of the NOBLEST prefaces in the English language. THOMAS HOLLIS."

197. The same version appears (1. 55) in "The Second Edition with Additions" of these *Familiar Letters*, London, 1697.

198. An edition of 1740 in folio is mentioned by Professor C. H. Firth in his article on Sidney in the *Dictionary of National Biography*. Since no other authority appears to mention an edition of 1740, and since Firth's list of editions omits the folio of 1704, I am inclined to think that his 1740 edition is simply a printer's error for 1704.

199. There is a copy of this catalogue in the library of the Massachusetts Historical Society. On circulating libraries in Boston at this period, see C. K. Bolton in *Publications of the Colonial Society of Massachusetts*, XI. 196 ff.

200. Brunet, *Manuel du Libraire*, Paris, 1864, mentions three editions.

201. On Jeremiah Gridley (1702–1767) see Appleton's *Cyclopædia of American Biography*; John Adams, *Works, passim*; J. T. Morse, Jr., in Winsor's *Memorial History of Boston*, IV. 574.

202. James Bowdoin (1752–1811), son of Governor James Bowdoin (1727–1790).

203. *Hollis Papers*, p. 25.

204. As is clear from the *Hollis Papers*.

205. 4 *Massachusetts Historical Collections*, IV. 412.

206. This copy, a part of the Sumner Bequest, was given to Sumner by George Livermore.

207. Mr. Lindsay Swift has pointed out that the Adams Library contains some books that have been added since the death of John Adams (*Catalogue of the Adams Library*, Boston, 1917, p. viii).

In addition to the Adams copy of the 1772 Sidney, the Boston Public Library has a copy given by Theodore Parker. In rebinding it all the original fly-leaves have been removed, and there is no clue to its history before 1864.

208. Thomas Hollis's note on these prints, written on the fly-leaf of the book containing them, is as follows:

"Years ago Mr. George Vertue made a Drawing of Algernon Sidney by permission of John the last Earl of Leicester of the Sidney Family, from the Original in Oils of Iustus ab Egmondt at penshurst; with the Intention to engrave a print by it, to be placed among the illustrious Men then publishing by Knapton. By a variety of Accidents no print however was executed. Long after a Gentleman purchased the Drawing; and that the Memory of so excellent a person might be still better preserved and extended, He caused a print to be made from it by the ingenious Mr. Jackson of Battersea, the same who studied many Years in Italy, and acquired Reputation by divers Works produced there, and afterwards in England. It is cut in Wood, on four Blocks, to receive four Impressions in Chiaro oscuro with Oyl; chiefly after the principles of Albert Durer, and Ugo di Carpi. The five first prints in this Book are compleat proofs from the four several Blocks of Mr. Jackson's print. The sixth is from the first and second Block only, and is curious for the outline. But all the six vary in some Respect each from the other. N. B. There are but four Sidney's of the large paper, in which these six prints have been bound up; neither is it now possible to bind another set in this same Manner, the Copys of that size being all already sold."

209. One can hardly mention Lucan without being drawn into the question of the source of our motto. After the vain efforts of Mr. George Birkbeck Hill (see the preface to his edition of *Gibbon's Autobiography*) I have thought it useless to search the Latin poets. Lucan, however, does contain (bk. vii, l. 348) an *ense petat* which Sidney

may have borrowed, for Sidney cites Lucan fully a dozen times in the *Discourses*. There seems to be no doubt that the motto *Manus haec inimica tyrannis* was in use by at least three families (Probyn of Bramton, Hunts; Tonson, Baron Riversdale; Tufnell of Boreham, Essex) before Sidney wrote the words in the album. But I cannot pretend to have gone with any thoroughness into either this question or the equally puzzling one of the relation between the Earl's version, the Molesworth version, and the Rochester version of what Sidney is supposed to have written. The inscription in the album at Copenhagen having been destroyed, and there being no clear light on the question whether the full line and a half can be found in any Latin author, I have thought it wisest to limit myself to the situation in Massachusetts from 1750 to 1775. There, unquestionably, the story as Molesworth tells it was accepted.

210. See bk. i, l. 128.

211. C. E. Merriam, *American Political Theories*, New York, 1906, p. 90.

212. *Memoir of Josiah Quincy, Jr., by his son, Josiah Quincy*, second edition, Boston, 1874, p. 289.

213. The Snare broken. / A / Thanksgiving-Discourse, / Preached / . . . . / In / Boston, N. E. Friday May 23, 1766. / Occasioned By The / Repeal / Of The / Stamp-Act. / By / Jonathan Mayhew, D.D. / . . . / [*motto*] / Boston / 1766.

214. John Adams, *Works*, x. 410. Editions of Sidney's *Discourses* appeared in New York and in Philadelphia in 1805.

215. *Works*, IV. 271 ff.

216. *Id.*, VI. 4.

217. The italics are mine.

218. Andrew Eliot had become minister of Fairfield, Connecticut, in 1774 (1 *Massachusetts Historical Collections*, x. 189).

219. Dr. Whiting I have not identified. Colonel Otis is of course James Otis of Barnstable (1702–1778). Major Hawley is Joseph Hawley of Northampton. Major Bliss is John Bliss of Wilbraham (1727–1809), on whom J. G. Holland has a little information (*History of Western Massachusetts*, II. 162). I find scattered accounts of these men (except Whiting), and a few of their letters; but nothing to throw light on the matter of the motto. It is greatly to be desired that those who have access to the papers of persons prominently mentioned in this article should search for some conclusive evidence.

220. See Honorable John Davis, *Life of John Winthrop*, Boston, 1811.

221. This, as Mr. Henry H. Edes has shown in *Publications of the Colonial Society of Massachusetts*, VII. 321 ff., is the first LL.D. granted by Harvard College.

222. Letter of Charles Chauncy to Ezra Stiles, May 8, 1768 (1 *Massachusetts Historical Collections*, x. 159).

223. Josiah Quincy, *History of Harvard University*, II. 223.

224. For John Winthrop's *Cogitata de Cometis*, see the *Philosophical Transactions* of the Royal Society, 1768, LVII. 132 ff. On Winthrop's not undisputed authorship of No. xxvi ("Dum servat stellas") in the *Pietas et Gratulatio* of 1761, see Justin Winsor, *Pietas et Gratulatio: an Inquiry into the Authorship of the Several Pieces*, Cambridge, 1879, p. 6. *Library of Harvard University: Bibliographical Contributions*, No. 4.

225. A. C. Potter and C. K. Bolton, "The Librarians of Harvard College, 1667–1877," Cambridge, 1897. *Library of Harvard University: Bibliographical Contributions*, No. 52.

226. Though these errata would alone seem to make this copy unique, it appears that a certain number of other copies were similarly annotated: H. M. Dexter (*Congregationalism of the Last Three Hundred Years*, Appendix, p. 68) suggests that they were fairly numerous: "Copies circulated by the author," Dexter writes, "contain nearly a page of errata on back of title." The Massachusetts Historical Society has a copy (given by John Cotton to Richard Mather) with the errata as in the Gay copy; but I have not thus far succeeded in finding any others. I am indebted to the assistant librarians of the John Carter Brown Library and of the Yale University Library for collations of the first edition of the *Singing of Psalms* with the second edition (1650). In the second edition only one of the errata noted by John Cotton has been corrected, that on page 51, line 7.

227. So far as I am aware, Shepard's authorship of this work has been asserted only by the Reverend John A. Albro, who on p. cxcii of the first volume of his edition of the *Works of Thomas Shepard*, 3 vols., Boston, 1853, includes *Singing of Psalms a Gospel Ordinance* in his list of Shepard's works. He gives no evidence of Shepard's authorship, however. It is, of course, possible that Albro may have seen the Gay copy of this book. Who owned the Gay copy in 1853 or thereabouts I am unable to learn. Cotton Mather (*Magnalia*, 1820, I. 255) mentions "a discourse about *singing of psalms*, proving it a gospel-ordinance" as

Cotton's; in his account (*id.*, pp. 343–357) of Thomas Shepard, Mather gives no indication that Shepard had any part in planning or writing this work.

228. *Miscellaneous Works of George Wither*, printed for the Spenser Society, 1872, Publications of the Spenser Society, Issue No. 12, First Collection, pp. 121–122.

229. Quoted in part by Phoebe Sheavyn, *The Literary Profession in the Elizabethan Age*, Manchester [England], 1909, pp. 81–82, where other interesting examples are given.

230. *Samuel Butler: Characters and Passages from Note-Books*, ed. A. R. Waller, Cambridge [England], 1908, p. 262.

231. *Perfect Diurnal*, No. 310, July 2–9, 1649, p. 2561.

232. Thomason (*Catalogue*, II. 125) says this pamphlet was published about the middle of August, 1655. He dates his copy August 20.

233. See, for instance, *London Gazette*, No. 886 (May 14–18, 1674); the *Compleat Library*, II. 220 (March, 1693).

234. Howell, *State Trials*, XIV. 1106–1107 (London, 1816).

235. For a full account of this matter, see J. F. Jameson's edition of Johnson's *Wonder-Working Providence*, New York, 1910, pp. 3–5.

236. *Magnalia*, I. 351.

237. Shepard's *Works*, I. clxxxvi.

238. *Magnalia*, I. 255.

239. *Plain Dealing*, ed. J. H. Trumbull, p. 52 note.

240. On Simmons, see Henry R. Plomer, *A Dictionary of Booksellers and Printers who were at work in England and Ireland from 1641 to 1667*, London, 1907, p. 164.

241. William H. Whitmore, Introduction to Dunton's *Letters from New England*, p. xxiv.

242. "To my only Brother Mr. Lake Dunton. Lately Return'd from Surat in the East Indies." The letter occupies pp. 20–55 of the Prince Society edition.

243. P. 43.

244. See Andrew D. White, *History of the Warfare of Science with Theology in Christendom*, I, chap. i, for a popular account, with many references, of the Physiologus and similar books. See also the article "Physiologus" in the *Encyclopædia Britannica*.

245. The / Travels / Of / Sig. Pietro della Valle, / A Noble Roman, / Into / East-India / And / Arabia Deserta. / In which, the several

Countries, together with the / Customs, Manners, Traffique, and Rites both / Religious and Civil, of those Oriental Princes / and Nations, are faithfully Described: / In Familiar Letters to his Friend / Signior Mario Schipano. / Whereunto is Added / A Relation of Sir Thomas Roe's Voyage / into the East-Indies. / London, / Printed by *J. Macock*, for *John Martin*, and *James Allestry*; and / are to be sold at their Shop, at the Bell in St *Paul*'s / Church-yard. 1665.

The Epistle Dedicatory to the Earl of Orrery concludes thus concerning the relation of Sir Thomas Roe's voyage: "The other Piece hath been judg'd fit to be adjoyned, as one of the Exactest Relations of the Eastern parts of the World that hitherto hath been publish'd by any Writer, either Domestick or Foreign; having been penn'd by one that attended Sir *Thomas Roe* in his Embassy to the Great *Mogol*; Than whom, 'tis acknowledg'd by one of that Country that trades most into those parts, none ever gave a more faithful Account thereof." This dedication is signed by G. Havers.

For a life of Pietro della Valle (1586–1652) and a bibliographical account of his *Viaggi*, see Edward Grey's edition of *The Travels of Pietro della Valle in India*, 2 vols., London, 1892 (*Hakluyt Society Publications*, Nos. 84 and 85).

246. There is an account of Sir Thomas Roe (1580 or 1581–1644) in the *Dictionary of National Biography* by Stanley Lane-Poole, who does not mention this relation. S. R. Gardiner mentions Roe frequently and with much respect: see the general index in the tenth volume of his *History of England, 1603–1642*.

247. Speculum / Mundi. / Or / A Glasse Re-/presenting The Face / Of The World; / Shevving both that it did begin, and must also end: / The manner Hovv, and time When, being / largely examined. / Whereunto Is / Joyned / an Hexameron, or a serious discourse of the causes, / continuance, and qualities of things in Nature; / occasioned as matter pertinent to the / vvork done in the six dayes of the / Worlds creation. / *The second Edition enlarged.* / Aug. in Ser. de Ascen. / *Qui se dicit scire quod nescit, temerarius est.* / *Qui se negat scire quod scit, ingratus est.* / Printed by Roger Daniel Printer to the / *Universitie of Cambridge*, 1643. / For *Troylus Adkinson*, Stationer in *Cambridge*.

Swan's *Speculum Mundi* was rather popular: the British Museum catalogue has editions as follows—Cambridge 1635, Cambridge 1643, London 1665, and London 1670. A recent bookseller's catalogue advertises a copy of the Cambridge edition of 1643 with a "fine frontispiece by W. Marshall." This is, of course, the well known William Marshall, on whom see the *Dictionary of National Biography*. Possibly this frontispiece is the "second title-page, engraved" referred to by the

British Museum cataloguer in describing their copy of the second edition.

The author of the *Speculum Mundi* may be the John Swan who entered Emmanuel College, Cambridge, as a sizar in the Lenten term of 1626–7 and proceeded A.B. in 1630–1 and A.M. in 1634. Another John Swan entered Queens College, Cambridge, as a pensioner in 1627 and was A.B. in 1630–1 and A.M. in 1634. Still another entered Trinity in 1622 and was A.B. in 1625–6 and A.M. in 1629 (Venn, *Book of Matriculations and Degrees*, 1913, p. 651).

248. The copy of Pell in the Harvard College Library is imperfect, the first six words of the title having been supplied in manuscript. The words so supplied are indicated below within square brackets. It appears, however, from the British Museum catalogue, Watt, the Thomason *Catalogue*, and other sources, that the first word of the title should be Πέλαγος, in part chosen, no doubt, for the sake of the pun upon the author's name. The full title of Pell's book should be, then, as follows:

[Πέλαγος Nec inter Vivos, nec inter Mortuos] Neither *Amongst the living*, nor / *amongst the Dead.* / Or, An / Improvement / of the Sea, / Upon the *Nine Nautical Verses* in the / 107. Psalm; / Wherein is handled / I. *The* several, great, *and* many *hazzards, that* Ma/riners *do meet withall, in Stormy and Tempestuous* / *Seas.* II. *Their* many, several, miraculous, *and* stupen/dious deliverances *out of all their helpless, and / shiftless distresses.* / III. *A very* full, *and* delightful description *of all those / many various, and multitudinous objects, which / they behold in their travels (through the* Lords / Creation) *both on Sea, in Sea, and on Land.* viz. / *All sorts and kinds of* Fish, Foul, *and* Beasts, / *Whether wilde, or tame; all sorts of* Trees, *and* / Fruits; *all sorts of* People, Cities, Towns, *and* / Countries; / With many profitable, and useful rules, and / Instructions for them that use the Seas. / By Daniel Pell, Preacher of the Word. / *London*, Printed for *Livewell Chapman*, and are to be / sold at the Crown in Popes-head Alley. 1659.

Pell dates his preface from his Study "at my Lady Hungerfords in Hungerford house upon the Strand, May 4, 1659." This was Lady Margaret Hungerford, wife of Sir Edward Hungerford. He died before 1659, as appears from Pell's separate dedicatory epistle to Lady Hungerford.

The publication of the book presumably occurred in November of 1659, according to the Thomason *Catalogue*, ii. 268.

A Daniel Pell, who may be our author, entered St. John's College, Cambridge, as a sizar, in Easter term 1651 (Venn, *Book of Matriculations and Degrees*, p. 520).

249. The contrary opinion is expressed in Dunton's *Athenian Mercury*, ii, No. 5, Question 5, where the question "Why a Dolphin fol-

lows a Ship until he is frightened away" is thus answered: "'Tis not from the same reason as Sharks, and other ravenous Fishes do, who expect a dead Body, or a Prey, but from the great love and kindness which these sort of Fishes bear unto Man."

250. This passage may indicate that Dunton had looked into Sir Thomas Browne's *Pseudodoxia Epidemica*, bk. v, chap. 2 ("Of the Picture of Dolphins"), wherein we read: "That dolphins are crooked, is not only affirmed by the hand of the painter, but commonly conceived their natural and proper figure, which is not only the opinion of our times, but seems the belief of elder times before us. . . . Notwithstanding, to speak strictly, in their natural figure they are straight, nor have their spine convexed, or more considerably embowed, than sharks, porpoises, whales, and other cetaceous animals" (*Works of Sir Thomas Browne*, ed. Simon Wilkin, London, 1852, II. 4–5).

251. *Publications of the Colonial Society of Massachusetts*, XIV. 253 [and p. 54 of this volume].

252. I have not taken into account the single sentence borrowed from Purchas.

253. Here I received the most generous assistance from our associate Mr. Samuel Henshaw.

254. See an article on the Fearing Collection, by our associate Mr. George P. Winship, in the *Harvard Alumni Bulletin* of November 3, 1915, XVIII. 92–94; and an article by Mr. Fearing in the *Harvard Graduates' Magazine* for December, 1915, XXIV. 263–274.

255. In 1902–03 Mr. Wendell gave the Clark lectures at Trinity College, Cambridge, and published them in 1904 as *The Temper of the Seventeenth Century in English Literature*. Though they left something to be desired, these lectures hardly deserved the severe handling which they received from the *Saturday Review*. Mr. Wendell believed the reviewer to be the late John Churton Collins.

256. Ra[lph] Johnson, *The Scholars Guide*, etc., p. 15.
For other definitions, see Overbury (1614) in his *Miscellaneous Works*, ed. E. F. Rimbault, London, 1856, pp. 168–169; S. Person, *An Anatomicall Lecture of Man . . . in Essays and Characters* (1664); Richard Flecknoe, *Fifty-five Enigmatical Characters* (1665); and *Seventy-eight Characters of so many Vertuous and Vitious Persons* (1677).

257. The number of characters of a prison is particularly large. Dekker tried the subject in 1607; one of the Overbury group in 1614; Fennor in 1617; Mynshul in 1618; Earle in 1628; the writer of *W. Bagnal's Ghost* in 1655 and of *The Captive Captain* in 1665; Kirkman

and Head, in *The English Rogue*, 1665; Head in *Proteus Redivivus*, 1675; Flecknoe in 1686; the author of *Hickelty-Pickelty* in 1708.

258. Note especially Donald Lupton's *London and the Country*, etc., 1632, which contains thirty-six characters, all but nine of which are of such inanimate objects as The Tower, St. Paul's Church, Play-Houses, Newgate, and the like.

259. Henry Morley, *Character Writings of the Seventeenth Century*, pp. 49–50.

260. See Sir R. C. Jebb's edition (revised by J. E. Sandys) of *The Characters of Theophrastus*, London, 1909, which contains the Greek text and an English translation. For a good critical essay on the influence of Theophrastus, see G. S. Gordon, "Theophrastus and his Imitators," in *English Literature and the Classics*, a group of essays collected by G. S. Gordon, Oxford, 1912.

261. G. S. Gordon, as cited above, pp. 64–65.

262. S. M. Tucker, *Verse Satire in England before the Renaissance*, New York, 1908 (Columbia doctoral dissertation); C. H. Herford, *Studies in the Literary Relations of England and Germany in the Sixteenth Century*, Cambridge (England) University Press, 1886.

263. Others who wrote characters during this period are Nicholas Breton (*The Good and the Bad*, 1616), Geoffrey Mynshul (*Essayes and Characters of a Prison and Prisoners*, 1618), Richard Brathwait (*Essaies upon the Five Senses*, 1619), John Taylor, the "Water Poet," Henry Parrot (*Cures for the Itch, Characters, Epigrams, Epitaphs*, 1626), R. M. (*Micrologia*, 1629), Wye Saltonstall (*Picturae Loquentes*, 1631), Donald Lupton (*London and the Country Carbonadoed, and Quartred into Seuerall Characters*, 1632), William Habington (*Castara*, 1634).

264. For a catalogue of this material, see the *Catalogue of the Pamphlets, Books, Newspapers, and Manuscripts relating to the Civil War, the Commonwealth, and Restoration, collected by George Thomason, 1640–1661*, 2 vols., London, 1908.

265. A few, taken almost at random, are *Anatomy of the Separatists*, 1641; *A Description of the Round-Head and Rattlehead*, 1642; *A Right Character of a true Subject*, 1642; *Character of an Antimalignant, or Right Parliamentier; expressing plainly his Opinion concerning King and Parliament*, 1645; John Geree, *The Character of an Old English Puritan*, 1646; *Character of a Cavalier*, 1647; *Character of an Agitator* 1647; *Character of a Time-serving Saint*, 1652; *The Character of France*, 1659; *A Character of England*, 1659; *A Brief Character of the Low Countries*, 1659; *The Character of Italy: or, the Italian Anatom-*

iz'd by an English Chirurgion, 1660; *Confused Characters of Conceited Coxcombs,* 1661; *The True Character of a Rigid Presbyter,* 1661; *Character of a Quaker,* 1671; *Poor Robin's Character of a Dutch-man,* 1672; *The Character of a Coffee-House, with the Symptoms of a Town-Wit,* 1673; *The Character of an Honest Lawyer,* 1676; *Character of a Town-Miss,* 1680.

266. Samuel Butler, *Characters and Passages from Note-Books,* ed. A. R. Waller, Cambridge (England), 1908. Butler wrote 187 characters.

267. This variety is of particular interest to the student of English fiction, who could hardly find a better example than the third paragraph in *Spectator,* No. 108, of the transition from the formal character to the novel of character.

268. *The English Theophrastus . . . being the Modern Characters of the Court, the Town, and the City,* 1692; *The Reformer, exposing the Vices of the Age, in Several Characters,* 1700; *Mars Stript of his Armour* (a collection of 24 military characters, such as a Major, a Captain, etc.) (By Edward Ward.) London, 1709; and others.

269. *Character of a Jacobite,* 1690; *The Trimming Court Divine,* 1690; *Character of a Whig,* 1700; *An English Monster; or, the Character of an Occasional Conformist,* 1703; *The Beau's Character,* 1706; *True Picture of a Modern Whig,* 1707; *The Character of a true Churchman,* 1711; *Character of an Honest Dissenter,* 1715; and many others.

270. Henry Morley, *Character Writings of the Seventeenth Century,* p. 255.

271. See *Publications of the Colonial Society of Massachusetts,* XIV. 213–257 [Reprinted in this volume, pp. 20–58].

272. This letter is owned by the Massachusetts Historical Society, the Librarian of which has kindly allowed it to be printed.

273. J. L. Sibley, *Harvard Graduates,* III. 61, No. 52.

274. January 7, 1698 (I. 246–247).

275. What reason Dunton had to expect to publish the *Magnalia* we do not know: he was quite capable of making the statement without any encouragement from the author. Note that in his *Letters from New England,* ed. Whitmore, p. 75, he says of Cotton Mather: "He has very lately finish'd the Church-History of New-England, which I'm going to print."

276. For Hackshaw see note 286. The Bromfield referred to seems to be Edward Bromfield of Boston, whom Sewall calls a merchant "well

known here and in England" (6 *Massachusetts Historical Society Collections*, I. 224). He was born in England in 1649, came to New England in 1675, was a member of the "South Church," and died in 1734. There is an extended notice of him in the *New England Weekly Journal* for June 10, 1734. More than once he was Mather's literary patron, as appears from the references to him in Mather's *Diary, passim.* Mather's *Memoria Wilsoniana*, 1695, was dedicated to him, and the address to him makes it plain that the book was published at his expense. Sewall records that "Capt. Mason sailed June 13th, and Capt. Foster June 14th, 1700. At 6 *mane*, Mr. Bromfield went off from Scarlet's Wharf. Mr. Elm Hutchinson and I accompanied him thither. I went and staid at his house till he was ready to goe" (6 *Massachusetts Historical Society Collections*, I. 239). Probably, then, Bromfield went to England in June, 1700. That he was back in Boston in 1703 is shown by Sewall's *Diary*, II. 72. The date when Mather records the sending of the *Magnalia* to England and the date of Bromfield's sailing are so close as to make it possible to wonder whether Bromfield was not trusted to carry the precious manuscript. Entry for June 8, 1700, in text on p. 135.

277. Was this Bromfield, or Quick, or someone else?

278. Presumably Hackshaw.

279. Presumably Parkhurst.

280. Arber, *Term Catalogues*, II. 400. One of the Harvard College Library copies has the following autograph inscription: "For my very Honoured Friend Elisha Cook Dr of Physick & one of ye Councill of New England at his House in Boston, from ye Publisher his very much obliged Friend & servant. John Quick. London, ye 6th. 24. 94." One would like to know more about Quick's relations with Cooke, of whom—see the index to his *Diary*—Cotton Mather did not approve.

281. See the sketch by Alexander Gordon in the *Dictionary of National Biography*, and in his *Freedom after Ejection*, p. 337; also the authorities mentioned at the end of these two sketches, and J. G. White's *Churches and Chapels of Old London*.

282. In a page headed "Advertisements" in Quick's *Serious Inquiry . . . Whether a Man may Lawfully Marry his Deceased Wife's Sister*, London, 1703, it is said: "Whereas there was about Three Years since Published by Mr. *Quick*, Proposals for the Printing his *Icones Sacrae*, being the Lives of Seventy Eminent Divines . . . the Reason of it's not Publication is this, the very next Week after the Death of his most noble Patron, who would have Printed his Works at his own Expences, it pleased God to visit Mr. *Quick* with those cruel Torturors of Scholars

the Stone and Gout . . . under which he has groan'd Night and Day for above these Three Years time, so that till the Lord shall please to restore him to his former Health, that he may be able to get in Subscriptions, or to raise up for him some other munificent *Mecænas*, the Publication is suspended."

283. K. B. Murdock, *Increase Mather*, p. 198.

284. *Diary*, 1. 364.

285. Samuel Mather, H.C. 1690, son of Increase Mather and brother of Cotton. For him see Mr. T. J. Holmes's paper, *Publications of the Colonial Society of Massachusetts*, XXVI. 312–322.

286. Excepting what appears in the letter I have found almost nothing about Robert Hackshaw, merchant, of London. Bromfield's letter of March 28, 1701 (*Diary*, 1. 400), speaks of him as "a very serious and Godly man." Cotton Mather (*id.*, 1. 550) includes in his list of his European correspondents in 1706 "Mr. Robert Hackshaw, Merchant, at Hogsdon [Hoxton], a suburb of London. A Robert Hackshaw was a cousin of Thomas Prince of Boston, and there are two letters from him to Prince in the library of the Massachusetts Historical Society, dated August 23, 1723, and August 1, 1726. In the first of these he says his family consists of a wife, son, and daughter, and speaks of his "Mother Buckle" as still alive, of his sister Robinson as dead, and of a brother Buckle. He says his own father died in October, 1722. Was the father Mather's Robert Hackshaw? The will of Robert Hackshaw, merchant of London, was proved in 1738. Presumably this was the son. See *New England Historical and Genealogical Register*, XLII. 401; *Memorial History of Boston*, II. 221 note, and W. H. Whitmore, *Catalogue of the Prince Library* (Wiggin and Lunt edition). In Hoxton, where Robert Hackshaw lived in 1706, there lived also the Reverend Edmund Calamy, and one or two other eminent nonconformist divines, and there was there "a noted college for training ministers of the Independent denomination" (Wheatley and Cunningham, *London Past and Present*, II. 246).

287. Of Thomas Parkhurst, whom John Dunton calls "the most eminent Presbyterian Bookseller in the Three Kingdoms," there is a short notice in the *Dictionary of National Biography*. The eulogistic notice of him by John Dunton, who had been his apprentice, is well known. See Dunton's *Life and Errors*, Nichols edition, 1. 205. Note that before the *Magnalia* Parkhurst had published at least five books for Cotton Mather. See Arber, *Term Catalogues*, II. 342, 521; III. 242, 271.

288. To the first of the two folio volumes of the *Whole Works of John Flavell* (1630–1691), the second edition of which was published

in 1716, there is prefixed a sketch of Flavell's life. No author's name is mentioned in connection with it, however, and therefore one is puzzled by Quick's statement. This edition of Flavell is among Parkhurst's books advertised at the end of the *Magnalia*.

289. Almanacs of the period often include, to show "The Dominion of the Moon in Man's Body passing under the 12 Signs of the Zodiack," a rude woodcut with short straight lines drawn from the different parts of the body to the names and signs of the various constellations in the margin. These lines do look like arrows. Indeed, some of the cuts (*e.g.* the one in Coley's *Merlinus Anglicus Junior* for 1700) show daggers or arrows instead of lines. Cf. G. L. Kittredge, *The Old Farmer and his Almanack*, pp. 53–61.

290. Quick does not quite accurately remember his Homer (*Odyssey*, bk. ix. 152 ff.).

291. On Raleigh's publisher, Walter Burre (fl. 1597–1621), see Arber, *Stationers' Register*, v. 224. He was made a freeman of the Stationers' Company on June 25, 1596 (*id.*, II. 716). Raleigh's *History* was entered April 15, 1611 (*id.*, III. 457), though not published until 1614. If Burre was as unsatisfactory as Quick suggests, it seems strange that Ben Jonson should have been content to have him publish *Every Man in his Humour*, *The Alchemist*, and *The Silent Woman* (*id.*, III. 169, 445, 498). On the legend, which Sir J. K. Laughton and Sir Sidney Lee reject, that Raleigh threw his manuscript into the fire, see John Aubrey, *Lives*, ed. Clark, II. 191. Aubrey apparently got the story from William Winstanley's *England's Worthies* (1660). In the second edition (1684) it occurs on page 300 (wrongly numbered 360 in the Harvard copy). The *Dictionary of National Biography* tells us that Winstanley's material was "principally stolen from Lloyd," but in Lloyd's *State Worthies* I do not find the story in the account of Raleigh.

292. As copy for the parts of the *Magnalia* that had already appeared in print Mather apparently sent over—as he naturally would—either the Boston or the London editions of the books in question. See, in Sibley's list, *Harvard Graduates*, III. 42–158, Nos. 5, 7, 32, 33, 52, 65, 66, 68, etc. Comparison of the text of these works as originally printed and as reprinted in the *Magnalia* would throw further light on the question of responsibility for the frequent misprints in the *Magnalia*. In sixteen cases, taken at random, where errors in the *Magnalia* are pointed out in the errata sheet found in a few copies of the *Magnalia*, the "prints" are correct in fourteen. That is to say, if given anything like the chance that an author now has of assisting in the correct production of his book, Cotton Mather would probably have shown himself, if not an impartial judge, at least the painstaking scholar that he was.

293. Joseph Dudley is said to have reached London some time before February, 1693, and to have sailed for Boston on April 13, 1702. See E. Kimball, *Public Life of Joseph Dudley*, pp. 65, 75. In the *Magnalia* (1702), bk. ii, p. 16, the elder Dudley is called a "Steward" to the Earl. The same is true of the earlier account in *Massachusetts Historical Society Proceedings*, XI. 207 ff., 212. On the differences between Mather's earlier account of Dudley and that in the *Magnalia*, see K. B. Murdock, *Selections from Cotton Mather*, p. xliv. Note the interesting passage in the *Magnalia* (1702), bk. ii, p. 16: "I had prepared and intended a more *particular Account* of this Gentleman [Thomas Dudley]; but not having any opportunity to commit it unto the *Perusal* of any Descended from him, (unto whom I am told it will be unacceptable for me to Publish any thing of this kind, by *them* not *Perused*) I have laid it aside, and summed all up in this more *General Account*."

294. Large paper copies of the *Magnalia* are to be found occasionally: the catalogue of the Church Library (No. 806) mentions seven besides its own. In the library of the Massachusetts Historical Society there are two copies not mentioned in the Church *Catalogue*, one being the copy that belonged to Samuel Mather and that was used by him while he was engaged upon an abridgment of the *Magnalia*. See Cotton Mather's *Diary*, II. 88, 142–143. This copy is about $14\frac{13}{8}$ inches high and $9\frac{13}{16}$ inches wide. Small paper copies are usually about 12 inches by 7¾ inches.

295. Strange as it may seem that an author's representative should unsuccessfully beg the privilege of seeing proof sheets, we must remember that in the seventeenth and early eighteenth centuries the author had nothing like the control of his text and front-matter that he now has. On this point see my article on John Cotton's "Singing of Psalms a Gospel Ordinance," in *Publications of the Colonial Society of Massachusetts*, XX. 241 ff. [Reprinted in this volume, pp. 89–97.]

296. Whether Quick here refers to the proposals for printing his own *Icones Sacrae* or those for the *Magnalia* is not clear. But we know that shortly before December, 1701, proposals for printing the *Magnalia* were issued over the names of Hackshaw and Parkhurst. Evidence of this is found in the following advance notice of the *Magnalia* in John Dunton's *The Post-Angel* for December, 1701 (II. 468), which on account of its rarity may perhaps be worth reprinting here: "Proposals were lately Publish'd for Printing *The History of New-England* from its first Plantetion [*sic*], in 1620. unto 1690. By *Cotton Mather, Pastor of a Church in* Boston, *in New-England, containing seven Books*. . . . As to the Author of this Elabrate History, HE IS A PERSON OF GREAT LEARNING AND PIETY: I had the Happiness formerly to be acquainted

with him, and have heard him Preach many Excellent Sermons in *New-England*, being once in his Company (which I took for Heaven; 'twas always so good and Spiritual) he shew'd me his *Library*, and I do think, he has one of the best (for a Private Library) that I ever saw: Nay, I may affirm, that as the *Bodleian Library* at *Oxford* is the Glory of that University, if not of all Europe: So I may say, Mr. Mather's *Library* is the Glory of *New-England*, if not of all *America*. I must own, I was greatly wanting to my self, if I did not learn more in that Hour I Enjoy'd his Company, than I cou'd in a Week spent in other mens: And therefore, none can doubt of an Extraordinary History, from an Author so well Provided with Books, and of such Great Parts; but I shan't Enlarge for the Work will recommended it self, for the Rich Variety of its Materials and for its most Exact Fidelity and Impartiality observed in its Collection. The whole containing 220 Sheets, or there abouts; it is to be Printed in Folio, on Paper and Print according to Proposals; deliver'd out by *Thomas Parkhurst*, at the *Bible* and Three *Crowns*, in *Cheapside*, near *Mercers Chappel*; and Mr. *Robert Hackshaw* Merchant in *London*. To Encourage Subscribers, to this Great and Useful Work, he that brings the first Payment for Six Books, —is promis'd a Seventh Gratis, in Larger or Smaller Paper; and it has already found, such great Encouragement, That the whole Book will be Finish'd about *Lady-Day* next." Parts of this are identical with Dunton's *Letters from New England*, ed. Whitmore, p. 75.

297. John Howe (1630–1705) lived on for four years more in spite of his severe labors. See *Dictionary of National Biography*; Calamy's "Memoir" prefixed to Howe's *Works*, 1724, and Gordon's *Freedom after Ejection*, pp. 287–288. In 1697 Howe and two others had signed the prefatory note recommending Cotton Mather's *Life of Sir William Phips* (Sibley, III. 64, No. 66). One of Howe's books is mentioned with approval in Mather's *Diary*, I. 56. George Hamond (Hammond)(1620–1705) was still lecturer at Salters Hall. See *Dictionary of National Biography*. For Vincent Alsop (1630–1703), see Gordon, p. 199. Perhaps "Mr. Griffyth" is Roger Griffith (*d.* 1708) (*id.*, p. 275). Mr. Bragge is presumably Robert Bragge (1627–1704), who was in 1702 the minister of a congregation in Pewterers' Hall, Lime Street, London (*id.*, p. 220; J. G. White, *Churches and Chapels*, Part II, pp. 17–18). At least two of these divines had known Increase Mather in England: see K. B. Murdock, *Increase Mather*, Index, *s.v.* Alsop and Howe.

298. Increase Mather's sermon on Ezek. ix. 3 is printed in his *Ichabod*, Boston, 1702, where appears also an "Epistle to yᵉ Reader" dated November 14, 1701, which explains how apt churches are to degenerate, that "Christians may be called to suffer for their Testimony unto

Truths which are not Fundamentals in Religion," and that there is reason to fear great calamities are impending for the English nation. I have not been able to find the sermons by Quick to which he refers; perhaps they were not published.

299. See, among other titles, Sibley, III. 51–157, Nos. 24, 41, 49, 52, 53, 55, 66, 68, 74, 77, 111, 118, 157, 159, 187, 213, 226, 250, 254, 261, 280, 301, 305, 307, 327, 330, 333, 338, 349, 362, 377, 394, 400, 419, 421, 423, 428, 429, 432, 441, 451.

300. See Harper's *Lexicon* and Du Cange.

301. The *Oxford Dictionary* also gives five examples—all in the seventeenth century—of "magnale" as a singular or "magnalls" as a plural form.

302. The Harvard College Library has a copy of this book.

303. The Harvard College Library has a copy of this book.

304. Edition of 1811, VII. 480.

305. The Harvard College Library has a copy of this book.

306. Page 89 has the following heading, printed like a chapter-title: God on the Mount, Or A Continuation Of Englands Parliamentary Chronicle.

307. Mr. Julius H. Tuttle is my authority for this statement.

308. Cf. his *Right Thoughts in Sad Hours* (1689) with Thomas Fuller's *Good Thoughts in Bad Times* (1645–46) and *Good Thoughts in Worse Times* (1647); note also Mather's *Balsamum Vulnerarium e Scriptura; or the Cause and Cure of a Wounded Spirit* (1691), as compared with Fuller's *The Cause and Cure of a Wounded Conscience* (1647). These resemblances are not the only ones between Mather's titles and those of certain predecessors: the kind of learning and word-play that he delighted to show lent themselves perfectly to this sort of thing. Nor are these the only examples of Cotton Mather's indebtedness to Fuller. That subject would, in all probability, be worth investigating.

309. See the *London Gazette*.

310. *Diary*, I. 433.

311. William Lee, *Daniel Defoe: His Life and Recently Discovered Writings* (1869), I. 155.

312. "The Author of this Paper now at Edinburgh" (*Review*, VI, London No. 70).

313. The letter is reprinted in Earl Stanhope's *History of England* (1872 ed.), II. 292–293.

314. A complete list of the variants is attempted below:

News from the Moon	Review, Vol. VII, No. 14 (Tuesday, May 2, 1710, Edinburgh)	Review, Vol. VII, No. 15 (Saturday, April 29, 1710, London)
P. 1, l. 7: for	by	by
P. 2, l. 5: their court	one of their courts	one of their courts
P. 2, ll. 20–21: with several	with the several	with the several
P. 2, l. 27: &	and	and
P. 3, ll. 2–3: the Drunkard	a Drunkard	a Drunkard
P. 3, l. 9: Streets	Street	Street
P. 3, ll. 16–17: There are Strict Laws, any Taylor making [sic]	[same]	[same]
P. 3, l. 18: &	and	and
P. 3, l. 19: Transgress	transgress	trangress
P. 4, l. 20: panting	Painting	Painting
P. 4, ll. 23–24: One said, that's at me	One said, d . . . m the Dog, that's at me	[same as Edin.]
P. 4, l. 28: That's such	That such	That such
P. 5, l. 1: L——	L——d	L——d
P. 5, ll. 4–5: it was far	far was it	far was it
P. 5, l. 5: the poor Author	the poor Author	tht poor Author
P. 5, l. 12: had bespoke	bespoke	bespoke
P. 5, l. 16: ones Eye-sight	one Eye-sight	one Eye-sight
P. 5, ll. 29–30: along the Streets	about Streets	about Streets
P. 5, l. 30: such Cases	such Gases	such Cases
P. 6, ll. 7–8: Prince Nobility	prime Nobility	prime Nobility
P. 6, l. 9: D——'s	Dog's	Dog's
P. 6, l. 11: begins	began	began
P. 6, l. 14: your Neighbour	my Neighbour	my Neighbour
P. 6, ll. 20–21: Lordship, and if	Lordship, you Dog, and if	Lordship, you Dog and if
P. 6, l. 27: in order to sent	in order to send	in order to send
P. 7, l. 1: That——has	That Dog has	That Dog has
P. 7, l. 7: was made for	was for	was for
P. 7, l. 27: &	and	and
P. 7, l. 29: &	and	and
P. 8 [omitted]	C. Did you make it for a Representer, or Character-Coat? T. Yes Sir.	[same as Edin.]
P. 8, l. 31: Their Guilt	Their own Guilt	Their own Guilt
P. 8, l. 35: to the 114 Gentlemen	to 114 Gentlemen	to 114 Gentlemen
P. 8, l. 39: Every one	Every Man	Every Man

315. The conjecture is presumably that of J. Hammond Trumbull.

316. *Massachusetts Historical Society Proceedings*, LVII. 340.

317. *Publications of the Colonial Society of Massachusetts*, XIII. 14.

318. The first of these works is in my own possession; the others are in the Harvard College Library.

319. Title-page reproduced in facsimile, showing the ornaments, in Andrew McF. Davis, *Colonial Currency Reprints*, II. 415.

320. Facsimile reproduction, showing ornaments, in *id.*, I. 367.

321. Mr. Davis's conjecture, *id.*, II. 18.

322. Facsimile reproduction of title-page, showing ornaments, in *id.*, II. 3.

323. Davis (*Colonial Currency Reprints*, II. 41–42) conjecturally ascribes the authorship to the Reverend Edward Wigglesworth. Facsimile of title-page, showing ornaments, in *id.*, II. 19.

324. First page, showing ornaments, reproduced in facsimile in *id.*, II. 97.

325. First page, showing ornaments, reproduced in facsimile in *id.*, II. 245.

326. Andrew Craigie, by the way, advertises his own wares in the *Boston News-Letter* of May 27, 1756.

327. For his autograph, see Winsor's *Memorial History of Boston*, II. 271.

328. *Boston News-Letter*, February 5, 1756 (p. 3, column 2).

329. John Franklin's ownership, if this really is his autograph, may —since the autograph appears not on a fly-leaf but on the page which contains the half-title of Vol. VI and the beginning of its preface— date from 1709 or 1710. The Preface ends with the words "Edinburgh. Printed in the Year MDCCIX." The final number (153) of Vol. VI is dated March 18, 1710, which means not 1710/11, but 1709/10.

330. *Dictionary of American Biography; New England Historical and Genealogical Register* (XI. 19), gives 1733.

331. *Publications of the Colonial Society of Massachusetts*, XIII. 3.

332. *American Bibliography*, I. 302.

333. *Massachusetts Historical Society Proceedings*, LVII. 340.

334. *Publications of the Colonial Society of Massachusetts*, XIII. 3, note I.

335. *Id.*, pp. 12–13.

336. It is reprinted in full in *Colonial Currency Reprints*, II. 266–270; the number of the *Review* from which it is taken is reprinted in *Publications of the Colonial Society of Massachusetts*, XIII. 6–10. I have used a photostat of *News from the Moon* kindly furnished me by the New York Public Library, the fortunate possessor of the only known copy.

337. April 29 (No. 15) in the London issue; May 2 in the Edinburgh issue.

338. The impeachment of Sacheverell in 1710 was one of the worst blunders on the part of the Whigs and one of the causes of their loss of power in that year. Sacheverell's famous sermon of November 5, 1709, had taken the extreme High Tory attitude toward the Dissenters, as Defoe had pretended to do in his *Shortest Way*. But although Sacheverell had been offensive enough in setting forth "the Heinous Malignity, Enormous Guilt, and Folly of this Prodigious Sin of False Brotherhood," and in his remarks on "such wilely Volpones" had quite clearly aimed at a great Whig minister, to allow him to become a martyr was bad judgment, as the Whigs discovered too late. For accounts of the episode, see Lecky's *England in the Eighteenth Century* (American ed.), I. 55 ff.; C. J. Abbey and J. H. Overton, *The English Church in the Eighteenth Century*, II. 379–381.

339. That is, pretending, as he had done in *The Shortest Way with the Dissenters* (1702), to be one of the extreme Tories, whose ecclesiastical policies he detested.

340. Nos. 9–12, 14.

341. No. 12.

342. "The Whiggs and all the Party may by this time see the ill Consequences of the Doctrine advanced by them of the Original of Government's being from the People, and their chief Writers, such as Hoadly, the *Review*, Kennett &c. ought to be punish'd with the utmost Rigour for maintaining such arguments as give the People a Power of taking up arms, when they shall think fit. If these Gentlemen could have been found out they had without all doubt felt the Effects of their Doctrine. The Mob would have either torn them in Pieces, or made them undergo very great Disgraces" (Hearne's *Collections*, *Oxford Historical Society*, II. 355).

See also Hearne's diary for April 10, 1710 (II. 371), in regard to an alleged slander against Dr. Sacheverell which "the scandalous, abominable, Author of the Paper call'd yᵉ *Review* has most maliciously asserted and publish'd in Print."

The force of the two passages cited above is increased when we remember Hearne's very low opinion of Sacheverell as a person. His diary for October 11, 1710 (III. 65), shows that he regarded Sacheverell as a "conceited and ignorant and impudent" man, "who, whatever good he may accidentally produce, is certainly a Rascal & Knave himself."

343. Sacheverell's famous sermon ("The Perils of False Brethren, both in Church and State," delivered November 5, 1709, and published in the same year) was inscribed to the Lord Mayor, who was said, though he denied the fact, to have urged its publication.

344. *Review*, No. 13 (London issue), April 25, 1710.

345. *Id.*

346. "Their last . . . Shift has been to tamper with the Publishers and Dispensers of it [the *Review*]. . . . We have now . . . put it into Hands, that will not be bias'd, terrify'd, or any way prevail'd upon to keep it back; and from henceforward, this Paper will be publish'd by Mr. Baker, as is printed at the Bottom in the usual Place" (*id.*).

347. My colleague Mr. Theodore F. M. Newton, who is engaged upon what bids fair to be the definitive study of Defoe's *Review*, has given me valuable help here. He it was who pointed out the significance of the "114" men, a nice little mystery which I could not have solved for myself.

348. According to the work of the same title for 1708, the civil government in that year was composed of the same number of men (pp. 686–688); the same source for 1711 gives the number as only ninety-seven (pp. 360–362). Chamberlayne's *Angliae Notitia: or, the Present State of England* for 1707 gives a total of 113 (pp. 644–648).

349. There is a possibility that the allusion to the "114" may have been instantly recognizable, especially with the help of the expression "Common Council," to Defoe's readers. Among numbers that were familiar enough to be political rallying cries one recalls the "Forty-five" that Wilkes made famous. Then there is the toast to "The Massachusetts Ninety-two," which was drunk (as the thirty-third toast) at a dinner in Philadelphia, in 1769, to commemorate Paoli's birthday (*Publications of the Colonial Society of Massachusetts*, XXVI. 191). And probably other instances could be collected.

350. The Boston Public Library has an almost complete set of the *Review*, except Vol. III. There are a few selections in George A. Aitken, *Later Stuart Tracts*, pp. 221–280. A complete facsimile reprint of the work is proposed by the Fascimile Text Society.

351. *Publications of the Colonial Society of Massachusetts*, XIV. 213 ff.

[Reprinted in this volume, pp. 20–58.] Those who find the explanation of the "character" too meagre as given here are referred to that earlier article, and especially to pages 232–236. For still further details see: for bibliography, Gwendolen Murphy, *A Bibliography of English Character-Books, 1608–1700* (1925); for texts, Henry Morley, *Character Writings of the Seventeenth Century* (1891); Gwendolen Murphy, *A Cabinet of Characters* (1925; with a good introductory essay); David Nichol Smith, *Characters from the Histories and Memoirs of the Seventeenth Century* (1920; with a good introductory essay on the Clarendon type of character); for the classical roots of the character, G. S. Gordon, "Theophrastus and his English Imitators," in *English Literature and the Classics* (1912).

352. The catalogue of the British Museum records a "fourth edition, corrected," in 1679. A "5th edition, corrected" (1699), was entered for publication (Arber, *Term Catalogues*, III. 128, 162). The Harvard College Library has the edition of 1665.

353. Reprinted in full in *Publications of the Colonial Society of Massachusetts*, XIV. 233 [and in this volume, p. 35].

354. Introduction (p. xli) to *A Life of Gilbert Burnet, Bishop of Salisbury*, by T. E. S. Clarke and H. C. Foxcroft (1907).

355. Italics mine.

356. The varied manifestations of the character in this period are not well represented in any volume of selections. See, however, Gwendolen Murphy's *Cabinet of Characters*, especially pp. 237–334; and the *Harleian Miscellany* and *Somers Tracts, passim* (see index). Halifax's *Character of a Trimmer* and his other works have been admirably edited by Miss H. C. Foxcroft in two volumes (London, 1898).

357. The device did not originate with Addison. Edward Ward's *London Spy* (1698–1700) makes less skilful use of the same method.

358. The technique of John Dunton in his *Letters from New England* is at times essentially like Addison's in the *Tatler*, No. 158. Observe how Dunton (see *Publications of the Colonial Society of Massachusetts*, XIV. 237 [and pp. 38–39 of this volume]) takes Thomas Fuller's abstract character of "The Good Merchant" (1642) and changes it to "Mr. Heath"; and how he takes Fuller's remark that justice to the buyer is a fundamental necessity in all trading, the neglect of which is "worse than open felony" because it is to "rob a man of his purse and never bid him stand," and makes it read: "and *I have heard him say* [italics mine] that such a Cozenage is worse than open Felony; because they rob a man of's Purse, and never bid him stand."

359. Italics mine.

360. Gwendolen Murphy, *Bibliography of English Character-Books*, p. 73.

361. These are, respectively, Nos. 39, 52, and 53 in *Enigmatical Characters* (1658).

362. In "A Brief History of the Times . . . in a Preface to the Third Volume of Observators" (1687). It is fair to say, however, that L'Estrange goes right on in the words quoted on p. 170 of the text.

363. Cf. also *Spectator*, Nos. 46, 567, and 568.

364. *Lives*, ed. G. B. Hill, II. 95.

365. *A Brief History of the Times.*

366. Thomas G. Wright, *Literary Culture in Early New England*, pp. 184–185.

367. *Diary*, II. 227 (7 *Massachusetts Historical Society Collections*, VII).

368. *Id.*, p. 74.

369. Cotton Mather frequently used the word "character" (in one or more of the meanings pertinent to this investigation) in his *Diary*: see, for example, II. 73 (May 16, 1711), where he resolves as he may have occasion to give "the Character" of a certain man who has injured him, still to treat him with goodness. See also *id.*, p. 561 (October 20, 1718), where he proposes to preach a funeral sermon on the Reverend Thomas Bernard, of Andover, "and add his Character in the close of it." And, especially, see *id.*, p. 562 (October 20, 1718), where, reviewing his own publications to see "how many Persons of Worth, a gracious God has employ'd . . . [his] poor Pen, publickly to exhibit unto the World, with an Advantageous History, or Character of them," he finds "no less than One hundred and fourteen men (whereof more than Four-score stand in the Church-History,) and above twenty Women; besides many more, who have more transiently and occasionally had an honourable Mention made of them."

370. Reprinted: Boston, 1692; London, 1694; Boston, 1741 (fifth edition). See J. L. Sibley's bibliography (No. 29) in *Harvard Graduates*, III. 53.

371. *The Ladies Calling by the Author of the Whole Duty of Man* (1673). For further information about this book, which John Dunton also made use of, see *Publications of the Colonial Society of Massachusetts*, XIV. 240, note 4 [and p. 266, note 119 of this volume].

372. His *Government of New England Churches* appeared in 1717.

373. *A History of the Congregational Churches in the United States* (1907 ed.), p. 211.

374. Letter to Robert Wodrow, September 17, 1715, *Diary*, II. 327.

375. *Id.*, 659. For many other entries see index, *s.v.* Small-pox.

376. Herbert L. Osgood, *The American Colonies in the Eighteenth Century*, III. 174–175.

377. See Worthington C. Ford, "Franklin's New England Courant," *Mass. Hist. Soc. Proc.*, LVII. 336–353.

378. *Manuductio* (1726), pp. 44–46, as quoted by Kenneth B. Murdock, *Selections from Cotton Mather*, pp. xxxvi–xxxvii.

379. Clyde A. Duniway, *The Development of Freedom of the Press in Massachusetts*, pp. 90–94.

380. *Id.*, p. 95.

381. *Id.*, pp. 102–103.

382. *Id.*, p. 92.

383. It is possible that the words, "*Letters, Postscripts, News, Dialogues*" were chosen with intention and refer more or less definitely to certain publications. That would, of course, make the advertisement more objectionable. Duniway (pp. 90–91) has some interesting remarks on that sort of propaganda in what purport to be advertisements.

384. For the whole passage see Davis, *Colonial Currency Reprints*, II. 118.

385. Davis, *Colonial Currency Reprints*, I. 133.

386. *Id.*, pp. 130–132.

387. "A very abusive Creature," wrote Cotton Mather (*Diary*, II. 397) on February 2, 1717, "in whom the three parts of the Satanic Image, Pride, Malice, and Falsehood, are very conspicuous, must be pittied and pray'd for. [I. Κολμαν]." The brackets are Mather's.

388. Davis, *Colonial Currency Reprints*, I. 407.

389. The whole passage (*id.*, 411–412) is extremely important: it helps to define the conservative type and by implication suggests the commercially unsubstantial and slightly disloyal nature, as the writer saw it, of the liberals.

390. Cotton Mather (*Diary*, II. 607) calls him "one who has been and would still have been the greatest Hinderer of good, and Misleader

and Enchanter of the People, that there was in the whole House of Representatives" (March 16, 1721).

391. Davis, *Colonial Currency Reprints*, II. 16.

392. *Id.*, pp. 97–107.

393. For example, the "Common Council" of London was just near enough to the Governor's Council in Massachusetts, and the "114" men who composed the City government of London were just near enough to the 119 men who constituted the House of Representatives in Massachusetts in 1721–1722, to be hardly actionable but decidedly spicy.

394. Bohn, VI, 529–532. Except on pp. 187–191 this text is followed.

395. Though omitted by Tickell (1721), Baskerville (1761), Hurd (1811), and Greene (1856), "The Play-House" is reprinted as by Addison in the collections of Anderson (1795), VII, 226; Park (1809), VI, 1–4; and Chalmers (1810), IX, 572, 573.

396. The names which follow are arranged in two columns; no attempt is here made to indicate their division into lines.

397. In the table of contents it bears the same title.

398. Which occurs in the same form in the table of contents and at the beginning of the poem.

399. The preface is signed H. D. Only the first part of the collection (Vol. 1, No. 1) is entered (Hilary Term, 1702) in the *Term Catalogues* (III, 289). Both the Harvard and the Yale libraries contain copies of this tract.

400. It is so given both in the table of contents and at the beginning of the poem. Again in 1703 the poem appears as "By T. G. Gent" at p. 374 of *Poems on Affairs of State. . . .* Vol. II. Printed *in the year* 1703. Still again in 1716 we have it as by T. G. Gent at p. 374 of *Poems of Affairs of State . . . Vol. II. The Second Edition. London, . . . M.DCC.XVI.*

401. Robert Gould († ca. 1708), *Poems Chiefly consisting of Satyrs and Satyrical Epistles* (London, 1689). In this "The Play-House. A Satyr. Writ in the Year 1685" occupies pp. 161–165. Gould's *Works* (2 vols., London, 1709) also contain the poem (II. 227).

402. E. Arber, *Term Catalogues*, III. 27.

403. Trent, in *The Cambridge History of English Literature*, IX. 468; William Lee, *Life . . . of Daniel Defoe* (London, 1869), I. xxix, No. 27, and pp. 56, 57.

404. *Op. cit.*, III. 114–124.

405. The Harvard College Library copy (shelf-mark, Gay 702.380.5) is of the eighteen-page issue.

406. Thirty-one lines, beginning "Such was our Builder's Art" and ending "They scarce cou'd bear the Lustre of these Eyes."

407. And remarkably filthy.

408. In a personal letter.

409. The broadside of 1706 is like the versions of 1707 and 1710.

410. They are: *grac'd, cast* (11–12); *on, stone* (48–49); *glass, face* (50–51); *warms, charms* (61–62); *fierce, verse* (67–68); *retreat, heat, sweat* (81–83); *cease, undress* (103–104); *boast, lost* (105–106).

411. For example, Addison rhymes *arms* with *warms*; *pierce* with *verse, rehearse* with *verse*; *forgets* with *heats*; *lost* with *most*, and *boast* with *most*. It is dangerous to attempt equations with such material; but one may fairly say that Addison, on this showing, seems capable of at least four of the eight questionable rhymes in "The Play-House."

412. Cf. in the version of 1702, vv. 45, 47, 49, 52–60.

413. Whereby two passages (vv. 10 and 110) become decidedly coarser than in the version of 1702.

414. The passage in *The Spectator*, No. 258 (being by Steele) is not in point: there Christopher Rich ("Kitt Crotchet") is rallied upon his trap-doors and his extraordinary success in "making his Army fight without Pay or Provisions." Cf. also (by Steele) *The Tatler*, No. 12 and *The Spectator*, No. 36.

415. On their general unreliability, see *The Cambridge History of English Literature*, VIII. 103, 104; for a specific case (the attribution to Dryden of the spurious "Satire on the Dutch"), see G. R. Noyes's edition of *Dryden's Poetical Works*, p. 71.

416. Though the argument is hardly worth pressing, it is, strictly speaking, "J. Addison," not Joseph Addison, who is charged with the authorship of "The Play-House" in 1707. There was a John Addison who published a very coarse translation of Petronius in 1736 and an Anacreon in 1735. But if he was the John Addison who was graduated B.A. from Queens College, Oxford, in 1731 (as seems probable), he comes too late for our purpose.

417. Through its donors, bibliographers, and officials, the American Antiquarian Society has done so much for students of our early almanacs that it has been a great pleasure to co-operate with them a little by attempting this preliminary study.

On the bibliography of New England almanacs see: for Maine, New Hampshire, and Vermont, Dr. Charles L. Nichols in *Proceedings of the American Antiquarian Society* for April, 1928; for Massachusetts, Dr. Nichols, *id.*, New Series, Vol. XXII, Part 1 (April, 1912); for Rhode Island, Howard M. Chapin, *id.*, April, 1915; for Connecticut, Albert Carlos Bates, *id.*, April, 1914.

One reason for the especially frequent use of the Ames almanacs throughout this article is that they had a wide circulation outside Massachusetts as well as within that province: see, for example, Albert Carlos Bates (*op. cit.*, pp. 6–7) on their circulation in Connecticut.

418. John Adams, *Novanglus and Massachusettensis*, Boston, 1819, p. 233.

419. Alice M. Baldwin, *The New England Clergy and the American Revolution*, Duke University Press, 1928.

420. Joseph T. Buckingham, *Personal Memoirs*, &c., Boston, 1852, I. 20.

421. Henry Morley, *Character Writings of the Seventeenth Century*, pp. 55–56.

422. Richard Brathwait, *Whimzies*, reprint of 1859, ed. James O. Halliwell, pp. 13–17.

423. The price of the almanac varied: usually single copies cost about five coppers; on large quantities the price was much reduced.

Almanacs seem to have gone to press early: Nathaniel Ames, the younger, sent his copy for 1769 on October 29 (Samuel Briggs, *Nathaniel Ames*, p. 34). And on November 1, 1760, the elder Ames notes in his diary (*Dedham Historical Register*, I. 113): "Almanacks for 1761 come out." But Edes and Gill's *North American Almanac for 1770* is advertised as "this day published" on March 8, 1770 (*Mass. Gazette*).

424. Ames, 1761.

425. Italics mine.

426. This phrase suggests, and was probably intended to suggest, Jonathan Mayhew's *The Snare broken, A Thanksgiving Discourse, . . . Occasioned by the Repeal of the Stamp-Act.* It was delivered in May, 1766, and published in that same year, with a dedication to Pitt, to whom, "under God and the King, grateful America chiefly attributes it, that she is now happily re-instated in the enjoyment of her former liberties and privileges."

427. John Mein's *Catalogue of his Circulating Library*, Boston, 1765, includes (p. 23) Salmon's *Geographical and Historical Grammar*

*. . . in which the History of England and other States is brought down
to the End of the Year 1763. 10s. 6d.*

Mein's note thus recommends the book: "Containing also the present State of all the Kingdoms of the Known World, with an Account of the Air, Soil, Produce, Traffic, Arms, Religion, Universities, Manners, Habits, Revolutions and memorable Events of the different States described; illustrated with Maps. A very useful Book, and Equally entertaining and Instructive."

428. In his diary for March 31, 1766, Ames notes: "Mr. Pitt that best of men and true Patriot engaged on b'h'lf of America." On July 2, 1766, Ames "went to Boston. Bespoke Pitt's Head for the Pillar of Liberty." Concerning this very interesting Pillar of Liberty, in Dedham, Massachusetts, see pp. 170–177 of the *Proceedings at the Celebration of the Two Hundred and Fiftieth Anniversary . . . Of the Town of Dedham . . .* Cambridge, 1887.

429. The *New-England Town and Country Almanack*, Providence, Rhode Island.

430. The subject is continued in the almanac for 1770.

431. *Cato's Letters; or, Essays on Liberty, Civil and Religious, and other important Subjects,* originally published, 1720–1723, in the *British Journal*, had reached a sixth edition in 1755.

432. "Throne" would be the word expected; perhaps "Town" was substituted to avoid legal consequences.

433. William Jackson, Theophilus Lillie, John Taylor, and Nathaniel Rogers.

434. With the following footnote to explain why no Captains of this Company are given for 1686–90: "Sir Edmund Andros upon his Arrival, turned out all the Magistrates, Judges, and Officers of the Militia, chosen by the People, and appointed others in their Room; he overturned by Degrees the whole Constitution; and stretched his Prerogative to such an Height, as made it impossible for the People to live under him; which prepared the Way for the Revolution that soon followed."

435. It also, of course, contains additional material of the various sorts already indicated. For instance (on the page for January), it boldly remarks that "Justice will overtake even KINGS."

436. See his diary (*Dedham Historical Register*, 1) for July 3, 6, and 14, 1758.

437. Misnumbered 415.

438. For evidence of Mrs. Macaulay's popularity in America in 1769, see *Publications of the Colonial Society of Massachusetts*, XXVI. 188, 191.

439. From Ames's diary for April 20, 1772.

440. Ames, for example, recommends Locke's *Essay on Government*, briefly but very strongly: "As it is unpardonable for a Navigator to be without his charts, so it is for a *Senator* to be without His, which is Lock's Essay on Government."

Ames also has a longish article (about a page and a half) on agriculture and wine-making, led up to by an important paragraph urging that such economic activities "will turn to infinitely greater profit than manufacturing, and . . . will, instead of discouragement meet with the protection of our Mother Country as soon as we have brought her to her former senses."

441. Note year. Was this a reprint? Of what?

442. Jonathan Shipley (1714–1788), Bishop of St. Asaph from 1769. He was an intimate friend of Franklin, who (*Works*, ed. Sparks, VIII. 40) declared in a letter written from London in 1773 that Bishop Shipley by his "liberal and generous sentiments, relating to the conduct of government here towards America" had "hazarded the displeasure of the court, and of course the prospect of further preferment." In his famous published (but undelivered) speech of 1774 Shipley said: "I look upon North America as the only great nursery of freemen left on the face of the earth." There is a picture of "The Patriotic Bishop, Dr. Jonathan Shipley" in Daboll's *New-England Almanack* (New London, Connecticut) for 1775.

443. Bickerstaff's Connecticut almanac for 1776 follows suit: its very title-page advertises as the first of its special features for the year "The Method of making Gunpowder, which at this Juncture may be carried into Execution in a small Way, by almost every Farmer in his own Habitation."

For further information on the manufacture of gunpowder in early New England, see William B. Weeden, *Economic and Social History of New England, 1620–1789*, II. 772–773.

444. Edward Ward, *London Spy* (fourth edition, 1753), Part XVI, p. 348.

445. Thomas Sprat, *The History of the Royal Society* (fourth edition, London, 1734), p. 64.

446. John Oldham, in *Poems and Translations*, p. 11.

447. G. Gregory Smith, *Elizabethan Critical Essays* (Oxford, 1904), I. 292, section 11.

448. S. Person, *An Anatomical Lecture of Man: Or a map of the little world, delineated in essayes and characters*, 1664.

449. Edward Everett Hale, while he was a Harvard undergraduate, entered in his diary for November 24, 1837, the fact that he "wrote some on a theme this morning. It is 'Draw a Character of a Misanthrope.' Sketching character was never my forte. I don't like the subject much" (Edward E. Hale, Jr., *The Life and Letters of Edward Everett Hale* [Boston, 1917], I. 33).

450. Thomas Wilson, *Arte of Rhetorique*, ed. G. H. Mair (Oxford, 1909), pp. 178–179.

451. This book reached a second edition in 1677.

452. Charles Hoole, in his well-known *New Discovery of the Old Art of Teaching Schoole* (ed. E. T. Campagnac, London, 1913, p. 159), recommends the use of "the pleasant *English Parnassus*" in the case of more advanced pupils in the grammar school "to furnish them with Rhymes, Epithites, and varietie of elegant expressions."

453. "Express their natures, qualities, conditions, practices, tools, desires, aims, or ends, by witty Allegories, or Allusions, to things or terms in nature, or art, of like nature and resemblance, still striving for wit and pleasantness, together with tart nipping jerks about their vices or miscarriages."

454. Johnson's book must have had a very considerable influence, for at least five editions of it had appeared by the end of the seventeenth century.

455. Here, as often, the epithets are contradictory.

456. Pages 41–42 in the edition of 1657.

457. Edward Arber, *Term Catalogues*, II. 190.

458. *The Works of John Dryden* (Scott-Saintsbury edition, Edinburgh, 1882–1893), VI. 267 ff., especially p. 269.

459. Reprinted in Joel E. Spingarn, *Critical Essays of the Seventeenth Century* (Oxford, 1908–1909), III. 282.

460. *Tragedies of the Last Age* (London, 1678), and *A Short View of Tragedy* (London, 1693).

461. For Bodin and other writers before Charron on this subject, see Robert Flint, *History of the Philosophy of History* (Edinburgh and London, 1893), p. 198.

462. According to the catalogue of the British Museum there would seem to have been at least fourteen editions in French by 1663.

463. The earlier translation, by Samson Lennard, appears to have gone through at least five editions by 1670.

464. *A Journey through England* (London, 1714), p. iii.

465. See George E. Hastings, "John Bull and his American Descendants," *American Literature*, 1 (March, 1929). 40–68. On Arbuthnot, see the admirable *John Arbuthnot: Mathematician and Satirist* by Lester M. Beattie (Cambridge, 1935).

466. J. C. Scaliger, *Poetices* (1561) recognizes (bk. iii, chap. xvii) "Natio, sive Gens" as one of the categories under which human beings differ, and gives lists of epithets for the principal nations of the world. For *Angli* his first epithet is *perfidi*.

467. Sir Sidney Lee, *The French Renaissance in England* (New York, 1910), p. 60. I have not been able to examine a copy of De la Porte's book.

468. *Études Critiques*, Fifth Series.

469. *Some Early Impressions* (London, 1924), p. 87.